REPRINTS OF ECONOMIC CLASSICS

THEORIES OF WELFARE ECONOMICS

THEORIES OF
WELFARE ECONOMICS

BY

HLA MYINT, Ph.D. (London)

Professor of Economics at the University of Rangoon, Burma

Published for

THE LONDON SCHOOL OF ECONOMICS
AND POLITICAL SCIENCE

(University of London)

REPRINTS OF ECONOMIC CLASSICS

Augustus M. Kelley, Bookseller
New York 1965

Original edition 1948.   Reprinted 1962 & 1965 by arrangement with Hla Myint.

Library of Congress Catalogue Card Number

65 - 16990

PRINTED IN THE UNITED STATES OF AMERICA

by SENTRY PRESS, NEW YORK, N. Y. 10019

PREFACE

THIS book is not a revision but a development of the ideas contained in my thesis " Postulates of Welfare Economics " submitted to the University of London for the Ph.D. degree in 1943.

I would like to express my deep gratitude to J. R. Hicks. Apart from the heavy debt I owe to his writings, I had the advantage of his constant advice and criticism in writing this book during my tenure of the Drummond Fraser Research Fellowship at Manchester University.

I would also like to thank Prof. Hayek who supervised my thesis and from whose mellow scholarship in the history of economic thought I have benefited, and Prof. Robbins for reading the manuscript and giving me kindly encouragement. None of my teachers is of course responsible for the errors that may remain in the book.

My thanks are due to the editors of the *Economica* for permission to use my article " The Classical View of the Economic Problem ".

H. M.

January 1948.

v

CONTENTS

INTRODUCTION . . . . PAGE xi

Plan of the work—Inquiry into the development and the relative practical usefulness of the theories of welfare economics from Adam Smith to the present day.

PART

PHYSICAL LEVEL

CHAPTER

I. THE CLASSICAL VIEW OF THE ECONOMIC PROBLEM ... 1

Inconsistency in the current interpretation of classical economics— Smith's labour-theory outlook and methods of increasing the size of the national dividend (i) by widening the scope of division of labour and exchange and (ii) by increasing capital accumulation and population—Ricardo's emphasis on diminishing returns and concept of Net Revenue—J. S. Mill's systematisation of the physical output approach —Quantitative importance of the physical level of analysis on economic welfare.

II. THE MEASURING ROD OF LABOUR 15

Smith's concept of the "quantity of labour commanded" as the measure (i) of current subjective income and (ii) of maximum physical output next year—Ricardo's "quantity of labour embodied" measure and the Cost and Output approach to the national dividend—Net Revenue as the measure of economic welfare.

III. THE MEASURING ROD AND THE GLUT THEORY . 34

Malthus's development of the "labour-commanded" measure of value into an Income approach to the national dividend—Malthus's measure of value and his theory of "intrinsic value"—Relation between the different measures of value and the Glut controversy.

IV. THE CLASSICAL THEORY OF FREE COMPETITION (A REINTERPRETATION) 53

The "allocative" interpretation of Smith's theory of competition based on very selective evidence—Classical theory of competition as an auxiliary instrument of dynamic expansion of economic activity, "widening" the scope of division of labour and opening up new investment opportunities—Ricardo's theory of Comparative Costs as a classic piece of optimum analysis at the physical level.

V. THE WELFARE SIGNIFICANCE OF PRODUCTIVE LABOUR 70

Smith's "storage" and "value" versions of Productive Labour— Their relation to the different measures of value—Doctrine of Productive Labour implies a fundamental weakness in the system of free choice in relation to saving, investment and level of economic activity —J. S. Mill's systematisation of the "storage" version—Reinterpretation of classical economics—Productive Labour doctrine as the mainspring of the classical theory of economic expansion.

vii

CHAPTER   PAGE
                          PART II

                    SUBJECTIVE LEVEL

 VI. MARGINAL   REVOLUTION   AND   THE   SCARCITY
     APPROACH   89
        Real significance of marginal revolution to be sought in the realm of
        welfare economics—(i) Extension of welfare analysis from the physical
        to the subjective level—(ii) Substitution of the Scarcity approach
        for the labour-theory outlook—Different development of welfare
        economic thought in England and on the Continent.

VII. THE THEORY OF THE GENERAL OPTIMUM   .   .   94
        Gaps in the classical theory of the competitive optimum—Marginal
        Utility theory and the Paretian formulation of the subjective optimum
        —Marginal Productivity theory and the technical or the physical
        optimum—Co-ordination of the subjective and the physical optima—
        Nature and Significance of the General Optimum.

VIII. CHARACTERISTICS   OF   NEO-CLASSICAL   WELFARE
      ECONOMICS   120
        Definition of Neo-classicism—(i) Compromise between the material and
        the subjective definition of wealth—(ii) Concern with the Optimum
        supply of factors—(iii) Concentration on concrete and *ad hoc* cases of
        exceptions to the general principle of laissez-faire—Sidgwick as a
        pioneer welfare economist—Background of Marshall's attitude towards
        the economic problem.

 IX. THE MARSHALLIAN SURPLUS ANALYSIS   .   .   .   142
        Need for a distinction between Marshall's broader views on the sur-
        pluses *in general* and his application of the *partial* surplus analysis—
        Essentially relative nature of Marshall's partial Consumers' Surplus
        analysis even in its original form—Modern reformulations and the
        principle of Compensation—Producers' Surplus as Differential rent—
        Asymmetry between the Consumers' and the Producers' Surplus—Mar-
        shall's practical applications of the Surplus Analysis mainly based on
        changes in Consumers' Surplus.

  X. PROFESSOR PIGOU'S " ECONOMICS OF WELFARE "   .   173
        Fusion between the English concrete particular approach and the
        Continental formal general approach—Neo-classical elements in Prof.
        Pigou's system—Substitution of Marginal Social Product analysis
        and the General Optimum for the Marshallian Partial Surplus
        analysis—Divergences between the Private and the Social Products—
        Mechanics of Prof. Pigou's Optimum—A comparative estimate of the
        practical usefulness of the Paretian Optimum, the Pigovian Optimum
        and the Marshallian Partial Surplus analysis.

                          PART III

                    ETHICAL LEVEL

 XI. TOWARDS A BROADER CONCEPT OF WELFARE?   .   199
        Distinction between the narrower economic welfare analysis at the purely
        subjective level and the problem of General Social Welfare at the ethical
        level—Knight and Clark on the Instability of wants—Knight on the
        inevitability of ethical and normative judgments—Clark on " Social
        Value "—In defence of a narrower scientific analysis of economic
        welfare on the assumption of given wants.

CHAPTER   PAGE

XII. CONCLUSION—DIFFERENT   LEVELS   OF   WELFARE
       ANALYSIS 229
          Three levels of welfare analysis and their place in a comprehensive study
          of the problem of human welfare—Special complementarity between
          the physical and the subjective level of analysis and the dangers of pre-
          occupation with one level of analysis alone—Problems to be tackled at
          the physical and the subjective level and the application of quantitative
          criterion of significance—The Economist and Ethics.

       SELECT BIBLIOGRAPHY 237

       INDEX OF AUTHORS   239

INTRODUCTION

THIS book traces the development of welfare economic thought from Adam Smith to the present day. It is not, however, merely an historical study. It also attempts to find out what types of welfare analysis are likely to prove most useful for the purpose of practical economic policy.

A history of welfare economics differs from a monograph on the development of a particular branch of economic theory in that its subject-matter is much the same as that of a general history of economic thought. The treatment, however, is different. Firstly, since a different standpoint is adopted, a rather different perspective is given to many familiar economic doctrines, particularly the classical economic doctrines. Secondly, since welfare economics by its nature is concerned with how efficiently the economic system works, even an historical study of it develops into a practical estimate of the relative usefulness of different theories of welfare economics.

In welfare economics at least, the better technique of modern economic analysis does not detract from the practical importance of the lessons to be learned from older types of analysis, for the following reason. A given type of welfare analysis cannot be discussed without reference to the particular problems it is designed to solve. These particular problems in their turn cannot be fully appreciated without considering the fundamental attitude towards the central Economic Problem which underlies them.

Now the nature and significance of economic activity may be viewed from different standpoints and it is not possible to demonstrate by logic which of these standpoints is right or wrong. The only available method of judging their relative merits is to consider how significant each of them is. Again many criteria of significance are possible and the one I have adopted is purely quantitative and free from value judgments. Thus I define economic welfare as consisting in the quantities of satisfaction of *given* individuals' wants, postulating that comparisons of economic welfare must proceed under the assumption of *constant wants* and that once the system of wants has changed, the problem is not one of *economic* welfare but of *general* social welfare which cannot be analysed in purely scientific and quantitative terms. I then assess the relative significance of the different views of the central economic problem according to the greater or lesser quantities of economic welfare involved in the problems suggested by each of them. On my criterion, therefore, older types of welfare analysis retain a great deal of practical importance if large quantities of economic welfare are still involved in the types of problems they have attempted to solve.

The plan of the book is as follows :

Part I deals with the type of welfare economic problems and the method of approach suggested by the classical labour-theory outlook or the " man-against-nature " view of the economic problem. I have described classical economics as welfare analysis at the Physical level since it implicitly assumes that quantities of satisfaction of given wants are roughly proportional to quantities of physical products, and concentrates on the methods of increasing the quantity and the physical productivity of resources as the most important means of increasing economic welfare. A considerable portion of the book has been devoted to Part I for two reasons : firstly, because my interpretation of classical economics differs from the conventional interpretation and has therefore to be substantiated in detail ; secondly, because I believe that the type of problems suggested by the classical view of the economic problem are still very important in their quantitative effect on present-day economic welfare.

Part II deals with welfare analysis at the Subjective level which provisionally assumes that there is no further possibility of increasing the total quantity of resources and concentrates on the possibilities of increasing economic welfare by a more efficient allocation of the *given* resources and by a better method of resolving the competing wants of different individuals which act as " obstacles " to each other. The subjective welfare analysis is closely related to the " scarcity " concept of the economic problem, although traces of the labour-theory outlook linger in the writings of the English Neo-classical economists. Part II covers most of the modern theories of welfare economics. In particular, it studies the relative practical importance of the different types of the problems which are dealt with by the Paretian theory of the General Optimum, the Marshallian Partial Surplus analysis and the Pigovian Marginal Social Product analysis.

Part III is made up of one long chapter which considers the various proposals to broaden welfare economic analysis to include the problem of general social welfare at the Ethical level. In the main, it is concerned with the question to what extent welfare economic analysis, based on the assumption of given wants, remains useful in a world of changing wants.

The scope of this book is limited in two directions. It is concerned entirely with the theories of Production Welfare Economics which deals with the size of economic welfare only. I have excluded discussions of how economic welfare should be distributed between different individuals since I feel that there is very little that can be said on the subject in a strictly scientific way without introducing value judgments. A logically satisfactory concept of Economic Equality is perhaps a lot more complicated than a simple equal distribution of incomes ; and although, speaking for myself, I am convinced by the arguments of Prof. Pigou and Mr. Lerner that economic welfare would be increased by a transfer of income from the rich to poor, I am bound to admit that these arguments still involve interpersonal comparisons of utility and cannot therefore be regarded as scientific propositions. I have further excluded discussions concerning how to maintain and stabilise economic welfare at a high level since this would lead to a review of trade cycle theories. Perhaps no justification is needed for this limitation. It should, however, be noted that the subject-matter of this book is not entirely " static " in that the means of increasing economic welfare by increasing investment and the total volume of economic activity are given a prominent place at the Physical level of welfare analysis.

PART I

PHYSICAL LEVEL

CHAPTER I

THE CLASSICAL VIEW OF THE ECONOMIC PROBLEM

THERE seems to be a fundamental inconsistency in the currently accepted opinions concerning the classical economists. We have been brought up on the belief that their main concern is to show that the equilibrium process of the free market will lead to a more efficient allocation of resources among different industries than State interference.[1] On the other hand, we have been frequently told that the classical analysis is vitiated by the labour theory which conceives the economic problem as the struggle of man against nature in producing material wealth. It has been said that the classical economists confuse the " economic problem " consisting in the choice between alternative methods of using given resources to maximise the satisfaction of given wants with the " technical problem " of physical productivity ; and that consequently they are guilty of a " materialist bias " (cf. Robbins, *Nature and Significance of Economic Science*, Chaps. I–III).

It will be seen that these two opinions, held implicitly and simultaneously by many economists, are inconsistent with each other. The first credits the classical economists with an essentially correct, if rather rough, solution of the problem of allocating scarce resources which, according to the second, they understand only imperfectly.

This inconsistency is fundamental, for the two opinions attribute to the classical economists two entirely different outlooks on the nature of the central economic problem.

When we say that the central problem of the classical economists is to allocate resources efficiently among different industries, we imply (i) that they start from the assumption of a given quantity of resources and (ii) that they are mainly concerned with the maximisation of consumers' wants as expressed by their market demands

---

[1] For recent examples of this belief see A. P. Lerner, *Economics of Control*, p. 67 ; T. d. Scitovsky, " A Note on Welfare Propositions in Economics ", *Review of Economic Studies*, Nov. 1941, pp. 77–8.

for different commodities. In short, we attribute to them what is known as the " scarcity " concept of the economic problem. The efficiency of the allocation of resources among competing uses cannot be judged except on the assumption of a given quantity of scarce resources and in terms of quantities of consumers' satisfaction.

On the other hand, the labour theory suggests an entirely different outlook on the economic problem. It starts from a fundamental contrast between land or natural resources, given once for all, and labour which is augmentable. Further, the problem of equilibrium adjustments to the consumers' demand is faded out and the analysis is largely confined to the physical level. Thus the amount of material wealth can be increased, either by raising the physical productivity of labour or by increasing the supply of labour.

The problem now is to determine which of the two viewpoints, the " scarcity " concept of the economic problem or the labour-theory outlook, should be regarded as the central principle which unifies the different aspects of classical economic thought into a coherent whole. In what follows it will be argued that the method of regarding the problem of allocating resources as the main concern of the classical economists fails to provide such a central unifying principle as it fails to explain a formidable array of things which are undoubtedly characteristic features of classical thought. It fails to explain, for instance, the classical " materialist bias " as typified by J. S. Mill's concept of the " economic man " and also the classical economists' preoccupation with the problem of capital accumulation which developed into the celebrated controversy over Malthus's Glut theory. It will be argued further that once we have learnt to steep ourselves in the labour-theory outlook and to regard the " allocative " problem as a subsidiary theme, all these apparently puzzling features sort themselves out into a coherent pattern and that this pattern is very different from what we normally understand by the " familiar tenets of the classical school ".

I

What then is the outlook on the economic problem suggested by the labour theory ? In its simplest form, the labour theory depicts a primitive agricultural community, self-sufficient, and having only a rudimentary system of exchange. In this setting it is natural to look upon production as the struggle of man against nature [1] and to measure wealth in terms of the physical product of

[1] Cf. Maurice Dobb, *Political Economy and Capitalism*, p. 20.

labour. This is the starting-point of Adam Smith's analysis ; from it he proceeded on the assumption that the more complicated structure of a developed economy may be reduced in its essential features to this basic model of the " early and rude state of society ". Thus he tried to show that behind the " veil of money " and complex relations of trade and industry, the essential nature of economic life remained the same ; that it consisted in the physical process in which commodities were annually produced and consumed. From this he derived his basic criterion of economic policy : it must be favourable to the greatness of the annual produce of labour.

In the " Introduction and Plan " to the *Wealth of Nations* Smith laid down two major determinants of the size of the annual produce or the national dividend : (i) " the skill, dexterity and judgment with which its labour is generally applied ", and (ii) " the pro-portion between the number of those who are employed in useful (or productive) labour and those who are not so employed ". Smith's conception of the economic problem in a developed economy may be best understood by following these two determinants.

(i) The first way in which the primitive economy may develop is by opening itself up for trade ; by extending the area of market and division of labour either within its own national boundary or beyond it. Starting from a technical concept of production as the transformation of natural resources into physical products, Smith was impressed by the striking possibilities of increasing pro-ductivity by the division of labour. He put it down as the most potent method of increasing the size of the national dividend (op. cit., Cannan ed., Vol. I, p. 5).

At this point it may be pointed out that one of the most powerful considerations behind Smith's desire for free trade is not the purely subjective consumers' gains from free exchange. He desired free trade mainly because it increases physical productivity by widening the scope of the division of labour and by bringing fresh natural resources into the framework of production. Thus, subjective gains apart, free trade is desired because it increases the annual produce of a country's labour even when considered at the purely physical level. In other words, free trade is a method of expanding the economic system horizontally so as to reap the advantages of increasing physical returns brought about by overcoming the tech-nical indivisibilities of production (cf. Allyn Young, " Increasing Returns and Economic Progress ", *Economic Journal*, 1928). Per-haps one may say that the difference between the modern concept of free competition and Smith's, is that the former is a method of

" tightening " up the allocative efficiency within a given productive framework, while the latter is a method of " widening " the area of the economy.

This does not, however, mean that Smith did not know the existence of the subjective consumers' gains in the modern sense. In analysing the mechanism of exchange which accompanies the division of labour, he became aware of the fact that on top of the increase in physical productivity, there was a further class of gains : " It gives a value to their superfluities by exchanging them for something else which may satisfy a part of their wants and increase their enjoyments " (ibid., p. 413). But this transition to the subjective level of analysis is neither clear-cut nor sustained and some of the modern interpreters are going too far when they would have us believe that Smith's central problem was to maximise the satisfaction of consumers' wants as expressed by their market demands for different commodities (e.g. M. Bowley, *Nassau Senior and the Classical Economists*, p. 67).

Perhaps a more balanced assessment of Smith's opinions on this point may be stated as follows. He would of course agree that the final aim of all production is consumption and that in the ultimate analysis wealth must consist in quantities of consumers' satisfaction. But he seems to assume implicitly that under normal conditions, i.e. in the absence of shortage or glut, the consumers' satisfaction from a commodity may be regarded as depending on its " value-in-use " as determined by its intrinsic physical properties. This amounts to assuming that quantities of satisfaction are roughly proportional to quantities of physical products. Granted this first approximation, he went on to develop the bulk of his analysis on the assumption that more substantial additions to the wealth of a nation could be made by increasing the volume of physical output rather than by making refined adjustments to the consumers' preference positions on the basis of a given volume of products. Thus the allocative problem became a subsidiary theme and however far Smith might have leant towards the demand approach, he could confine himself to the physical level of analysis suggested by his initial labour-theory outlook. In the exchange economy, as in the primitive economy, the first major determinant of the size of the annual produce is the technical conditions governing the physical productivity of labour.

(ii) The second major determinant of the wealth of the nation, according to Smith, is the proportion in which its labour is used between " productive " and " unproductive " purposes. Deferring a more detailed discussion of the meaning of " productive " labour to Chapter V below, we may provisionally define it in general terms as that labour used for investment purposes. Now, in Smith's time, fixed or durable capital played only a very small part in economic life and the bulk of investment was in the form of circulating capital or " advances to labour ". Thus, broadly speaking, " productive " labour may be regarded as that labour which produces material necessities or wage goods which enables society to maintain a greater quantity of labour for future production. An increase in saving thus increases the size of the wage fund which raises wages above the subsistence level and stimulates the growth of population. Thus the greater the proportion of resources used in " productive " purposes, the greater will be the supply of labour available to society.

This again clinches with the labour-theory outlook, which starts from a fundamental contrast between land, the passive and non-augmentable factor and labour, the active and augmentable factor. Given the natural resources and average productivity of labour, the size of the national dividend may be regarded as being determined by the major variable, the supply of labour. Thus the second way in which our initial model of the primitive economy may develop is to expand itself vertically, by increasing its capital accumulation and population.

The two methods of increasing the size of the national dividend, horizontally by widening the area of the market and the division of labour and vertically by increasing the supply of labour are complementary, and not competitive. However, Smith seems to think capital accumulation as the more important mainspring of economic progress. Without capital accumulation, division of labour cannot be carried out to any considerable extent and the new investment opportunities offered by a greater freedom of trade cannot be fully utilised. On the other hand, a mere increase in capital accumulation resulting in an increase in population can by itself open up enormous scope of increasing returns for labour, not only due to the " abridging of labour " by machinery, but also due to the overcoming of technical indivisibilities. Here, not having a clear idea of the principle of diminishing returns from land, Smith appears to think that a mere increase in population will increase the productivity of labour. Comparing society to a private workshop, Smith wrote : " The greater their number, the more they naturally divide themselves into the different classes and sub-divisions of employment " (ibid., p. 88).

To sum up : the labour-theory outlook systematically shifted Smith's focus of attention from the problem of allocating *given* resources among different industries to maximise the consumers' satisfaction, to the problems of increasing the physical productivity of labour and the total volume of economic activity. The subjective level of analysis was pushed to the background by the broad assumption that quantities of consumers' satisfaction are roughly proportional to the quantity of physical product. The assumption of a given quantity of resources was undermined by Smith's interest in the possibilities of increasing the national dividend by increasing the degree of the division of labour and the total supply of labour.

II

After Adam Smith, the classical outlook on the economic problem moved further and further away from the problem of allocating given resources efficiently among different industries.   It is true that J. B. Say, an important disciple of Smith, made important advances in the demand approach and even initiated a minor tradition of the marginal utility and productivity analysis, which included such considerable figures as Montifort Longfield and Nassau Senior (cf. M. Bowley, op. cit., Chap. II, secs. v and vi).   But these economists exerted little influence on the main stream of classical economic thought.   Malthus also might be regarded as a demand economist.   But again his interest was centred on the influence of the total Effective Demand on the volume of employment and not on the allocative mechanism of relative demand for particular products in different markets.   To him the wastages due to the collapse of general economic activity and the " glut " were overwhelmingly more important than wastages due to the mal-distribution of resources.   When, however, we come to the mainstream of classical economic thought dominated by the Ricardian tradition we find the physical output approach of the labour theory firmly established almost to a complete neglect of the allocative problem.   It continued to be so until the " marginal revolution ".

It is significant that the development of economic thought after Adam Smith should be given its initial impetus by a simultaneous discovery of the principle of diminishing returns from land by many economists, notably by West, Anderson and Malthus.   This discovery was brought to a head by Government inquiries into the state of British agriculture.   But even without that external stimulus, it would probably have been discovered since it is the next step of generalisation to be arrived at by the logic of the man-against-nature view of the economic problem. It laid down a basic relation between the constant factor, land, and the variable factor, labour, and set a determinate limit to the process in which additional doses of labour can be applied to a given quantity of natural resources.

Perhaps the way in which this development affected the classical analysis can be illustrated by adopting the expository device suggested by Smith, viz. to regard society as one giant firm, employing one main type of variable factor, labour, and producing a single " commodity ", which we may call " corn " after Ricardo, meaning by it a more or less homogeneous physical mass of " material necessities " or wage goods. Smith had pictured this giant firm as working under increasing returns ; as being capable of almost unlimited expansion either by free trade or capital accumulation.

What the Ricardian theory of Distribution in fact did was to curb this expansive optimism by showing that society as a giant firm would be working, on the contrary, under conditions of diminishing returns and that there would be a determinate limit ʋo which population could expand marked by the stationary state. Ricardo argued that the increase in population brought about by progressive capital accumulation would extend the margin of cultivation to poorer lands where a greater quantity of labour would be required to produce a standard unit of " corn ". The price of " corn " would then rise and a higher rent would be claimed by the owners of the better-grade land. Since real wages could not fall below the minimum subsistence level, money wages would rise which would in turn lower the rate of profit. Expansion would come to a stop when the marginal product of labour had fallen so low as to leave nothing for the capitalists after wages and rents had been paid off ; for at this point, there would be no further incentive to accumulate capital and expand economic activity. Thus the emphasis was shifted from the absolute scale of social production to the social net product or the " Net Revenue " which increases at a diminishing rate as the scale of production is expanded. Thus Ricardo argued that it was not enough to infer the wealth of society from the Gross Revenue as Smith had done ; we must further examine the balance sheet of the giant firm to find out how much net product in terms of " corn " has been left, after the wages of labour have been paid off. " Provided its net real income, its rents and profits be the same, it is of no importance

whether the nation consists of ten or twelve millions of inhabitants "
(Ricardo, *Principles of Political Economy*, Everyman's ed., pp. 234–5).
The aim of economic policy was thus to increase the net social out-
put rather than the absolute scale of social production.

Malthus's contribution consisted in showing that it was not
sufficient to regard society merely as a giant producing unit ; and
that it should also be studied as a giant consuming unit. He
believed that there was no automatic synchronisation of society's
capacity to produce and its capacity to consume ; and that an
attempt to expand economic activity by capital accumulation would
result in a breakdown and a glut, long before the extreme limit of
Ricardo's stationary equilibrium was reached.

We have not simplified the essential features of the classical
analysis by suggesting the analogy of a giant firm producing a single
commodity, " corn ", with a single variable factor, labour. In the
light of economic conditions existing at that time, there is much
to be said for such a method of abstraction. In those days, wage
goods in fact consisted of a few primary products which could
be lumped together under the head of a single commodity, " corn ",
and the output of " corn " could then be used as a convenient
index of the output of consumers' goods in general. At the subsistence level of real wages, " determined by the habits and customs
of the people ", a given output of " corn " could maintain a determinate quantity of labour. Labour, being a versatile factor, could
then be turned to the production of all sorts of articles, both " necessities " and " luxuries ", particularly so, when the bulk of the luxury
consumption was in the form of direct personal services. The
concept of labour as the single variable factor is again a justifiable
assumption. As we have pointed out, fixed capital played a relatively unimportant part in the economic life of that time and investment was mainly in the form of " advances to labour ". Since
land was assumed to be fixed in supply, social output could then
be treated as the function of a single major variable, the quantity
of labour.

It might at first sight be thought that an economic system
supposed to produce a single " commodity " with a single variable
factor could not give rise to any economic problems as we understand them nowadays ; that once it is assumed that quantities of
satisfaction are proportionate to the quantities of physical products,
all problems of production would be of a purely technical nature.
This, however, is not true. For even when we have completely
faded out the problem of allocating given resources among com-

peting industries (and this extreme measure is not adopted by the classical economists), there still remains a major problem of choice : the choice between using labour directly for present consumption, or using it indirectly or " productively " so as to increase its own supply and thus increase future consumption. Here, the modern economist, working at the subjective level of analysis, would say that resources should be allocated between present and future consumption, according to the time preferences of the consumers. The classical economists, however, were working at the physical level of analysis. Since they believed that quantities of satisfaction are proportional to quantities of physical product, they arrived at the following interesting conclusion : optimum allocation between present and future would be attained when the physical product of direct labour is equal to that of indirect or " stored up " labour. That is to say, so long as the " roundabout method " of production yields a greater physical product than direct labour, additional investment would increase the economic welfare of society. Thus the stationary equilibrium at which the rate of profits is reduced to zero may be regarded as the point of optimum investment, according to Ricardo, although he was far from being cheered by its prospect.

Thus again we have a shift of the centre of attention from the problem of allocating *given* resources among different consumers' goods industries, to the broader problem of distributing the resources between the consumers' goods and the producers' goods sectors of the economic system with a view to expand the total volume of economic activity. Ricardo and Malthus might not be able to agree on the ideal " balance of production and consumption " ; but they did agree that the key to economic prosperity depended on this balance. Malthus, with his Effective Demand approach, might not be able to accept the physical output approach of Ricardo, but he devoted the whole Book II of his *Principles of Political Economy* to the problem of Economic Progress and not to the problem of Economic Equilibrium. The fact that the " glut controversy " became the foremost issue of those times is a sufficient indication how far the centre of attention had shifted away from the equilibrium adjustments of relative consumers' demand in different industries to the savings-investment nexus (cf. J. S. Mill, *Principles of Political Economy*, Ashley ed., p. 747).

III

The triumph of the Ricardians in the " glut " controversy was such that even that fragment of subjective element contained in Malthus's Effective Demand theory disappeared from classical economic thought. With J. S. Mill, technological considerations became predominant and the physical output approach was completely systematised.

This is apparent from the celebrated arrangement of the contents of his *Principles*, which set the tradition of dividing the subject-matter of economics into Production, Distribution and Exchange. In Book I, under the heading of Production, were considered those topics, later on to be repeated *ad nauseum* by the old-fashioned text-books, e.g. advantages of division of labour, different laws of returns in agriculture and industry, relative merits of large- and small-scale production, etc., all bearing on the technical efficiency of the producing unit in the best tradition of scientific factory organisation. The underlying idea of this book is that the size of the national dividend is determined entirely by technology and the laws of changes in the supply of factors, almost independently of the equilibrium process of the market.

When Distribution and Exchange were introduced in Books II and III, they merely played a secondary rôle of parcelling out this predetermined block of wealth, national dividend, among different individuals according to the prevailing system of economic organisation. It was not thought that Distribution and Exchange could directly affect the size of the national dividend.

Hence followed Mill's famous distinction between the laws of Production, which are immutable physical laws, and the laws of Distribution and Exchange which pertain to existing social institutions.

The laws and conditions of Production of wealth partake of the character of physical truths. There is nothing optional or arbitrary in them. Whatever mankind produce, must be produced in the modes and conditions imposed by the constitution of external things and by the inherent properties of their bodily and mental structure. The opinions, the wishes which may exist in these matters do not control the things themselves (J. S. Mill, *Principles of Political Economy*, Ashley ed., pp. 199–200).

Having absorbed Rae's theory of saving as the choice between present and future consumption, Mill appears to be rather uneasy about the fact that the quantity of capital accumulation, a major determinant of the physical output, would depend on human choice. But he heroically stuck to his deterministic theory of production by arguing that the " excess of production above the physical necessaries of the producers " not only offered the upper limit to savings, but also partly contribute to " determine how much would be saved " (ibid., p. 164 ; cf. p. 175).

With this deterministic theory of production, there was a shift of emphasis from Adam Smith's concept of wealth as a flow of " annual produce " or the national dividend to the concept of wealth as a stock, the national capital. Since the size of the physical output was supposed to follow as a determinate technical function from a given stock of resources and technique, the wealth of society could simply be measured by measuring the physical magnitude of its capital stock. Hence, more than any other classical economist, Mill made it a principle to exclude immaterial services from his " philosophically correct " definition of wealth as " instruments, meaning not only tools and machinery alone, but the whole accumulation possessed by individuals and communities for the attainment of their ends " (ibid., pp. 8–9).

> It is essential to the idea of wealth to be susceptible to accumulation ; things which cannot, after being produced, be kept for some time before being used are never regarded as wealth, since however much of them may be produced or enjoyed, the person benefited by them is no wise richer, is no wise improved in circumstances (ibid., p. 47).

Thus the tendency of the nineteenth-century statisticians like Giffen to give pride of place to the calculation of the national capital rather than that of national income was in line with the economic theory of their time (cf. Giffen, *The Growth of National Capital*).

Finally, it may be noted that once wealth was defined in a thorough-going materialistic fashion, Mill's much-maligned concept of the " economic man " became the necessary logical prop to support the whole approach. It was merely a more explicit and courageous formulation of the idea which was implicit in the minds of most of the classical economists, viz. quantities of consumers' satisfaction might be assumed as being roughly proportional to quantities of physical product and that therefore a greater quantity of physical product or material wealth would be normally more preferable than a lesser quantity.

IV

Our interpretation of the classical outlook on the economic problem, if accepted, seems to cast a serious doubt on the practice of taking it for granted that the central problem of the classical economists was to demonstrate the " allocative efficiency " of the equilibrium adjustments to consumers' demand in the free market. We have seen that they were concerned, not as much with the problem of maximising consumers' satisfaction in the modern sense, as with the problem of increasing the total physical output. The central principle, which successfully unifies the various classical economic doctrines from Adam Smith to J. S. Mill, embodies the following fundamental proposition : viz. the economic welfare of society can be more effectively promoted (i) by increasing the physical productivity of labour, and (ii) by increasing the total volume of economic activity,[1] rather than by tamely accepting the given quantity of productive resources and making refined adjustments in allocating them among different industries. From this follow the two major canons of classical economic policy, (i) free trade which extends the scope of division of labour and brings fresh resources into the productive framework, and (ii) capital accumulation which enables society to maintain a greater quantity of labour.

What we have said above does not of course mean that none of the classical economists were ever concerned with the " allocative " problem. This would be going to the other extreme. A careful reading of the *Wealth of Nations* would reveal that Smith's analysis of this problem was on the whole confined to two odd chapters, Book I, Chapters VII and IX ; but that within this narrow compass Smith had succeeded in showing that the equilibrium process of the competitive market will lead to an optimum allocation of resources among different industries, whether or not we share his metaphysical optimism concerning the working of the " invisible hand ". Again, Ricardo's theory of Comparative Cost (as distinct from Smith's theory of increasing returns from expansion of international trade) might be regarded as a classic piece of optimum reasoning, although Ricardo confined himself to the physical level of analysis and was concerned only with the technical

---

[1] This is quite compatible with Ricardo's emphasis on Net Revenue since expansion in total economic activity will increase the absolute size of the Net Revenue, although at a diminishing rate.

optimum and not with the subjective optimum.[1]   Finally, we might consider J. S. Mill's theory of reciprocal demand in international trade as opening up the whole avenue of demand approach.

All these points should be admitted.   But even so, it is a far cry from this to the belief that the " allocative " problem was the *central* preoccupation of the classical economists.   As we have tried to show, the truth of the matter was that, taking classical literature as a whole, considerations concerning " allocative " efficiency were eclipsed by broader considerations concerning the means of raising the physical productivity of labour and expanding the total volume of economic activity.   Once this is admitted, to exalt the " allocative " problem into the central problem of classical economics seems to be nothing short of reading our latter-day preoccupation with the " allocative " problem into the classics through the distorting spectacles provided by the General Equilibrium economists of the Marginal Utility school.   It is time we learned to cure ourselves of this theoretical anthropomorphism and to approach the classical economists in the context of their own intellectual climate.

Were the classical economists then guilty of a confusion between the " technical " and the " economic " problem ?   If we accept their method of analysis at the physical level, the answer on the whole is no.   It is true that the less-gifted followers of the classical economists frequently got themselves lost in the niggling details of technological efficiency.   But none of the major classical economists, with the possible exception of J. S. Mill, seems to be guilty of the " confusion between the technical and the economic problem ", at least in the sense in which the present writer understands the phrase.   That is to say, unlike the full-blooded technocrats they were not bemused by the purely technological or engineering possibilities of increasing output divorced from the economic calculus based on the relation between cost and output.   If they got different results from us (e.g. they would advocate saving beyond the time-preferences of the savers so long as indirect labour yields a higher physical product than direct labour), it is because they were applying the economic calculus to physical quantities of labour and physical quantities of output.   Perhaps Henry Sidgwick restated the classical position most clearly when he explained that

the use of a more efficient machinery would not always result in the efficiency of labour as a whole : since the better instrument might require more labour

---

[1] Cf. Chap. IV, sec. III below.

to make and to keep in repair, and it is possible that this extra labour might be more productive if applied in some other way. Thus an invention *technically* successful may fail *economically* (*Principles of Political Economy*, 3rd ed., pp. 124–5).

Of course, it is certainly true that a full distinction between the " technical " and the " economic " problem is not possible unless we can take into account the consumers' wants ; unless we can choose among the many technically efficient ways of production a particular method which maximises the consumers' satisfaction according to the existing relative prices of .the factors and the products. But may we not start with the physical level of analysis as a first approximation, always remembering that a second and more closer approximation can be attained only by a further analysis at the subjective level ?

After all, even when the economic welfare of society is regarded as consisting in the satisfaction of individuals' wants, it cannot be denied that this subjective economic welfare is as much quantitatively affected by the techno-institutional factors as by the equilibrium process of the market. Or perhaps even more. Therefore, it is not surprising that after decades of work on the " allocative " problem many modern economists should have turned their attention to such problems as output per man hour, the extent of unused capacity, the socially desirable rate of investment, etc., problems having a distinctly classical flavour.[1]

[1] Cf. Colin Clark, *Conditions of Economic Progress*.

CHAPTER II

THE MEASURING ROD OF LABOUR

IN order to appreciate how the labour-theory outlook is bound up with the welfare analysis of the classical economists it is necessary to inquire into their ideas concerning the nature of the " annual produce " or the national dividend and its relation to the economic welfare of society. This is perhaps the least-explored part of their writings, partly because their opinions on the subject are frequently too amorphous to be easily reducible into clear-cut propositions and partly because the term " value ", as they have used it, has the disconcerting habit of changing its meaning from one context to another. But these disjointed notions concerning the measure of " value " and " wealth " deserve a patient study for they seem to lurk at the back of the minds of the classical economists, pervading their whole approach to welfare economics.

I

The common starting-point of all the classical economists may be summarised by the following propositions : (i) Since the essence of the economic process consists in the application of human labour to natural resources, all items of wealth, with negligible exceptions, originate from labour. In transforming natural resources into finished products labour confers " value " on them and it is the possession of " value " which ear-marks the economic goods from free goods. Labour, therefore, may be regarded as the source and measure of value and wealth and the economic goods relevant for social accounting should be confined to the products of labour. (ii) Labour is a more significant measure of value and economic welfare than money. While money is merely a " nominal " standard, a " veil " over the real or the physical processes of production and consumption, labour is intimately and automatically connected with these processes. Thus, while value in terms of money might be inflated or deflated without corresponding changes in the amount of real goods, value in terms of labour would be less subject to such distortions.

However, when it came to the problem of establishing a precise relationship between the measuring rod of labour, " value " and economic welfare, the classical economists were divided into two main camps.

Ricardo and his followers, approaching the subject from the side of Cost and Production, believed that the " value " of a commodity could be most significantly measured by the " quantity of labour embodied " in its production ; that is to say, by the quantity of labour required to overcome the technical obstacles facing its production (cf. M. Dobb, *Political Economy and Capitalism*, p. 20). Accordingly, they proposed to measure the value of the social output as a whole by the aggregate quantity of labour " embodied " in its production. To them, therefore, " value " is the measure of the difficulty of production and should be sharply contrasted with " riches " or economic welfare. If anything, value might be regarded as the inverse index of changes in economic welfare.

Malthus, on the other hand, approaching the subject from the side of Income and Effective Demand, believed that the " value " of a commodity should be measured by the " intensity " of demand for it. This, as we shall see, is not the same thing as the modern concept of the marginal utility of the commodity. Amongst other things Malthus believed that the " intensity of demand " could be more accurately measured by the effort and sacrifice which the consumer is willing to undergo for the commodity rather than by the amount of money he is willing to pay for it. Since he assumed with Adam Smith that the disutility of performing an average unit of labour is constant and identical for everyone, he came to the conclusion that the most significant measure of the value of the commodity is the " quantity of labour commanded " in exchange for it. To him, therefore, " value " is the positive index of economic welfare ; the economic welfare of society cannot be increased unless the increase in the physical magnitude of social output and the increase in its value (resulting from increasing Effective Demand) go hand-in-hand with each other.

The " quantity of labour commanded " measure needs a little more explanation. For ordinary purposes it may be defined as the money value of social output divided by the existing money wage rate (Malthus, *Principles of Political Economy*, 2nd ed., pp. 304–5). Thus the " quantity of labour commanded " by the social output should be equal to the number of wage-units contained in it. Malthus, however, did not always strictly adhere to this definition of the " quantity of labour commanded " and he attached more than an arithmetical significance to it. In the first place, he regarded it as the index of the total volume of employment.

Furthermore, to him the fact that the labourers were willing to give so many units of labour in exchange for a given social output meant that the constituent products of that output represented a subjective income equivalent to the aggregate disutility of performing that number of units of labour. This argument was sustained by the assumption that the disutility of performing an average unit of (unskilled) labour is constant and identical for everyone.

The writings of Adam Smith represent the formative stage of both these Income and the Cost approaches. They served as a half-way house from which Ricardo and Malthus travelled in opposite directions. Thus, while Smith was the originator of Malthus's " labour-commanded " measure of value, he implicitly assumed with Ricardo that the quantity of labour " commanded " by the social output would always at least be equal, if not more than the quantity of labour " embodied " in its production.

It will be helpful to start with a broad outline of the main issues involved in the controversy over the appropriate measuring rod of labour. Adam Smith argued, if a little too implicitly, that in the " early and rude state of society " it did not matter whether we measured " value " by the quantity of labour " embodied " in the production of the commodities or by the quantity of labour " commanded " by them. Labour, being assumed to be the only scarce factor of production, would receive the entire social output as its wages. Therefore the quantity of labour " commanded " would be equal to the quantity of labour " embodied " since they were merely reciprocal aspects of the same transaction. In a developed economy, however, capital and land would become scarce factors and would therefore claim a share of the social output. Thus then the quantity of labour " embodied " would measure the value only of that part of output paid out in the form of wages. In order to obtain the full value of the national dividend, including not only wages, but also rents and profits, we should measure it by the aggregate quantity of labour it could " command " as a whole at the given wage rate.

Ricardo, however, thought that Smith was inconsistent on this point. Following a strictly technical view of production and subsuming capital under the heading of stored up labour, he maintained that even in a developed economy, the value of the gross social output should be measured by the quantity of labour " embodied " in its production. According to him, the sharing of the national dividend merely meant that after the quantity of labour " embodied " had been paid off at the given wage rate, a

Net Revenue would be left over for rents and profits. This did not in any way impugn on the usefulness of the " labour-embodied " measure as the index of the difficulty of overcoming the technical obstacles facing social production. In fact, the size of the Net Revenue on which, he believed, the economic welfare of society depended, could not be calculated except on the basis of the quantity of labour " embodied " or used as outlay in social production.

Malthus advocated the " labour-commanded " measure, but for a different reason from Smith's. He believed that the quantity of labour " embodied " in the production of social output would diverge from the quantity of labour " commanded " by it in the event of a failure in the Effective Demand. The quantity of labour " embodied " would depend on the amount of savings or " advances to labour " and an increase of savings beyond a certain point would result in a collapse of the Effective Demand and a general glut of commodities. Since wages would be normally " sticky " and could not anyhow fall below the subsistence level, prices and incomes would fall much more than any possible reduction in wages. Thus, in such a case, social output would *command* a much lesser quantity of labour than that which had been embodied in its production. Thus the economic welfare of society should be measured by the present value of the social output, by the quantity of labour it could currently command ; the quantity of labour embodied in its production in the past should be dismissed as irrelevant.

From this it will be seen how intimately the different concepts of the measure of value and wealth were bound up with the far-reaching issues of classical economics. The Glut controversy cannot in fact be fully appreciated except in terms of the opposing concepts of the measure of value. In adopting the " labour-commanded " measure of value, Malthus denied the fundamental proposition inherent in Smith's and Ricardo's approach, viz. that the quantity of labour " embodied " in a commodity can always reproduce its own equivalence and generally a further net product and that, therefore, so long as a greater quantity of labour is embodied in social production by a greater amount of saving, the wealth of society cannot fail to increase.

II

What Adam Smith had to say on the subject of the measure of value would have been fairly simple had it not been for his vacillations between the Cost or Output approach and the Income approach to the national dividend.

The first point which has puzzled many students is Smith's change-over from the " labour-embodied " to the " labour-commanded " measure of value (*Wealth of Nations*, Book I, Chap. IV). The explanation, as we have seen, is that Smith considered these two terms to be interchangeable only under the special conditions of the primitive economy where labour is the only scarce factor of production and therefore absorbs the entire national dividend as its wages. In a developed economy, however, Smith believed that the quantity of labour " embodied " could only measure the value of that part of the dividend belonging to wages ; it would fall short of the full value of the dividend by the extent of the shares going into rents and profits. Thus the general measure of the value of the national dividend valid for all types of economy should be the quantity of labour " commanded " by it and not the quantity of labour " embodied " in its production.

> The real value of all the different component parts of price, it must be observed, is measured by the quantity of labour which they can, each of them, purchase or command. Labour measures the value not only of that part which resolves into rent, but also of that which resolves itself into profit.

What then does the " real value " of the " annual produce ", measured by the quantity of labour it can " command ", signify ? It is here that we have to face a more serious difficulty of interpretation, for Smith wavered between two different meanings of the term " value ".

(I) First of all, there is what may be described as the subjective Income approach. This is suggested by the following passage.

> The real price of everything, what everything really costs to the man who wants to acquire it, is the toil and trouble of acquiring it. What everything is really worth to a man who has acquired it and wants to dispose of it or exchange it for something else, is the toil and trouble which it can save to himself, and which it can impose on other people. What is bought with money or with goods is purchased by labour as much as what we acquire by the toil of our own body. They contain the value of a certain quantity of labour which we exchange for what is supposed at the time to contain the value of an equal quantity. Labour was the first price, the original purchase money that was paid for everything (op. cit., Vol. I, Cannan ed., p. 32).

This passage would suggest that Smith considered the essence of man's struggle against nature as consisting in the outlay of subjective disutility rather than, as Ricardo would say, in the physical units of labour. Since outlay and return must be comparable, the statement implies that Smith was trying to arrive at a subjective concept of income as distinct from Ricardo's concept of objective physical output. This impression was strengthened when Smith put forward a basis of measuring the " value " of the social output.

Equal quantities of labour, at all times and places, may be said to be of equal value to the labourer. In his ordinary state of health, strength and spirits ; in the ordinary degree of his skill and dexterity, he must always lay down the same proportion of his ease, liberty and happiness. The price he pays (in terms of disutility of labour) must always be the same, whatever the quantity of goods he receives in exchange for it (ibid., p. 35).

The argument contained in the above two passages may be illustrated by an arithmetical example. Let us suppose that a given social output can " command " 1000 units of labour at the existing price and wage-level ; i.e. the money value of the social output ÷ by the money wage rate = 1000. If the disutility of performing an average unit of labour which is constant and identical for everyone can be measured by k, then the commodities making up the social output should contain that quantity of satisfaction or subjective income which is the equivalent of $1000 \times k$.

(II) However, as we have seen in Chapter I, the main part of Smith's fundamental ideas on the ideal organisation of the economic system were based on a physical level of analysis, that is to say, by assuming that quantities of satisfaction are proportional to quantities of physical product. This would, therefore, suggest a physical output approach (which is not essentially different from Ricardo's) rather than a subjective Income approach. Here the term " real " seems to be identical with the physical quantity of goods. According to this trend of thought it would appear that Smith considered labour as the ideal measure of " real value " simply because he believed that while the purchasing power represented by a given sum of money might depreciate to any extent, that represented by a given quantity of labour could not fall below the amount of real goods that labour would yield when turned to direct production. Thus while the fact that the social output of a given year can command £1000 might not mean very much, the fact that it can command 1000 units of labour does mean that if all these labour units be used " productively " society would be assured of the physical product of 1000 units of labour in the succeeding year. The significance of this argument will be appreciated if we remember Smith's proposition that in a developed economy the quantity of labour " commanded " by the national dividend exceeds the quantity of labour " embodied " in its production by the extent of that part of the dividend paid out in the form of rents and profits.

To illustrate, let us say that the current social output which commands 1000 units of labour is also made up of 1000 units of physical output in terms of the general wage goods W and that out of this, 600 W units are paid out as wages and 200 W units each paid out as rents and profits. Then according to Smith this state of affairs means that : (i) the current social output of 1000 W units is the product of only 600 units of labour " embodied " in its production although it now commands 1000 units of labour and (ii) if the entire amount of labour commanded were used in " productive " purposes, i.e. if the 400 W units making up rents and profits have been saved up entirely and reinvested or " embodied " in the next year's production, the social output of that year would be raised very appreciably. Thus, assuming labour yields a constant return, if 600 units of labour can produce 1000 units of wage goods W, then 1000 units of labour can produce $\dfrac{1000 \times 1000}{600} = 1666$ W units approximately. Assuming that the supply of labour remains elastic at the wage of 1 W unit per unit of labour, then this would give society a command over 1666 units of labour, which is equivalent to a command over the amount of real goods in general which that quantity of labour can be made to produce. Thus the " value " of the social output measured by the quantity of labour " commanded " in the second sense is not the measure of the subjective social income contained in the output ; it is the measure of the maximum possible amount of physical output which can be anticipated next year if all the labour commanded had been used in " productive " purposes. In conjunction with his broad assumption that quantities of satisfaction are proportional to quantities of the physical product, Smith then made use of this second version of the measure of " value " as a cast-iron argument to show that the economic welfare of society could be invariably increased by increasing the amount of saving (op. cit., Vol. I, p. 56).

Smith's first line of approach, which we have called the subjective income approach, petered out and was superseded by the physical output approach. Nevertheless, it deserves some attention for it throws a considerable light not only on Malthus's theory of the measure of value, but also on the dual elements in Smith's doctrine of productive labour (cf. below, Chap. V, sec. II).

Can we seriously maintain that if a given social output commands 1000 units of labour then it must represent a quantity of satisfaction or subjective income to the labourers equivalent to their aggregate disutility in performing these 1000 units of labour ?   Even granting the basic assumptions that quantities of satisfaction are measurable in an absolute sense and that the disutility of performing a standard unit of labour is constant and equal for everyone, there are many difficulties to a satisfactory interpretation of this proposition.   These difficulties can be seen by returning to our example where the given social output which commands 1000 units of labour is made up of 1000 units of wage goods W out of which 600 W units are paid out as wages and 200 W units each are paid out as rent and profit.

(a) Let us assume that the landlords and capitalists decide to consume their entire share of 400 W units by advancing them to " unproductive " labourers who produce " luxury " services.   How does the quantity of labour commanded as the measure of the subjective income work ?   The 600 W units presumably paid out as wages to the " productive " labourers do not give much trouble. At the rate of 1 W unit per unit of labour, the wages bill will command 600 units of productive labour, which will produce 1000 W units next year and the productive labourers will enjoy a subjective income equivalent to the disutility of performing 600 units of labour. But what about the 400 W units advanced to " unproductive " labourers ?   These labourers will also enjoy a subjective income equivalent to performing 400 units of labour ; but, in addition to this, the landlords and capitalists will also receive a certain amount of subjective income from the " luxury " services rendered to them. Thus it would seem that under the condition we have assumed, the total subjective income of society must exceed the equivalence of the disutility of performing 1000 units of labour by the amount of income derived from " luxury " services or unproductive consumption.   Thus Smith could maintain his proposition only by excluding " luxury " services which runs contrary to the whole income approach.

(b) Let us, on the other hand, assume that the landlords and capitalists decide to reinvest their entire (net) income of 400 W units.   Here, since no " luxury " services are produced, the subjective social income may be measured by the equivalence of performing 1000 units of " productive " labour.   But what will happen to the quantity of labour commanded next year ?   At constant returns, the 1000 units of " productive " labour " embodied " in production this year will yield $\dfrac{1000 \times 1000}{600} = 1666$ W units approximately next year.   This will not command 1666 labour units unless the supply of labour is perfectly elastic at the wage rate of 1 W unit. In the short run this assumption is not likely to be fulfilled unless we start from a position with a considerable reserve of unemployed labour. If, for instance, the 1000 units of labour commanded in the first year represent a position of full employment, then the increase of the social output to 1666 W units in the second year would not increase the quantity of labour commanded or volume of employment. Assuming that the entire social output is exchanged for the available supply of labour, it would merely have the effect of raising the wage rate from 1 W unit to $\dfrac{1666}{1000} = 1\frac{2}{3}$ units of W. Thus we have the conclusion that the " value " of the social output measured by the quantity of labour it can " command " will be determined by the given supply of labour, 1000 units in our example, whatever the physical magnitude of the social output and consequently whatever the size of the corresponding subjective income.

Smith's method of getting out of this difficulty was to shift his argument into long-term co-ordinates. Thus in our example (*b*) he would say that since the wage rate is raised to $1\frac{2}{3}$ W units in the second year, it will have the effect of stimulating population. After a suitable (and rather lengthy) time-lag, the increase in social output and income will be registered by an increase in population and the quantity of labour " commanded ". Thus it is not the quantity of labour commanded in a given year, but the *trend* of the quantities of labour commanded year after year which should be regarded as the index of the *trend* in the variation of the social income. The economic welfare of society will be increasing, constant or decreasing as it " commands " an increasing, constant or decreasing quantity of labour year after year. " The most decisive mark of the prosperity of any country is the increase in the number of its inhabitants " (ibid., p. 72).

So much for Smith's concept of the " labour-commanded " measure of " value " as the index of the subjective social income. We have endeavoured to state it as coherently as the textual evidence permits. Once this is got out of the way, what Smith had to say concerning the measure of value in terms of the physical output approach is fairly simple and is crystallised in the following passage.

As in a civilised community there are but few commodities of which the exchangeable value arises from labour only, rent and profit contributing the far greater part of them, so the annual produce of its labour will always be sufficient to purchase or command a much greater quantity of labour than what was employed in raising, preparing and bringing that produce to market. If the society were annually to employ all the labour it can purchase, as the quantity of labour will increase greatly every year, so the produce of every succeeding year would be of a vastly greater value than the foregoing. But there is no country in which the whole annual produce is employed in maintaining the industrious. The idle everywhere consume a greater part of it ; and according to the different proportions in which it is annually divided between those two orders of people, its ordinary or average value must either annually increase, diminish or continue the same from one year to another (ibid., p. 56).

The argument here may again be illustrated by returning to our numerical example where the social output of a given year which commands 1000 units of labour consists in 1000 W units out of which 600 W units are paid out as wages, leaving 400 W units as rents and profits or the net income of the landlords and capitalists. Starting from this situation, there are three possibilities which may be taken as type cases. (i) The capitalists and landlords might decide to reinvest their entire net income of 400 W units and to advance them to " productive " labourers. In this case, as we have seen, the social output in the next year will be increased to 1666 W units approximately calculated at constant returns. (ii) The capitalists and landlords might decide to consume their net income of 400 W units and to advance them to " unproductive " labourers rendering perishable services. Here, since 600 units of " productive " labour is " embodied " in production as before, the social output in the next year will remain constant at 1000 W units. (iii) The capitalists and landlords, instead of merely consuming their net income of 400 W units, might decide to " eat into their capital ". Let us say that now 600 instead of 400 W units are advanced to " unproductive " labourers, leaving only 400 W units for the " productive " ones. On the basis of constant returns, this will reduce the social output of the second year to $\dfrac{1000 \times 400}{600} = 666$ W units approximately.

As indicated by the above passage, Smith believed that it was too much to expect that the capitalists and landlords would reinvest their entire net income in " productive " purposes. Therefore, in practice, the economic system would not attain the upper limit marked by case (i). On the other hand, he pointed out that

the uniform, constant and uninterrupted effort of every man to better his condition, the principle from which public and national, as well as private opulence is originally derived, is frequently powerful enough to maintain the natural progress of things towards improvement, in spite of both the extravagance of government, and of the greatest errors of administration (ibid., p. 325).

Thus again the economic system would not probably sink to the lower limit marked by case (iii), but would fluctuate between the stationary condition of case (ii) and the upper limit of case (i). He then concluded that a fundamental principle of good economic policy was to encourage saving so as to force up the economic system as near as possible to the upper limit marked by case (i) which denoted the condition of the maximum rate of economic progress.

It will be seen that Smith's concept of the quantity of labour " commanded " as the index of potential increase in social output and economic welfare is based on the following assumptions :

(a) It assumes that the supply of labour is perfectly elastic and that an increasing quantity of labour can be commanded year by year so long as an increasing proportion of the social output is laid aside for the wage-fund. This suggests that Smith was concerned with the long-term *trend* or the " ordinary or average value " of the social output rather than with its precise measurement for a given year. Or, at the least, Smith's argument implies that the economic system is in the middle of an expanding phase with a steadily increasing population (cf. op. cit., p. 56).

(b) In our arithmetical example, we have based our calculations on the assumption that labour works under constant returns. This is in fact an understatement of Smith's contention. In contrast to the later classical economists who were preoccupied with the principle of diminishing returns from land, Smith believed that an increase in population by itself would raise the average physical product of labour by overcoming technical indivisibilities. " The greater their number, the more they naturally divide themselves into different classes and subdivisions of employment " and this makes " a smaller quantity of labour produce a greater quantity of work " (ibid., p. 88).

(c) Perhaps the most interesting assumption in Smith's argument is that once a certain quantity of labour is " embodied " in production, it is always capable of producing a social output which can generally command more (or at least never less) than its own equivalence in economic welfare and this surplus product is equal to the share paid out in the form of rents and profits. This implies three things :

(i) It implies that even if the economic welfare of society consists in quantities of satisfaction, these quantities of satisfaction may be regarded as increasing roughly proportionately to the quantities of physical product.

(ii) It implies that there is no appreciable divergence between the physical social output and social income ; that is to say, production and consumption are synchronised and that there are no Malthusian Gluts.

(iii) It finally implies the Marxian proposition that labour creates a "surplus" value and is therefore "exploited" in a developed economy. This is worth pointing out as a refutation of the popular socialist view that Smith was an apologist of the rising capitalist class of his time (cf. E. Roll, A History of Economic Thought, 1st ed., pp. 152–3). A careful reading of Smith's account of the transition of society from the primitive to the developed state would seem to confirm rather than deny the Marxian argument (Smith, op. cit., Book I, Chap. VI). If Smith did not develop the exploitation argument at length it was perhaps because he was more concerned with the changes in the aggregate economic welfare of society as a whole rather than with its distribution among the various classes of the community. Or, as the modern economist would say, he was concerned with the Production Welfare economics, rather than with the Distribution Welfare economics. In any case, before one dubs Adam Smith as a partisan in the class war, one should recall this vigorous passage :

> Is the improvement in the circumstances of the lower ranks of the people to be regarded as an advantage or as an inconveniency to the society ? The answer seems at first sight abundantly plain. Servants, labourers and workmen of different kinds make up the far greater part of every great political society. But what improves the circumstances of the greater part can never be regarded as the inconveniency to the whole. No society can surely be flourishing and happy, of which the greater part of the members are poor and miserable (op. cit., p. 80).

III

Ricardo's approach to the national dividend differed from Smith's and Malthus's in that it was based on a purely materialistic concept of the economic problem, without a leavening consideration of the subjective demand element in any form. Thus he regarded production simply as the technical transformation of resources into finished products and measured Cost, not by the disutility of effort, but by the number of physical units of labour required to overcome the technical obstacles of production.

While Smith and Malthus looked upon "value" in one sense or another as an index of social Income, Ricardo regarded "value" as the index of scarcity, or the difficulty of production, and identified it with social Cost. Hence his sharp contrast between "riches" and

" value ". According to him, the true economic welfare of society or " riches " depends on the abundance of commodities and on the physical magnitude of the social output, whereas " value ", determined by the quantity of labour " embodied " in production, measures the cost of producing that output. If anything, " value " as understood by Ricardo may be regarded as an inverse index of the physical productivity of labour. Thus a technical development which enables the same quantity of labour to produce a greater quantity of products will increase the " riches " ; but it will lower the (average) " value " of these products since they now require a smaller quantity of labour " embodied " per unit in their production (Ricardo, *Principles of Political Economy*, Chap. XX, pp. 182–3, Everyman's ed.).

Having started from this concept of cost or " value " as consisting in the outlay of physical units of labour, Ricardo matched it by a corresponding concept of output or return as consisting in physical units of wage goods which he sometimes referred to under the collective heading of " corn ". He assumed that the rate of wage in terms of " corn " was fixed at the minimum subsistence level determined by " the habits and customs of the people ". Thus given the aggregate quantity of labour " embodied " in social production, he could reduce social output and social cost into the common denominator of " corn ". The difference between the two gave him the " Net Revenue " which he regarded as the most significant measure of the economic welfare of society.

Ricardo's argument can be illustrated by returning to our example in the previous section where a social output of 1000 W units (or " corn ") is produced by 600 units of labour " embodied " and where the rate of wage per unit of labour is equal to 1 unit of W. As we have seen, Smith would have said that (a) the " value " of the social output should be measured by the 1000 units of labour " commanded " by it and that (b) this " value " should be taken as a positive index of the economic welfare of society. In contrast, Ricardo would say that (a) the " value " of social output should be measured by the 600 units of labour " embodied " in its production and that (b) the economic welfare of society would depend, not on the " value " of the gross social output, but on the physical magnitude of the Net Revenue which would be left after the 600 units of labour " embodied " had been paid off at the given wage rate. The Net Revenue in our example is equal to 1000 W units of social output minus 600 W units paid out as wages, i.e. 400 W units which form the share of profits and rents.

Adam Smith constantly magnifies the advantages which a country derives from a large gross, rather than a large net income. Provided its net real income, its rents and profits be the same, it is of no importance whether the nation consists of ten or twelve millions of inhabitants (op. cit., pp. 234–5).

So far, except for the emphasis on the Net Revenue, Ricardo's argument is not significantly different from Smith's second line of approach, i.e. the physical output approach. In the next step, however, Ricardo set a determinate limit to Smith's vision of an almost indefinite economic expansion by introducing the principle of diminishing returns from land. Let us say that the capitalists and landlords in our example decide to reinvest their entire net income of 400 W units. Thus altogether the advances to labour will be 1000 W units and at the one-to-one wage rate 1000 labour units will be available for the next year's social output. At this juncture we have seen Smith's argument that an increase in the quantity of labour would overcome technical indivisibilities and raise average productivity; and that, even at constant returns, the 1000 units of labour turned to " productive " purposes this year should yield $\dfrac{1000 \times 1000}{600} = 1666$ W units next year. Ricardo, however, pointed out that the expansion of production would bring poorer grades of land under cultivation and that consequently social output next year would be considerably less than 1666 W units, let us say 1500 W units. The subsistence fund to be claimed by 1000 units of labour " embodied " being 1000 W units, the net revenue next year would be 500 W units, only 100 units more than this year's Net Revenue. Ricardo further pointed out that, out of this, a larger share, say 225 W units, would be claimed by the landlords since the extension of the margin of cultivation would raise the rents on better grades of land. This would thus leave only 275 W units for profits showing a clear fall in the rate of profit. While 200 W units were obtained from an investment of 600 W units this year, i.e. $33\frac{1}{3}$ per cent., only 275 W units would be obtained by an investment of 1000 W units next year, lowering the rate of profit to $27\frac{1}{2}$ per cent.

Thus Ricardo characterised economic expansion by the falling rate of interest due partly to the diminishing physical returns from land and partly to an ever increasing share of the Net Revenue appropriated as rents. When the expansion had gone far enough, in the absence of technical progress, the rate of profit would tend towards zero and the economic system would come to a rest at the stationary equilibrium, since at that point there would be no incentive to increase saving and expand the volume of economic activity any further (op. cit., pp. 71–7 ; cf. also Chaps. II and X). From this analysis, the quantity of labour " embodied " in social production emerges as the key to social accounting. It determines the Gross Social Output, the Social Cost of producing it and consequently the difference between the two, the Net Revenue, which Ricardo regarded as the true measure of the economic welfare of society. (a) With given land and capital equipment, the size of the Gross Social Output in terms of physical units of " corn " (or wage goods in general) follows as a determinate technical function of the quantity of labour " embodied " in its production. (b) The Social Cost of producing that output can also be determined by multiplying the number of labour units " embodied " with the current rate of real or " corn " wage. (c) The Gross Social Output minus the subsistence fund for labour gives us the Net Revenue, again in units of " corn ". But, as Ricardo explained, the command over the Net Revenue of " corn " means a command over the quantity of labour it can maintain at the current wage rate and that labour may be used for the production of " luxuries ", for " maintaining large fleets and and armies ", or for the production of more " corn " so as to enable society to maintain a greater quantity of " productive " labour in future (op. cit., pp. 268–9).

Granted that the economic welfare of society lies in its Net Revenue, it follows that the main aim of economic policy is to increase the size of that Net Revenue. According to Ricardo, there are two ways of increasing it :

it may be increased by employing a greater portion of the revenue in the maintenance of productive labour, which will not only add to the quantity, but to the value of the mass of the commodities ; or it may be increased, without employing additional labour, by making the same quantity more productive, which will add to the abundance, but not to the value of the commodities (op. cit., p. 186).

The first method, i.e. increasing saving, will add to the " value " of the social output since it increases the quantity of labour " embodied " in its production. Due to the principle of diminishing return from land, the size of the social output will increase but at a diminishing rate. But so long as the additional labour yields some net product over and above its subsistence wage, the absolute size of the Net Revenue will be increased. The second method, i.e. technical progress, will keep the " value " of social output constant since it enables the same quantity of labour " embodied " to produce more. Thus the Gross Social Output being increased with the same outlay of subsistence fund, the Net Revenue will be correspondingly increased.

" Of these two modes of increasing wealth," wrote Ricardo, " the last must be preferred, since it produces the same effect without the privation and diminution in consumption which can never fail to accompany the first mode." However, he pointed out that, apart from the fact that technical discoveries could not be relied on to occur at will, they would not be an unmixed blessing unless introduced gradually so as to serve as an outlet for capital already accumulated and not to divert the existing capital already employed in the maintenance of labour. A sudden and widespread adoption of labour-saving machinery might be frequently " very injurious to the interest of the class of labourers " (op. cit., Chap. XXXI, pp. 265, 270). Thus in practice he had to fall back on the first method of increasing the Net Revenue, i.e. increasing saving. Thus, in the Ricardian system the stationary equilibrium at which there is no incentive for additional saving also denotes the point of maximum welfare since it marks the maximum possible extent to which the absolute size of the Net Revenue of society can be increased.

Let us now turn our attention to a number of minor points which have frequently obscured Ricardo's essentially straightforward approach to the national dividend.

(i) It has become fashionable nowadays to say with J. M. Keynes that Ricardo, unlike Malthus, was concerned only with the Distribution and not with the absolute " amount of national dividend ". The following extract from his letter to Malthus, dated 9th October, 1820, has been cited to support this view (Keynes, *General Theory*, p. 4 n.).

> Political Economy, you think, is an inquiry into the nature and causes of wealth. I think it should be called an inquiry into the laws which determine the division of produce amongst the classes which concur in its formation. No law can be laid down respecting its quantity, but a tolerably accurate one can be laid down respecting proportions. Every day I am more satisfied that the former inquiry is vain and delusive and the latter only the true objects of the science (cf. Ricardo's " Original Preface " to the *Principles*).

This statement, decisive as it sounds, requires careful interpretation. It is true that Ricardo was never interested in the size of the Gross Revenue or the total volume of economic activity for its own sake, but only for its effect on the size of the Net Revenue. This does not, however, mean that Ricardo was not concerned with Production Welfare economics pertaining to the size of the national dividend as distinguished from the Distribution Welfare economics. In the third edition of the *Principles* issued just a year later after the above letter, in 1821, there still remain considerable fragments of what may be regarded as Production Welfare economics concerned with the size of the Net Revenue, as an absolute magnitude and not merely as a proportion (op. cit., Chap. XX, and p. 235, Chap. XXVI, quoted above). It is not possible to tell how far these fragments would be modified had Ricardo been able to revise his writings thoroughly, but, as they stand, a more balanced interpretation would be that Ricardo's denial of the possibility of laying down accurate laws concerning the quantity of wealth does not preclude him from being actively concerned with the means of promoting the economic welfare of society as measured by the absolute size of the Net Revenue. From one point of view it may be said that the significance of the Ricardian Theory of Distribution lies, not as much in explaining how the social output is shared, as in setting a determinate limit to the possibility of increasing social output by increasing capital accumulation and population.

(ii) The second difficulty arises from Ricardo's attempt to qualify his pure labour theory of value by putting a gradually increasing emphasis on the use of machinery and the unequal durability of capital and the different rapidity of the circulation of capital through the process of production in different industries (cf. *Principles*, 3rd ed., Chap. I, secs. iii, iv and v). These qualifications are very damaging to his labour theory in the narrower sense, but they do not create any serious difficulties for his " labour-embodied " approach to national dividend which subsumes durable capital goods used in production under the heading of stored-up labour. Thus the Net Revenue can still be derived by subtracting from the Gross Social Output (*a*) the subsistence fund required to maintain the direct labour used in its production and (*b*) the subsistence fund required to maintain the indirect labour used in repairing or replacing the wear and tear of capital goods used in its production (cf. op. cit., Chap. I, sec. v). However, apart from these later emendations, Ricardo had not given a prominent place to the allowance for the depreciation of capital goods in his social accounting. This is perhaps due to the fact that in the economic life of his times " circulating capital " or " advances to labour " played a quantitatively more important part than durable capital goods. It may also be partly due to the fact that here again Ricardo had not been able to revise his analysis in the light of his later refinements. It was left to J. S. Mill to give a clear formulation of the Marshall-Pigou concept of " maintaining capital intact " (cf. Mill, *Essays on Unsettled Questions of Political Economy*, p. 89).

(iii) The third source of obscurity is created by the perennial difficulties raised by the concept of labour as the "invariable standard of value ", a legacy of Smith. As we have seen Smith had maintained that labour should be treated as possessing invariable " value " because the disutility of performing a standard unit of labour is constant and identical for everyone " at all times and places ". Ricardo, on the other hand, contended that since value is determined by the quantity of labour " embodied ", only that commodity which always required a constant objective quantity of labour in its production could possess invariable value and that no commodity, not even labour, could fulfil this condition ; for the quantity of labour required to produce a given bundle of wage goods which would maintain a labourer at the minimum subsistence level would vary not only with changes in technique but also with the shift in the margin of cultivation (op. cit., Chap. I, sec. vi).

For Adam Smith and Malthus or for anyone who regards " value " as one of the dimensions of wealth, this denial of an invariable standard of value would seem to preclude comparisons of social wealth at different periods of time. For Ricardo, however, this did not follow. Having sharply contrasted " value " with " riches " he could go on to compare the riches of society at different periods of time by comparing the number of physical units of wage goods contained in the respective Net Revenues at two periods. It should be noted that in Ricardo's terminology only the Gross Social Output has a " value " ; the Net Revenue, by definition, is a purely physical magnitude the size of which could be measured in standard units of wage goods. Thus the constant which served as a basis of his comparisons of wealth at different times is the assumption that a given bundle of wage goods would continue to support a labourer at the minimum subsistence level for the periods of time under comparison. Ricardo seemed to believe that even when the subsistence level is interpreted, not as a physiological minimum, but as a social minimum determined by the habits and customs of the people, it would remain fairly stable for long periods. Thus the bundle of subsistence wage goods might require different quantities of labour to produce it at different periods, but it would continue to maintain the same quantity of labour. The weakness in this argument lies in the fact that, accepting that wealth should be measured in physical terms and that the Net Revenue which contains the same number of wage units can maintain the same quantity of labour, this quantity of labour will not represent the same amount of physical wealth to society unless it can also be assumed that the physical productivity of labour has remained constant in the periods under comparison. Ricardo had denied this last assumption when he maintained that no commodity could serve as an invariable standard of value since it would require different quantities of labour to produce it at different periods.

(iv) Fourthly, there is the question whether we should interpret Ricardo's proposition that the " value " of a commodity is determined by the quantity of labour embodied in its production in a relative or an absolute sense. Sometimes Ricardo went out of his way to be a relativist (cf. op. cit., p. 29). But some sort of absolute concept of " value " seems to be necessary in his social accounting. Thus let us say that in a given situation commodities A and B require, respectively, 4 and 6 units of labour to produce them. In a relative sense this proposition merely means that 3 units of A will exchange for 2 units of B. Assuming that each unit of labour requires 1 unit of wage goods W, Ricardo would say that the combined cost of producing A and B was 10 units of wage goods W and this cost would vary in an absolute sense with the absolute quantities of labour required to produce A and B. Suppose that due to technical progress A and B can now be produced by 2 and 3 units of labour respectively. Their relative exchange rate will be unchanged. But Ricardo would say that the social gain consisted in the reduction of the " value " of A and B together from 10 units to 5 units of labour " embodied ".

Finally, the relation between Ricardo's physical Cost approach and the Glut controversy may be briefly outlined. The whole of the Ricardian approach is based on the assumption that a given quantity of labour " embodied " would reproduce a net product in excess of its subsistence fund at any point before the stationary state where it would still reproduce its own upkeep and that the economic welfare of society would increase *pari passu* with an increase in the physical size of its net revenue. This excludes the possibility of maladjustments in transforming social output into social income whence follows the conclusion that the economic welfare of society could be increased so long as labour could produce a net physical product. This perhaps was the most important reason why the Ricardians fought so fiercely to maintain the so-called " Say's Law " significantly enough first expounded by James Mill. For with the fall of " Say's Law " their basic postulates concerning the relation between the physical Net Revenue and the economic welfare would have to be revised and this almost involves the whole of the Ricardian theoretical system.

CHAPTER III

THE MEASURING ROD AND THE GLUT THEORY

ONE of the manifold results of the " Keynesian revolution " is a revaluation of the history of economic thought. It has been suggested that economic theory might have been better served if the Ricardians had not triumphed so completely, as they did, over Malthus in the famous Glut controversy (cf. Keynes, *Essays in Biography*, pp. 139–47 ; *General Theory*, pp. 362–4). This newly found enthusiasm is, however, not without its dangers. It frequently leads to an attempt to draw a sharp contrast between the Malthus and the Ricardo stem of thought, almost to the exclusion of the fact that both stems of thought have grown out of the common parent trunk of Smith's *Wealth of Nations*.

In this chapter we hope to show that the Glut controversy instead of being a disturbance caused by an alien element outside the main stream of classical thought is in fact closely related to the question of the correct measure of value ; and that the process of thought which led Malthus to the Glut theory cannot be fully appreciated without reference to the " labour-commanded " measure of value which he took over from Smith. It is true that Malthus introduced many changes into Smith's measure of value and these will be considered in detail. But he retained enough of Smith's essential premises to justify saying that the continuity of thought had not been broken.

I

The changes which Malthus introduced into the " quantity of labour commanded " measure of value when he took it over from Smith may be grouped under three heads :

(i) Smith had not made any special effort to tighten the relation between his measure of value and his normal cost of production theory of price. He had been content to state merely that although in a developed economy the price of a commodity would be made up of normal wages, rent and profit, labour could measure not only that part of price paid out as wages, but also those parts of price paid out as rent and profit (Smith, op. cit., Vol. I, p. 52). Malthus, on the other hand, seems to give special twists to his theory of value to fit it in with the " labour-commanded " measure of value.

(ii) Smith was frequently guilty of mixing up his measure of value with the measure of Price, Social Output and Social Income. Malthus consistently used it as the measure of the "intensity of demand" for the commodity. Thus he was able to avoid some of Smith's confusing vacillations between the Output and the Income approach and to develop the latter approach more consistently.

(iii) As we have seen, Smith was driven by various difficulties to use the "labour-commanded" measure of value mainly as the long-term index of the secular changes in the wealth of society. In contrast, Malthus incorporated it into a short-period analysis which culminated in the Glut theory.

Malthus's interest in the short-run economics, as contrasted with Ricardo's long-run normal equilibrium, had a decisive influence on his choice of value theory. He concentrated on the market equilibrium and arrived at the conclusion that "the great law of demand and supply is called into action to determine what Adam Smith calls natural prices, as well as what he calls market prices" (Malthus, *Principles of Political Economy*, 2nd ed., L.S.E. Reprints, Book I, Chap. II, sec. iii, p. 71). He relegated the normal cost theory to the background and maintained that

The cost of production itself only influences prices of these commodities as the payment of cost is the necessary condition of their continued supply to the extent of the effectual demand for them (op. cit., p. 71).

He did not regard this indirect influence as decisive since, if the cost of production were to rise,

without the increase in the intensity of demand—the commodity would cease to be produced, that is, the failure of the supply would be contingent upon the will or power to make a greater sacrifice for the object sought (ibid., p. 65).

He next drew a sharp distinction between the "extent of demand" and the "intensity of demand". According to him, the "extent of demand" merely determines the quantity demanded which, in equilibrium, is always equal to the quantity supplied ; the price of the commodity, on the other hand, is determined by the "intensity of demand" (ibid., pp. 62–3).

He defined the "intensity of demand" as follows :

Demand has been described as the will to purchase, combined with the means of purchasing. The greater degree of this will, and of these means of purchasing when directed to any particular commodity wanted, the greater or more intense may be said to be the demand for it (op. cit., p. 63).

It is difficult to say how far this concept of the "intensity of demand" should be regarded as a development in the direction

of the marginal utility theory.   Nassau Senior's path-breaking work
on the subject was known to Malthus.   But in his desire to contrast
it with the " extent " of demand Malthus frequently spoke of the
" intensity " of demand for a commodity as though it were given
by tastes and purchasing powers of the consumers alone, almost
independently of the quantity involved.

Thus we are told that even if the " extent " of the demand were
doubled (presumably at the previous equilibrium price) with the
given supply, price need not necessarily rise unless the " intensity "
of demand is also increased ; and conversely that even if the
quantity available were halved, price need not rise unless the
" intensity " of demand is also increased (op. cit., p. 64).   It does
not require a great knowledge of the modern theory of value to
show that, other things remaining the same, both examples given
by Malthus necessarily imply an increase in the marginal " intensity " of demand and a rise in price ; unless of course we assume
the extreme case of a perfectly elastic or horizontal demand curve.
Malthus missed the essential point of the principle of diminishing
marginal utility when he regarded the " extent " and the " intensity " of demand as separate variables each of which may change
without involving a change in the other (cf., however, op. cit.,
p. 69 n.).

Malthus's theory does not admit of a consistent interpretation
even on the basis of the assumption of a perfectly elastic or horizontal
demand curve.   For, a little later taking the case where the cost of
production is doubled, Malthus argued :

> The quantity of the commodity brought to the market under these circum-
> stances might be extremely different.   It might be reduced to the supply of a
> single individual, or might remain precisely the same as before.   If it were
> reduced to the supply of a single individual, it would be proof that only one of
> the former purchasers was both able and willing to make an effectual demand
> for it at the advanced price.   If the supply remained the same, it would be proof
> that all the purchasers were in this state, but the expression of this intensity of
> demand had not been rendered necessary on account of the facility with which
> the article had been previously produced (ibid., p. 65).

The first part of this argument admits the possibility of different
buyers having different intensities of demand for the same commodity, but does not mention the possibility of the same buyer
having different intensities of demand for successive units of the
commodity.   The second part implies a perfectly inelastic or vertical
demand curve, for under no other condition would the quantity
demanded remain " precisely the same as before " after the cost of
production and price has been doubled.

On the whole it seems, therefore, fair to say that Malthus has failed to grasp the principle of diminishing marginal utility and the related concept of the continuous forward falling demand curve. He has failed in particular to understand the equilibrium mechanism which adjusts the " intensity " of demand to price *at the margin* by a simultaneous adjustment of the " extent " of demand to the given supply.

However, the motive underlying Malthus's emphasis on the " intensity of demand " as the main determinant of value is not difficult to guess. All his seemingly diffuse arguments seem to lead to the following proposition, viz. if the

intensity of demand for the commodity [at some unspecified point on its demand curve][1] is below its cost of production then it will cease to be produced ; the failure of the supply would be contingent on the failure of the will or power to make a greater sacrifice for the object sought (ibid., p. 65).

Malthus realised that one of the necessary conditions of effective demand is the adaptation of the commodities to the wants of the consumers in suitable quantities. He pointed out that the supply of different commodities should be " so *proportioned* as to give them their *proper* value " and that value is " not only the great stimulus to production of all kinds of wealth, but the great regulator of the forms and relative quantities in which it shall exist " (ibid., pp. 301–2). But while not neglecting this " allocative " aspect of the problem, what impressed him more was that even if there was the will to consume, the " extent " of demand or the consuming capacity would not be effective, unless the " intensity " of demand was raised to the required degree by an adequate purchasing power.

At this point we can see how Malthus's sophistry brought the two divergent parts of his value theory, the one which implies a perfectly elastic demand and the other which implies a perfectly inelastic demand, to serve a common purpose. With a perfectly elastic or horizontal demand curve and assuming, as Malthus always implicitly did, constant cost, the commodity would not be produced if the cost of production rises above the ceiling of the demand price. But if it were equal to or less than the full " intensity of demand ", then the output of the commodity would be determined by the total amount of purchasing power in the hand of the consumers. In either case equilibrium output will be equal to $\frac{\text{total purchasing power}}{\text{average cost of production}}$. With a perfectly inelastic or vertical

---

[1] Parentheses mine.

demand curve, even if a given output at a given cost is equal to the " extent " of the demand, it will not be cleared off the market unless the total purchasing power of the consumers is equal to the volume of output × average cost. In short, the net effect of Malthus's emphasis on the " intensity of demand " which is not a strict function of the amount of the commodity is to focus on purchasing power as the chief determinant of output and the effective demand for it.

II

Let us now trace how this peculiar value theory of Malthus dovetails into the " labour-commanded " measure of value. To do so, we must start from Malthus's distinction between the " extrinsic " and the " intrinsic " value borrowed from Nassau Senior (cf. Senior, *Political Economy*, Library of Economics, p. 20).

Malthus defined the " extrinsic " value of a commodity as its general purchasing power over all other commodities, i.e. what we normally understand by its exchange value. He pointed out that this " extrinsic " value would vary, not only with the intensity of demand for, and the cost of production of, the particular commodity in question, but with all the general equilibrium forces operating on the economic system at large. This being so, he frankly admitted that it was not possible to find an accurate measure of value in this sense. He, however, added that even if it were possible to measure the " extrinsic " value, it would not be a significant measure since it would not tell us how much a given commodity is capable of contributing to the economic welfare of society on its own merits alone (Malthus, op. cit., pp. 57–8).

Thus in order to isolate the real significance of a particular commodity from the viewpoint of society as a whole, undistorted by random general equilibrium forces, he proposed to concentrate on its " intrinsic " value. This he defined as the purchasing power of the commodity as determined by those causes directly arising out of its own particular conditions of production and consumption. He believed that so long as the " intensity of demand " for a given commodity and the technical difficulties of producing it remained unchanged, its " intrinsic " or " real " worth to society would remain constant, regardless of whatever variations that might have taken place in its " extrinsic " or " nominal " rate of exchange with other commodities (ibid., p. 57).

As we have seen, Malthus considered the " intensity of demand " to be the more fundamental determinant of value than cost of production. Thus the problem of measuring the " intrinsic " value resolved itself into the problem of measuring the " intensity of demand ". The " intensity of demand " for a given commodity, he maintained, could only be measured by the amount of sacrifice in terms of labour disutility which the individual would be willing to make in order to acquire it. Since he assumed, with Adam Smith, that the disutility of performing a standard unit of labour is constant and identical for everyone at all times and places, he then arrived at the proposition for which he had been building up his arguments, viz. the " intensity of demand " for a given commodity and consequently its " intrinsic " value should be measured by the quantity of labour which the individual would be willing to exchange for it ; in other words, the quantity of labour which it can " command " (cf. ibid., Book I, Chap. II, secs. i–v).

From this the rest of the argument follows. The disutility of labour being postulated to be invariable, the willingness to continue exchanging a constant quantity of labour for a given commodity must always be counterbalanced by the prospect of a similarly constant quantity of economic welfare from the commodity. Thus so long as the commodity continues to exchange for the same quantity of labour, its " intrinsic " worth to society remains unchanged, irrespective of whatever changes which may take place in its relative or " extrinsic " rate of exchange with other commodities. It is only when the commodity " commands " a different quantity of labour that its " intrinsic " value may be considered to have undergone a real change. In all such cases, labour being considered to be invariable in " value " by virtue of its constant disutility, the causes of the change in the exchange rate between labour and the commodity must originate from the side of the commodity. It must mean a change in the " intrinsic " conditions of its production and consumption as reflected by a change in the " intensity of demand " for it (cf. ibid., p. 99).

It is not difficult to see that Malthus's theory of the " intrinsic " value will not withstand a critical examination. Amongst other faults, it is based on a very rigid absolute concept of value. Thus to the modern reader it must appear quite arbitrary to say that whenever a change in the exchange rate between labour and the commodity occurs, it is the value of the commodity which has changed and not the " value " of labour. This is particularly so when such a change can be easily due to causes apparently operating on the side of labour, such as changes in the demand and supply for labour, or in its physical productivity resulting in a change of the level of wages. One plausible defence that can be put forward for Malthus is to say that the value of labour, i.e. the general wage level, being relatively more stable than the value of any one commodity, a given change in the quantity of labour " commanded " by that commodity is more likely to reflect a change in its particular conditions of production and consumption rather than a change in the general purchasing power of labour.

However, rightly or wrongly, Malthus believed that in concentrating on the " intrinsic " value measured in terms of labour as opposed to the " extrinsic " value measured in terms of money or general purchasing power, he had arrived at the key to the fundamental working of the economic system and its relation to the economic welfare of society. He claimed that his concept of " intrinsic " value emphasises the relation, not between one commodity and another, but between the commodity and man in his rôle as producer and consumer. It attempts to measure to what extent a given commodity is adapted to the wants of the consumers, the majority of whom are labourers, and what amount of sacrifice in terms of labour effort they are willing to make in order to acquire the commodity. On this basis Malthus tried later on to show that the fundamental condition of a successful transformation of society's productive resources into economic well-being depends on the smooth exchange, not as much between commodities and commodities, as between " the mass of commodities " on one side, and human labour on the other. Thus he maintained that the fatal weakness of Say's Law lay in the fact that while it insisted that " productions are always bought by production ", it neglected the more important relation between commodities in general and human beings as producers and consumers (ibid., pp. 316–17).

III

From the quantity of labour " commanded " by the commodity as the measure of its " intrinsic " value, Malthus proceeded to argue that the value of the national dividend or the Gross Revenue should be measured by " the quantity of standard labour which the whole yearly produce would exchange for, according to the actual money prices of the labour and the commodities at the time " (ibid., pp. 304–5). In opposition to Ricardo's physical output approach he pointed out that the wealth of a country does not " increase in proportion to the mere quantity of what comes under the denomination of wealth, because the various articles of which this quantity is composed may not be so proportioned to the wants and powers of the society to give them their proper value ". On the other hand, he conceded that " an increase in value may take place under an actual diminution of commodities ". Thus

> It appears then that the wealth of a country depends partly upon the quantity of produce obtained by labour, and partly upon such adaptation of this quantity to the wants and powers of the existing population as is calculated to give it value. Nothing can be more certain than that it is not determined by either of them alone (ibid., p. 301).

In reiterating this Smithian " labour-commanded " measure of value, Malthus carried out the Income approach more consistently than Smith had done. As we have seen, Smith's Income approach petered out since instead of consistently regarding the aggregate quantity of labour " commanded " by the social output as the measure of *current* social income, Smith went on to use the quantity of labour " commanded " this year as the measure of potential physical output *next year*, if the whole of the available labour had been turned to " productive " uses. It was left to Malthus to develop the concept of the quantity of labour commanded as the demand price which the consumers-cum-labourers are willing to pay for the commodities contained in the current social output.

The relation between Malthus's theory of " intrinsic " value and his Income approach to the national dividend may be illustrated by using a numerical example. Let the physical social output of a given year be made up of 1000 units of commodity A and 1000 units of commodity B, both belonging to the general category of " necessities " or wage goods denoted by the symbol W in our previous examples. Let the money costs of production per unit of A and B be equal to the wage of 2 and 3 units of labour respectively at the current rate of money wage.

In this example Malthus would say that the " extrinsic " rate of exchange between A and B will be 3 : 2. But this side of the situation would not interest him very much. Even his statement that the relative outputs of the commodities should be " so proportioned to the wants and powers of society to give them proper value " remains vague since, as we have seen, he had not completely grasped the equilibrium adjustments of relative outputs and prices at the margin. But what would interest him more would be the " intrinsic " value of each commodity and the conditions of the aggregate effective demand for the whole social output.

Thus he would argue that the commodity A would not be produced unless the "intensity of demand" for each unit of it is strong enough to counterbalance the disutility of the effort of 2 units of labour. Similarly, the commodity B would not be produced unless the "intensity of demand" for it counterbalances the disutility of 3 units of labour. Thus the first condition of effective demand for the whole social output would be that the consumers are willing to undergo the disutility of 2000 plus 3000, i.e. 5000 units of labour in order to consume 1000 units of A and 1000 units of B. In Malthus's own words : "where wealth and value are perhaps most nearly connected is in the necessity of the latter to produce the former" and " it is the sacrifice of labour or labour's worth, which the people are willing to make in order to obtain them, that in the actual state of things may be said to be *almost the sole cause* of the existence of wealth " (ibid., pp. 301–2).

But even when there is the will to consume, the demand will not be effective unless backed up by purchasing power. The majority of the consumers of wage goods being labourers, having no other source of income than their own wages, their demand will not be effective unless they are employed. Thus, in order that the whole output of A and B should effectively command the required 5000 units of labour in our example, the total volume of employment must be at least 5000 units of labour. This is the second condition of effective demand.

Let us now suppose that the commodities A and B have been produced by labour in co-operation with other factors of production and that although the money cost of producing 1000 units of A and 1000 units of B is equal to the money wages of 5000 units of labour, only 3000 units of labour has been actually used in their production ; that is to say, the remaining part of the cost, equivalent to the wages of 2000 units of labour, has been paid out as rent and profit. Then, assuming that the non-labouring classes have no demand for the wage goods A and B, the total wages paid out in their production will fall short of the purchasing power required to purchase the whole output of A and B by that amount equivalent to the wages of 2000 units of labour. It is at this point that Malthus advocated " unproductive " consumption in the form of direct personal services and " material luxuries " as distinct from wage goods. He argued that unless the gap in purchasing power is filled by " unproductive " consumption creating employment for 2000 units of labour, the " value " of 1000 units of A and 1000 units of B would be less than their " cost ", both magnitudes measured in wage units. And then the incentive to continue the same output of A and B would collapse, creating a Glut of these commodities and dragging down the economic system into a severe depression.

This illustration will bring out the double function of the " labour-commanded " measure of value in Malthus's scheme of thought. In the first place, it is a measure of the " intensity of demand " for commodities contained in a given social output. Thus, if the disutility of performing a standard unit of labour, assumed to be constant and identical for everyone is k, and if the consumers are willing to exchange 5000 units of labour for the given output, then it must contain a subjective income equivalent to $5000 \times k$. In the second place, it implies the far-reaching proposition that the economic welfare of society should be measured by the total volume of employment it can generate each year. Malthus believed that while Ricardo's " labour-embodied " physical output approach could merely measure the productive capacity of society, his " labour-commanded " approach had succeeded in measuring to what extent this productive capacity is actually transformed into consumption and income by the Effective Demand.

In spite of these developments, however, Malthus's " labour-commanded " measure is still subject to the drawbacks inherent in Smith's original formulation of the idea (cf. above, Chap. II, sec. II). In particular, the " quantity of labour commanded " seems to refer only to that part of the social output consisting of wage goods. Even assuming that social output in those days was in fact mainly made up of wage goods or " necessities " and that subjective income can be treated as the reciprocal of disutility, the " quantity of labour commanded " calculated upon the Smith-Malthus plan will not measure the full amount of social income accruing in a given year, except under the special conditions of the primitive community where the entire social output is paid out as wages. To return to our previous example, where the cost of producing 1000 units of A and 1000 units of B is equal to the value of 5000 units of labour, out of which the value of 3000 units of labour is paid out as wages, and that of 2000 units of labour is paid out in the form of rent and profit. Then, as we have seen, in order that the whole output of the wage goods A and B should " command " the required 5000 units of labour, 2000 units of these would have to be given employment by " unproductive " consumption on the part of the landlords and capitalists. Thus the 5000 units of labour " commanded " merely measure the income represented by the output of wage goods A and B. The additional income rendered in the form of " material luxuries " and personal services by the 2000 units of " unproductive " labour to the landlords and capitalists is not included in the measure.   Since Malthus himself declared that " luxuries are a part of wealth as well as necessities ", the " labour-commanded " measure is clearly inadequate.   This sort of underestimate will always occur so long as rents and profits form a part of the cost of production of the wage goods so that some "unproductive " consumption is necessary to create enough employment and purchasing power to pay for the total cost of the wage goods.

Further it will be seen that once the limit of full employment is reached, the quantity of labour " commanded " by the social output will remain constant ; further increase in the size of social output, say due to increase in physical productivity, will result in a rise in wages and not in an increase in the quantity of labour " commanded ".   And yet there would have been a definite increase in the economic welfare of society from any point of view.   It was this difficulty which led Smith to shift his analysis into long-term co-ordinates and to argue that the rise in wages would stimulate population so that the initial increase in the wealth of society would be registered after a suitable time-lag by its ability to " command " a greater quantity of labour than before.   Malthus, with his insistence on the short-period analysis, could not even make use of this way of escape and his attempt to cover up the difficulty is distressingly weak.   Thus we are told :

> It will be readily understood that the labour which the commodities command or purchase is used entirely as a measure, and has little more relation to the actual quantity of labour employed in the country, than a thousand feet in length has to the number of foot rules existing in the town where the length may be measured (ibid., p. 307).

The falseness of this analogy, of course, lies in the fact that the size of the wage unit is not given once for all like that of a foot rule, but is determined by the available quantity of labour on the one side, and the size of the social output with which it is to be exchanged on the other.   In talking of a hypothetical quantity of labour society could command, which apparently has no relation to the actual number of labour units available, Malthus seems to be thinking in terms of a constant wage rate which remains unaffected by changes in the demand and supply of labour.   It is rather surprising that he should fail to apply his famous Law of Population in this connection.   This does not, however, affect the main part of his argument which is concerned with situations below the full employment level.

IV

We are now able to outline the relation between the different concepts of the measure of value and the Glut controversy. Whatever his original intentions, Smith had ended by using the " labour-commanded " measure of value as the long-term index of the secular changes in the wealth of society. He could, therefore, ignore the time-lag between the increase in savings and the size of the wage fund and the subsequent increase in population. Thus, assuming an elastic supply of labour, he argued that so long as the net revenue, measured by the excess of the quantity of labour " commanded " by the social output over that which had been " embodied " in its production, was reinvested in the wage fund, there would always be more productive labourers forthcoming who would add to the quantity of the social output. Profits need not fall, for wages in this " progressive " state of society would be rising and the increasing population would generate enough Effective Demand to absorb the increasing output it was helping to produce in its stride. Since labour was assumed to work at least under constant, if not increasing, returns, this process of expansion could go on almost indefinitely so long as an increasing rate of accumulation was maintained. Thus Smith concluded : " The most decisive mark of the prosperity of any country is the increase in the number of its inhabitants " (Smith, op. cit., Vol. I, p. 72).

Ricardo, although holding a formally different measure of value from Smith, had also arrived at a similar conclusion. His principle of diminishing returns from land did not negate Smith's theory of economic expansion ; it merely set a determinate, if rather remote, limit to that expansion at the stationary equilibrium. Before that limit was reached, every additional amount of saving would add to the wealth of society. Progressive accumulation and the extension of the margin of cultivation would lower the rate of the net productivity of investment ; but capital accumulation would nevertheless add to the absolute size of the Net Revenue and consequently the economic welfare of society, although at a successively diminishing rate.

We have already noted the reason why Smith and Ricardo arrived at the same conclusion concerning the beneficial effect of saving while holding formally different measures of value. It is because they started from the common assumption that once a certain quantity of labour is used or " embodied " in production the resulting output would always have a " value " which is at least equal, if not more than, the " value " represented by the original quantity of labour " embodied " in it.   Both Smith and Ricardo denied the possibility of the " value " of an output falling below the " value " represented by the quantity of labour " embodied " in its production.   Granted this, capital accumulation would always add to the wealth of society because the investment of a certain quantity of labour would under all circumstances reproduce at least its own equivalent of wealth.   It was left for Malthus to show that if saving is carried beyond a certain critical point, the social output would " command " less labour than the quantity originally " embodied " in its production.   The " value " of social output would then be less than its cost of production.

Malthus must not be looked upon as an out-and-out opponent of saving.   Essentially a moderate man, he believed in the importance of the correct proportion, the correct " balance between production and consumption ".   While his main theme was to show that a Glut would result if saving is carried too far, he readily admitted that the wealth of society could not increase if the entire Net Revenue was consumed " unproductively " (ibid., p. 235). What he really objected to was Smith's and Ricardo's uncompromising dictum that saving offered an infallible motive power of economic expansion under all circumstances.   He believed that they, particularly Ricardo, had arrived at a wrong conclusion, since they were too preoccupied with the extreme long-term limit of economic expansion without pausing to consider what *regulates* the actual step-by-step process of expansion, and whether the motive power of expansion might not break down before the extreme limit of the stationary equilibrium is reached (ibid., Book I, Chap. V, secs. ii and iii).

Malthus's criticism of the Smith-Ricardo theory of economic expansion may be summarised as follows :

First of all, he pointed out that they assumed an elastic supply of labour which responds to an increase in demand for it without any time-lag, whereas in real life " an increase of labourers cannot be brought to market, in consequence of a particular demand, till after the lapse of sixteen or eighteen years " (ibid., pp. 319–20). Thus even when considered in purely physical terms, capital accumulation, however great, cannot expand economic activity beyond the point marked by the full employment of the existing supply of labour.   Further, even assuming that the supply of labour is expanding as the result of past high wages, " a country is always liable to increase in the quantity of funds for the maintenance of labour faster than the increase in population " (ibid., p. 320). Thus, economic expansion, instead of being continuously stimulated by increasing accumulation as Smith and Ricardo supposed, will be tripped up and checked by the short-term limit of full employment long before the extreme limit of the stationary state is reached (ibid., p. 402).

Next he proceeded to argue that when we pass from the consideration of the maximum possible physical output to the consideration of maximum possible social income, the limit to the desirable amount of saving will be still further and more drastically reduced. The optimum amount of saving required to maximise the social income, he believed, is always less than that which is required to maintain all the available supply of labour in " productive " employment ; for, long before the entire supply of labour could be transferred to " productive " uses, the Effective Demand would have collapsed, leaving the economic system in a state of Glut, sharply contracting the quantity of labour " commanded " by the social output.

Malthus's concept of the optimum amount of saving which would enable the social output to " command " the greatest possible amount of labour is, however, rather vague. It seems to be governed by the following two conditions :

(i) To begin with, it is clear that there must be enough saving to maintain a sufficient number of " productive " labourers to produce basic wage goods, not only for themselves, but also for other labourers catering for the " unproductive " consumption of the landlords and capitalists. Malthus believed that the proportion of this necessary amount of saving to the total resources of society would vary with its productive capacity. In a primitive society with low productivity, the whole population may be needed for the production of necessities, whereas in a technically developed society a large surplus of labour would be left after a sufficient amount of wage goods has been produced (ibid., pp. 305–6). This surplus labour would have to be given employment somehow or other by consumption on the parts of the landlords and capitalists. Otherwise, the surplus labourers would lack the purchasing power to buy the wage goods and this would result in a reduction of employment among the " productive " labourers themselves in the wage-goods industries which might spread a depression to other sectors of the economic system.

(ii) This is, however, not the end of the story. Malthus's

attitude towards any sort of physical output, whether it consists of basic wage goods or of articles of luxury and comfort is almost like that of the story-book murderer's towards the body of his victim : it has to be disposed of without a hitch. Thus he proceeded to draw a distinction between consumption in the form of " material luxuries " and consumption in the form of direct personal services. The former although catering for " unproductive consumption " involves the problem of disposing of the output, of creating a sufficient Effective Demand, while the personal services are consumed directly as they are produced, leaving no physical output behind. In his terminology consumption in the form of material luxuries adds to the size of the annual produce but may or may not create a corresponding " value ", whereas consumption in the form of direct personal services creates " value " but does not add to the physical magnitude of social output. Since the ideal condition of economic progress requires both an increase in " value " and in physical output, he advocated a correct balance between these two modes of using the surplus revenue. Thus :

if the net revenue of a country could only be employed in the maintenance of menial servants and soldiers, there is every reason to think that the stimulus to production in modern states would be greatly diminished, and that the cultivation of the soil would be carried on with the same kind of indolence and slackness as in the feudal times.

On the other hand, if the whole surplus beyond what was required for the support of those who were employed in the production of necessities could be spent in no other way than in the production and purchase of *material* luxuries and conveniences, if no menial servants can be kept to take care of houses, furniture, carriages, horses, etc., it is quite clear that the demand for material luxuries would very soon abate, and the owners of land and capital would have very slender motives to employ them in the most productive manner.

It is clearly then the operation of both stimulants, under the most favourable proportions, which is likely to give the most effective encouragement even to the production of necessaries (ibid., pp. 235-6).

This passage throws a new light on the frequently quoted statement of Malthus that the resources of political economy are unequal to determine " what the proportion is between the productive labourers and those engaged in personal services, which affords the greatest encouragement to the continued increase of wealth " (Malthus, ibid., p. 399 ; Keynes, *General Theory*, p. 363). Apparently, in speaking of a happy medium between the two extremes, Malthus was not merely thinking of the proportion between saving and consumption in the ordinary sense, but also of the proportion between consumption in the form of " material luxuries " and consumption in the form of direct personal services. In the above context, where he contrasted " productive " labourers and those engaged in personal services, the labourers producing " material luxuries " are classified under the head of " productive " labour since they are producing a tangible physical output (cf. Malthus, ibid., p. 35).

Let us now consider some of the detailed points in Malthus's argument to show that if saving is carried beyond the optimum limit, it must depress general economic activity irrespective of whether it is invested in the wage-goods industries or in industries producing " material luxuries and conveniences ".

He began from the case where the additional saving is invested in the wage-goods industries. This is what Smith and Ricardo had regarded as the normal mode of economic expansion ; they had argued that by increasing the output of wage goods, society would be able to maintain a greater number of productive labourers who would in their turn produce more wage goods and this process of expanding the social output could go on up to the limit of the stationary state. Malthus considered this argument fallacious since, in the short run, population cannot increase sufficiently enough to absorb the additional output of wage goods, and the demand for wage goods will remain fairly inelastic. Thus additional saving directed towards the expansion of the output of wage goods must sooner or later result in a Glut of these articles and the consequent depression will be all the more intensified because the surplus income of the landlords and capitalists which should have been used in creating employment and purchasing power by consumption has been diverted to saving.

In this context he complained of Ricardo's inconsistency in arguing that savings can never be redundant because human desire for luxuries and new commodities is unlimited. He pointed out that the actual effect of saving which Ricardo prescribed was to transfer resources from the production of secondary and tertiary commodities to the production of primary wage goods and to reduce the variety of commodities available for consumption (ibid., pp. 324–6).

It is to found a doctrine upon the *unlimited* desire of mankind to consume ; then to suppose this desire *limited* in order to save capital, and thus completely alter the premises, and yet still maintain that the doctrine is true (ibid., p. 402).

But what will happen if the more enterprising capitalists decide to use the additional saving in the production of semi-luxury articles instead of wage goods for the labourers ?   Here Malthus admitted that " a new commodity thrown into the market " might stimulate some demand though allowance must be made for the difficulty of " fabricating " such a commodity, the slow growth of tastes for luxuries and the possible preference of the labourers for " indolence " to a higher standard of living (ibid., pp. 318, 320).

He also seems to believe that so long as the luxury goods are aimed at labourers only, the total Effective Demand forthcoming will never be sufficient to make such investments profitable.   The expected receipts of the producers in this case might at the most be equal to their advances to the labourers, but never more than it to leave a net profit.

A man whose only possible possession is labour has, or has not, an effective demand for produce according as his labour is, or is not, in demand by those who have the disposal of the produce.   And no productive labour can ever be in demand with a view to profit unless the produce when obtained is of greater value than the labour which obtained it.   No fresh hands can be employed in any sort of industry merely in consequence of the demand for its produce occasioned by the persons employed (ibid., pp. 311–12).

He thus concluded that

there must be something in the previous state of demand and supply for the commodity in question, or in its price, antecedent to and independent of the demand occasioned by the new labourers, in order to warrant the employment of an additional number of people in its production.

And this " something " must be created either by the direct demand of landlords and capitalists for the luxury articles or the demand for personal services which enables the persons so employed to purchase some of the luxury articles.

Malthus did not pay much attention to the case where the additional saving is invested in the production of durable capital goods.   In this, like most of the classical economists, he was thinking in terms of his contemporary economic life where the circulation capital or " advances to labour " played a quantitatively more important part than investment in fixed capital goods.   He agreed with Ricardo that a gradual introduction of durable capital goods would be generally beneficial, but like any other cause which increases the productive capacity, he did not believe that it could by itself provide a basis for a continual economic expansion.   Since the introduction of machinery enables society to produce the necessary wage goods with a smaller quantity of labour, it must be counterbalanced by an increase in " unproductive " consumption (ibid., pp. 236–8, 351–4).

On the whole, Malthus's concept of " Economic Progress ", to which he devoted the whole of his Book II, must appear rather discouraging to the modern reader (though perhaps not more so than Ricardo's). He would perhaps concede that in the long run, with the growing prosperity and development of tastes for new commodities on the part of the masses of the people, the " luxury " industries might be able to offer an increasing outlet for new savings, thus shifting the optimum amount of saving beyond that which is required to finance the production of wage goods only. But even if the labourers increase their standard of living instead of their numbers, there would be many obstacles before the increase in the productive capacity of society could be transformed into an increase in the standard of living of the masses. For one thing, so long as rents and profits form a considerable share of the national dividend, earnings in the form of wages by itself would not provide the necessary effective demand for the entire social output ; and the gap in purchasing power would have to be filled by consumption on the part of the landlords and capitalists. Further, he believed that " an efficient taste for luxuries and conveniences, that is, such a taste as will properly stimulate industry, instead of being ready to appear at the moment it is required is a plant of slow growth " (ibid., p. 321). Thus a rapid increase in saving with a view to investment in the mass production of secondary and tertiary goods would strain the gradual process of the diffusion of wants to a breaking point and cause a Glut. Thus, according to him, the only reliable alternative left was to make use of the firmly rooted demand of the landlords and capitalists for " material luxuries " and personal services (which he incidentally regarded as complementary goods) and to allocate the surplus revenue judiciously among these two modes of consumption. This would provide a gradual but continuous stimulus for economic progress.

It seems, therefore, fair to say that Malthus's concept of Economic Progress is of a negative character. It does not offer a solution for increasing the standard of living of the masses of the people at least in the immediate future. It seems to be concerned mainly with the prevention of economic retrogression in the form of Gluts and mass unemployment. The only people who are able to enjoy a positive increase in economic welfare seem to be the landlords and capitalists and even when Malthus spoke of " Distribution " as a stimulus to Production, he seems to be thinking of " Distribution " not in the sense of equalisation of incomes, but in the sense of

" circulation of goods " induced by better transport, opening up of commerce and brisk buying and selling in a general sense (ibid., Book II, secs. vii–ix).

To summarise Malthus's arguments : he maintained that if saving is carried beyond the optimum point necessary to finance that physical output of wage goods and " material luxuries " for which there is a sufficient effective demand, there would be a general decline in profits and employment leading on to a Glut and a depression. In terms of the measuring rod of labour, this means that the social output would now " command " a much lesser quantity of labour than the equivalent of the quantity of labour " embodied " in its production. The shrinkage in social income and purchasing power would be proportionate to the reduction in the quantity of labour " commanded ". It is only when the social output " commands " the entire existing supply of labour that an efficient synchronisation between society's capacity to produce and to consume is attained. Ricardo had missed this fundamental point due to his " labour-embodied " physical output approach which considered " value " merely as a measure of the technical obstacles of production and not as a measure of the " intensity " of demand for the product. It is only in the light of Malthus's " labour-commanded " measure and his concept of the " intrinsic " value that we can fully appreciate Malthus's famous reply to the Ricardians :

In the first place, they have considered commodities as if they were so many mathematical figures, or arithmetical characters, the relations of which were to be compared, instead of articles of consumption, which must of course be referred to the numbers and wants of the consumers.

If commodities were only to be compared and exchanged with each other, then indeed it would be true that, if they were all increased in their proper proportions to any extent, they would continue to bear among themselves the same relative value ; but, if we compare them, as certainly we ought to do, with the means of producing them, and with the numbers and wants of the consumers, then a great increase of produce with a comparatively stationary number or with wants diminished by parsimony, must necessarily occasion a great fall of value estimated in labour, so that the same produce, though it might have *cost* the same quantity of labour as before, would no longer *command* the same quantity ; and both the power of accumulation and the motive to accumulate would be strongly checked.

. . . Their [commodities'] relation to each other may not have changed ; but their relation to the wants of society, their relation to labour, may have experienced a most important change (ibid., pp. 316–17).

CHAPTER IV

THE CLASSICAL THEORY OF FREE COMPETITION
(A Reinterpretation)

IT is generally taken for granted that the sole concern of the classical economists was to show that free competition will lead to the most efficient allocation of the *given* resources of society among different industries according to the existing consumers' demand. This apparently well-established belief has not, however, been borne out by our more detailed inquiry into the classical ideas concerning the nature of the economic problem and the measurement of the national dividend. There we have seen that the classical economists were not in the habit of thinking in terms of a static framework where the available amount of resources is given once for all throughout the whole analysis. Smith and Ricardo assumed that the supply of labour can be increased by increasing saving, and Malthus was acutely aware that different volumes of employment might result from a given supply of labour. We have further seen that irrespectively of whether they approached the problem from the Cost side or from the Income side, they all agreed that the main determinant of the wealth of society is the total volume of economic activity in general, rather than its allocation in particular proportions among different industries.

In this chapter, we hope to show that (i) a purely " allocative " interpretation of the classical theory of free competition is based on very selective evidence and that (ii) it is only when free competition is further reinterpreted as an auxiliary instrument of dynamic economic progress that it fits in with the fundamental classical outlook on the economic problem and gives an organic unity to their theoretical system as a whole.

Our proposed reinterpretation, although it upsets the established current opinion, can be traced back to the works of the older generation of the Neo-classical economists (cf. Marshall, *Principles*, pp. 5–10 ; Pigou, *Memorials of Alfred Marshall*, pp. 9, 307 ; Allyn Young, " Increasing Returns and Economic Progress ", *Economic Journal*, 1928 ; Taussig, *Principles*, Vol. I, Chaps. III–IV). There it will be found that free competition, significantly described as " free enterprise ", was not regarded as an abstract model of analysis

53

possessing certain logical properties leading to the most efficient allocation of resources. It was treated as a precept of economic policy which merely states that, taking the economic system as it exists in practice, the state should not interfere with free entry into industry or the profit motive. Free enterprise was desired not merely for the static advantages of allocative efficiency. It was further supposed to promote the " growth of economic freedom " as an historical tendency and therefore to give the freest rein to the mainsprings of economic progress. Thus a free economy was thought to encourage thrift, enterprise and initiative which promote a greater division of labour, expansion of market, accumulation of capital, etc. In fact, it is plausible to argue that the main objection of the economists of the eighteen-nineties against State interference rests on the fear that it will undermine the incentive to save and embark on new enterprise rather than on the more familiar argument that it will lead to a maldistribution of resources.

The " allocative " interpretation of free competition in its fully developed version as we know it nowadays did not become current until a generation later. It was only then that the concept of the General Equilibrium under Perfect Competition as formulated by Walras and the Austrian School began to percolate through the main stream of economic thought. Of course, no economist ever imagined that Perfect Competition could be attained in real life, but the study of the working of the competitive forces under stringently formulated ideal conditions profoundly moulded their theoretical outlook. More consciously than ever, they learned to look upon the facilitation of allocative efficiency as the most essential characteristic of any fairly competitive system in real life. This change in outlook can be clearly seen by comparing Pigou's concept of free competition with Marshall's definition of it as " Freedom of Industry and Enterprise " (cf. Pigou, *Economics of Welfare*, Part II, Chap. I ; Marshall, *Principles*, p. 9).

Viewed in this perspective, the " allocative " view of the classical theory of free competition no longer appears as authoritative as we have been usually brought up to believe it to be. It would then seem desirable to probe behind the familiar façade of free trade policy and to separate more carefully the arguments originally employed by the classical economists from those which have been imputed to them by the latter-day economists. Only then can we hope to get an accurate idea of how the classical economists really looked upon their theory of free competition unbiased by our contemporary modes of thought. Indeed, when one considers the question in a detached way, it seems hardly credible that two schools of thought, so widely differing in the method of approach and technique of analysis as the classical and the modern General Equilibrium economists, should arrive at the same conclusion concerning economic policy for precisely the same reasons. To presume too readily that the classical economists put forward a cruder but an essentially similar version of the modern theory of competition is to be guilty not only of anthropomorphism, but also of intellectual pride. In what follows we hope to show that the so-called " familiar tenets of the classical school " are far from being familiar to the average economist.

I

The main source of textual evidence for interpreting the classical concept of competition as the allocator of resources within a given closed economy is the *Wealth of Nations*. After Adam Smith, none of the major classical economists developed this trend of thought in any significant way. Ricardo and Malthus were content to accept Smith's theory of competition without further modification and amplification as far as its application to domestic trade within the closed economy was concerned (Ricardo, *Principles*, Everyman's ed., p. 50). The forerunners of the marginal analysis such as Senior and Longfield had important contributions to make to the theory of competitive equilibrium. They, however, exerted little influence on the main stream of classical tradition which continued undisturbed until Cairnes introduced his idea of " non-competing groups " within the domestic economy.

Even with Smith, the exposition of the working of the competitive equilibrium within the closed system was confined to a very narrow section of his book, particularly to Chapters VII and X, Book I. In fact, we hope to show that the allocative interpretation of competition can be maintained only by considering these two chapters *in vacuo*. But within that narrow compass Smith's achievement was very considerable. Taking Political Economy at its stage of " primitive generalisation and particular inquiries " he transformed it into a coherent analysis of how the economic system works as a whole.

Chapter VII contains his well-known demonstration of how free competition in the product market will equate the demand and supply of each commodity and eliminate abnormal profits in any particular industry. In the short run, with a given supply of the commodity, its price will be determined "according as the acquisition of the commodity happens to be of more or less importance" to the consumers. If this market price is above the "natural" price, equal to the cost of production including normal profits, there will be an increase in supply until price is lowered to its "natural" level. If the market price is below the "natural" price there will be a decrease in supply until price is raised to its "natural" level.

> The natural price, therefore, is, as it were, the central price to which the prices of all commodities are continually gravitating. Different accidents may sometimes keep them suspended a good deal above it, and sometimes force them down even somewhat below it. But whatever may be the obstacles which hinder them from settling in this centre of repose and continuance, they are constantly tending towards it.
> The whole quantity of industry annually employed in order to bring any commodity to market, naturally suits itself in this manner to the effectual demand. It naturally aims at bringing always that precise quantity thither which may be sufficient to supply, and no more than supply that demand (op. cit., Cannan ed., Vol. I, p. 60).

Next, monopoly is introduced into the discussion as one of the permanent obstacles to the attainment of this competitive equilibrium.

> The monopolists, by keeping the market constantly under-stocked, by never fully supplying the effectual demand, sell their commodities much above the natural price and raise their emoluments, whether they consist in wages, or profit, greatly above their natural rate (ibid., p. 63).

It may be noted that Smith was here mainly concerned with denouncing the monopoly price as the "highest that can be squeezed out of the buyers". It was only at a much later stage that we are told that monopolies "derange more or less the natural distribution of the stock of society" (op. cit., Vol. II, p. 130).

It was not until two chapters later, in Chapter X, that Smith introduced the analysis of free competition in the factor market. Like most other classical economists before Cairnes, he implicitly assumed that permanent immobility of factors within a country is mainly the result of artificial restrictions. Granted free entry into industry, he believed that sooner or later, the factors will be allocated among different industries in such a way as to equalise not only the money earnings but "the whole advantages and disadvantages" in all these industries. He, however, mentioned three qualifications.

> First, the employments must be well known and long established in the neighbourhood ; secondly, they must be in their ordinary, or what may be called

their natural state ; and thirdly, they must be the sole or the principal employments of those who occupy them (ibid., p. 116).

The first two qualifications show Smith's awareness of the intimate relation between the assumption of perfect knowledge and mobility of factors. If knowledge is imperfect, a time-lag must intervene before the frictions are smoothed out and equilibrium is attained. The third qualification is a quaint one suggesting that part-time work may reduce the flexibility of wages and labour market. Here we may also recall Smith's famous saying that the " overweening conceit of some men " leading them to overestimate their own chances of gain may frequently result in a flow of factors into certain industries more than the risks involved would justify (ibid., p. 109). Elsewhere he indicated that a better standard of education by reducing inertia and irrational estimates may facilitate mobility and correct adjustments in the labour market (op. cit., Vol. II, p. 268).

This is about all the textual evidence available to show that Smith looked upon free competition as the allocator of resources within the closed system. But it is sufficient to demonstrate that free competition will allocate the " right " amounts of resources among different industries and will, therefore, lead to the production of the " right " quantity of every commodity existing in the economic system. Of course, applying strictly modern standards, this formulation is not stringent enough in many respects. For instance, Smith has not shown how the " right " quantities of factors allocated to the production of different commodities will be combined in " right " proportions. This was beyond the theoretical equipment of his time. Nevertheless, taking it by and large, in the two odd chapters (VII and X, Book I), Smith succeeded in outlining a broadly workable allocative concept of competition which could stand independently of his metaphysical optimism concerning the benevolent working of the " Invisible Hand ".

But it is a far cry from this to the currently accepted proposition that the allocative concept of competition is the central essence of Smith's welfare analysis. Once we stop reading the above two chapters in isolation and try to fit them into the general framework of the *Wealth of Nations*, we will get an entirely different view of their significance. We will then see that the allocative axiom breaks down rather badly when we try to use it as the central unifying thread of Smith's argument. We will further discover that the various parts of the book hang together as a significant whole only when we abandon the Scarcity concept of the economic problem

postulated by the allocative interpretation and adopt the labour-
theory outlook we have described in previous chapters.

Let us review the *Wealth of Nations* impartially from its beginning
chapters in Book I. Chapter I lays down the fundamental proposition that the wealth of a nation depends on the annual product
of its labour and is, therefore, determined by the number and
productivity of its labourers. In Chapters II and III it is shown
how the division of labour is the most far-reaching method of
increasing physical productivity and how its operation is "limited
by the extent of the market". These foreshadow the dual theme
of the book, viz. the wealth of a nation can be increased (*a*) by
increasing the number of its labourers by saving up a greater amount
of wage fund to maintain them and (*b*) by extending the area of
the market and promoting further division of labour. Skipping
Chapter IV on "Money" and Chapters V and VI (dealt with
above under the heading of the "Measuring Rod of Labour"),
let us reconsider Chapters VII and X, this time together with the
two intervening chapters. The first thing to strike us is the pervading idea that the equilibrium process of the market should be viewed
against the background of the secular tendency of the economic
system to be in an "advancing, stationary or declining condition".
This robs a great deal of self-sufficiency and determinateness from
the competitive equilibrium. Thus at the end of Chapter VII
itself we are told that the natural price previously described as the
"centre of repose and continuance"

itself varies with the natural rate of each of its component parts, of wages, profit
and rent ; in every society this rate varies according to their circumstances,
according to their riches and poverty, their advancing, stationary or declining
condition (ibid., p. 65).

Chapter VIII resumes the important theme of the supply of
labour for society and states that population can be kept increasing
by maintaining a rising level of wages and that, above the minimum
subsistence level, the normal wage will vary with the rate of accumulation and the state of general economic activity. "It is not the
actual greatness of national wealth, but its continual increase, which
occasions a rise in the wages of labour." The conclusion is that
continuous accumulation must be maintained because the lot of
the labouring poor, "the far greater part of every political society",
will be "hard" and "miserable" in the stationary and declining
state of economic activity and will be "cheerful" and "hearty"
in the advancing state. Chapter VIII contains a further significant

argument which maintains that a mere increase in population may by itself raise the average physical productivity of labour by breaking down technical indivisibilities and by stimulating inventions. The economic system is likened to a firm enjoying the economies of large-scale production.

> What takes place among the labourers of a particular workhouse, takes place, for the same reason, among those of a great society. The greater their number, the more they naturally divide themselves into different classes and subdivisions of employment. More heads are occupied in inventing the most proper machinery for executing the work of each, and it is, therefore, more likely to be invented (op. cit., p. 88).

Smith's interest in indivisibilities may appear strange when we approach his analysis from the static viewpoint, for his was an age of small-scale production units where such difficulties would not normally arise. But taken together with his preoccupation with the dynamics of economic expansion it has an added significance (cf. Allyn Young, loc. cit., *Economic Journal*, 1928).

By now it will be apparent that the allocative approach to Smith is rather out of focus and that we should interpret his theory of competition as something more than an instrument of economic equilibrium making allocative adjustments within a static framework. Chapter IX on " Profits " indicates how it can be looked upon more importantly as an instrument of economic prosperity facilitating the dynamic process of economic expansion. Continuous capital accumulation within a country will, sooner or later, exhaust investment opportunities and lower the rate of profit resulting in a stagnation of economic activity with its undesirable consequences. Therefore, in order to maintain a continuous state of economic expansion, fresh outlets for investment must be found.

> The acquisition of new territory, or of new branches of trade, may sometimes raise the profits of stock, and with them, the interest of money, even in a country fast advancing in the acquisition of riches (op. cit., p. 95).

Thus a further and more important function of free competition emerges ; it is a method *par excellence* of widening the area of the market and of investment opportunities which will rejuvenate the economic system even when it is approaching a state of stagnation.

Book II, perhaps the most important part of the *Wealth of Nations*, further and more seriously undermines the allocative concept of competition. It contends that although the process of the expansion of the market and capital accumulation must go hand in hand, the latter must be regarded as the more important mainspring of economic progress. " The accumulation of stock must, in the nature of things, be previous to the division of labour ", and without a sufficient amount of capital the new investment opportunities offered by fresh markets cannot be fully exploited (ibid., p. 259).

> The number of its productive labourers, it is evident, can never be much increased, but in consequence of an increase of capital, or of the fund destined for maintaining them. The productive powers of the same number of labourers cannot be increased, but in consequence either of some addition or improvement to those machines and instruments which facilitate and abridge labour ; or of a more proper division of labour and distribution of employment. In either case an additional capital is almost always required.
>
> When we compare, therefore, the state of a nation at two different periods, and find, that the annual produce of its land and labour is evidently greater at the latter than at the former, that its lands are better cultivated, its manufactures more numerous and more flourishing, and its trade more extensive, we may be assured that its capital must have increased during the interval of those two periods and that more must have been added to it by the good conduct of some, than had been taken away from it either by the private misconduct of others, or by the public extravagance of government (op. cit., pp. 325–6).

Book II reaches its climax in the doctrine of Productive Labour, which exalts capital accumulation above all other things as the life blood of the economic system. Postponing a detailed consideration of this doctrine to the next chapter we can clearly see its disruptive influence on the concept of allocative efficiency. It frankly proposes to interfere with the given time-preference of the savers and the free allocation of resources between the capital and consumers' goods industries in order to increase savings and expand the total volume of economic activity. To Adam Smith and his followers it was evident that the dynamic gains from expanding economic activity would be so great and widespread as to swamp all the wastes from interfering with the static allocative equilibrium. Accordingly they were willing to throw the allocative considerations overboard without compunction should these considerations interfere with the accumulation of capital.

The allocative aspects of Smith's theory of competition in foreign trade is well known. There is the famous argument showing how the " spirit of monopoly " which engineers the Mercantilist restrictions can benefit only those in the protected industries whose interest is " directly opposed to the great body of the people " (op. cit., Vol. I, p. 485). There is the equally famous argument showing how the free play of self interest will automatically lead to the enormous benefits of the international division of labour (ibid., pp. 422–3). These are important points and should not be belittled. But, as some authorities have found out long ago, it is only a half-truth to assume that Smith advocated free trade purely on the ground of consumers' gains (cf. Gide and Rist, *History of Economic Doctrines*, pp. 99–100). In fact, when we examine the textual evidence carefully, the following is the only sustained passage where Smith explicitly links consumers' gains with foreign trade and it looks stronger than it really is isolated from the context.

> It carries that surplus part of the produce of their land and labour for which there is no demand among them, and brings back in return for it something else for which there is demand. It gives a value to their superfluities, by exchanging them for something else which may satisfy a part of their wants and increase their enjoyments (ibid., p. 413).

For the rest, a country is supposed to benefit from foreign trade in its rôle as the producer. Foreign trade, by overcoming the " narrowness of home market " increases the " exchangeable value of the annual produce of its industry ". Since, however, as we have seen in Chapter II above, " value " is to be measured by the quantity of labour commanded, this means that the main advantage of foreign trade is that it enables a country to employ a greater number of productive labourers *internally*, by opening up new markets to dispose of their surplus product. Far fetched as it may sound, one of Smith's arguments against protection is that by reducing a country's total income and consequently its capacity to save, it will reduce internal employment ! (ibid., p. 423). Hence this revealing analogy : " As a rich man is likely to be a better customer to the industrious people in his neighbourhood, so is likewise a rich nation " (ibid., p. 485).

Here again this line of argument would have been apparent at the outset had we paid more attention to the important Book II, particularly Chapter V, instead of implicitly accepting the conventional free trade argument viewing the problem purely from the standpoint of consumers' demand and in terms of static allocation of resources throughout the international economy. There it is stated that the prosperity of a country depends not only on its total accumulation but also on how it is distributed among (i) Agriculture, (ii) Manufactures, and (iii) the Carrying trade between countries, which are carefully listed according to their capacity to create internal employment, in a descending order. If the country has not sufficient capital to maintain all these three types of industries, it should restrict its investment to the first two, almost irrespectively of the terms of the international division of labour.

When the capital of any country is not sufficient for all three purposes, in proportion, as a greater share of it is employed in agriculture, the greater will be the quantity of productive labour which it puts into motion *within that country* ; as will likewise be the *value* which its employment adds to the annual produce of land and labour of the society. After agriculture, the capital employed in manufactures puts into motion the greatest quantity of productive labour, and adds the greatest value to the annual produce. That which is employed in the trade of exportation, has the least effect of any of the three (ibid., p. 346).

Thus, with insufficient capital, care must be taken to ensure that capital " resides within the country " and creates internal employment. Only when accumulation has increased beyond the needs of domestic investment, should capital " naturally disgorge itself " to the carrying and export trade. Thus it is only to those countries where the investment opportunities at home have been exhausted that foreign trade offers the greatest advantage by finding new outlets for exports and investments. It would be quite logical for Smith to oppose free trade on gold standard if it leads to a reduction in internal employment.

If our interpretation is correct, free competition as conceived by Adam Smith was not primarily a " tightening " process delving inwards into a given static framework to make finer readjustments of given resources to given wants, but a " widening " process which facilitates the expansion of economic activity. Only thus will free competition increase the economic welfare of society in terms of the measuring rod of labour and fit in as an organic part of the general structure of Smith's analysis.

The concept of competition as the allocator of resources within the closed system was not much further developed by Ricardo and Malthus. Both were content to accept Smith's formulation of the idea in general terms and to turn their attention to new developments in other directions such as the theory of Distribution and the theory of Effective Demand. In the sphere of Foreign Trade and Comparative Costs theory, however, there were some significant developments towards the idea of allocative efficiency. These will be considered separately in the next section.

Ricardo's neglect of the allocative concept of competition within the closed system is only to be expected in the light of his technological Cost approach to the economic problem. In adopting the " quantity of labour embodied " theory of value, he pushed the whole equilibrium process of the market to the background. According to him, whatever the temporary market conditions, the relative values of the commodities in the long run will be determined by the relative quantities of labour required to produce them. In thus trying to determine price without quantity, he missed out the essence of the allocative process as consisting of commodities produced to suit the relative demand for them. This, however, is quite logical if we accept the full implication of his method of measuring the wealth of society by the size of social output at the purely physical level. The technical optimum implicit in that approach to the economic problem requires no other condition than that every commodity should be produced with the minimum quantity of labour possible under given technical conditions. In modern terminology, this means that optimum will be attained at any point on the technically determined " opportunity cost curve ", whether or not it is tangential at that point to the consumers' indifference curve (cf. below, Chap. VI, sec. IV). There is thus an indeterminate range of possible optima rather than a definite point of optimum. Further, since imperfections in the product market need not lead away to a position off the opportunity cost curve, they should be considered as being compatible with optimum in technical terms. It is only when there are imperfections in the factor market also that there will be divergencies from the optimum.

There is a further element in the Ricardian system which complicates the formulation of the optimum in the modern sense. It is his assumption of constant returns in every industry except in agriculture. It may be noted that in the Ricardian system diminishing returns from land merely seems to serve as a limit to the total volume of economic activity ; once the available quantity of labour with a given margin of cultivation is given, it may be allocated among different branches of economic activity without being subject to diminishing returns ; i.e. changes in the relative outputs of different commodities will not alter their technical cost ratios, or the relative average quantities of labour required to produce them. Thus the marginal rate of transformation between any two commodities will be constant and the opportunity cost " curves " will be straight lines. Under these conditions, if we follow the method of illustrating the optimum conditions by " sitting " two opportunity cost curves (keeping their axes parallel) so that they just touch each other, we will find that so long as the rates of transformation between the two commodities are different in the two producing units, each producing unit will be specialising on one of the commodities only (cf. J. R. Hicks, " Foundations of Welfare Economics ", *Economic Journal*, 1939, pp. 701–5).

But Ricardo was not troubled by these considerations ; he

was concerned with the determinants of a different sort. From his point of view it did not matter whether or not there are determinate adjustments at a point of time, for that is merely a phase in the relentless tendency of the economic system towards the stationary equilibrium. In the long run, wages will tend towards subsistence level and profits towards zero. The stationary equilibrium will then be only too determinate and it is cold comfort to allocate labour nicely among competing uses so as to equalise their marginal products when population is increasing towards the subsistence level. Nor does the allocation of capital among different industries appear very exciting with the prospect of a zero rate of profits. Thus, the Smithian " natural price " had at last achieved determinateness at the cost of being stripped of its penumbra of optimism, and the consequences of the dynamic mechanics of the economic system reduced the static considerations of allocative efficiency to comparative insignificance.

Turning to Malthus, we might have expected that with his Income and Demand approach, he would have more to contribute towards the concept of allocative efficiency than Ricardo. But he again was concerned more with the total volume of Effective Demand than with its relative strength for different particular commodities. There are passages in which he lightly touched on allocative efficiency. Thus he stated in passing that the various articles which make up social output should be " so *proportioned* as to give them their proper value " and that demand is " not only the great stimulus to the production of all kinds of wealth, but also the great regulator of the *forms* and *relative quantities* in which it shall exist " (*Principles*, 2nd ed., L.S.E. Reprints, pp. 301–2). But, as we have seen, in his anxiety to maintain that " value " is determined by the " intensity of demand " for a commodity, independently of its cost of production and available quantity, he built up his whole analysis of market on contradictory assumptions concerning the shape of the demand curve (ibid., Book I, Chap. II, sec. ii ; cf. Chap. III, sec. I above). His inability to grasp the equilibrium mechanism, adjusting the " intensity of demand " to price *at the margin* by a simultaneous adjustment of the " extent " of demand to the given supply, did not favour the development of the idea of optimum allocative efficiency.

On the subject of the determinateness of competitive equilibrium within the closed economy, the later classical economists did not get much beyond the generalisation that while the law of diminishing returns characterises agriculture, increasing returns may operate in manufacturing industries. Indeed, the labour-theory outlook with its emphasis on the so-called dynamic laws of changes in the supply of labour and labour operating on given natural resources seems almost to be inimical to the allocative approach. The important place which J. S. Mill gave to his formula of the " Equalisation of Demand to Supply " in Book III of his *Principles* may appear as a revival of interest in the equilibrium process of the market. But, as Marshall has pointed out, this is largely illusory, depending on the peculiar arrangement of the contents of Mill's *Principles*. In his Book I, " On Production ", he expounded a very deterministic theory of production based on the Ricardian technological cost analysis. Thus in Book III, " On Exchange ", he was able to give the impression of emphasising the market phenomenon, by a " curt reference to Book I " (*Memorials of Alfred Marshall*, p. 122). Further, even in Book III, Mill's reverted to the Ricardian labour theory in his Chapter IV on " Ultimate Analysis of Cost of Production ".

II

The Ricardian theory [1] of Comparative Costs is perhaps the only branch of classical economic analysis which gradually freed itself from the concept of absolute technological cost implied by the labour-theory outlook on the economic problem. We will, therefore, try to assess how far it actually enabled the classical economists to move towards the concept of allocative efficiency aimed at the satisfaction of given consumers' wants.

Smith's case for free trade on allocative grounds never got beyond the stage of pointing out in general terms the gains from international division of labour. It was merely stated that, without free trade, some of the imported commodities could not be produced at home at all or could be produced only at costs absolutely greater than those at which it could be produced abroad. Free trade would enable commodities to be produced in those countries where the absolute real costs were lowest.

It was Ricardo who first gave due emphasis to the doctrine that the profitability of foreign trade does not depend on absolute costs but on comparative costs. Thus take his celebrated illustration in which wine can be produced in England by the labour of 120 men

---

[1] Cf. Jacob Viner, *Studies in the Theory of International Trade*, Chap. VIII, for a very comprehensive account of this doctrine and also for the details of the controversy whether Ricardo or Torrens was the originator of this doctrine.

and in Portugal by 80 men, while cloth can be produced in England by 100 men and in Portugal by 90. He showed that although Portugal can produce both cloth and wine at lower absolute labour costs, it will still be profitable to her to import cloth and export wine in the production of which she has a comparative advantage. Similarly, although England can produce both wine and cloth at higher absolute labour costs, it will be profitable to her to import only wine and export cloth in the production of which she has a comparative advantage. The comparative cost ratios do not determine the actual rate of exchange ; they merely serve as the upper and lower limits to the zone of profitable exchange to both parties. Thus as long as Portugal can get more than 1 unit of cloth for 9/8 unit of wine, it will be profitable to her to continue exchanging wine for cloth. Similarly, as long as England can get more than 5/6 unit of wine for 1 unit of cloth, it will be profitable to her to continue exchanging cloth for wine. This indeterminateness of equilibrium is very important for our argument. For one thing, it led J. S. Mill to the reciprocal demand analysis in his attempt to fix the actual rate of exchange (cf. Ricardo, *Principles*, Chap. VII).

Perhaps the best way to assess the allocative significance of this construction is to find out how far it will fulfil the optimum conditions of international trade. With no pretence of stringency, the workable conditions of optimum may be stated as follows : (i) The " right " quantities of different commodities should be purchased by each country and produced by each country. (ii) The " right " quantities of commodities purchased by each country should be apportioned in " right " amounts among its individual consumers. (iii) The " right " quantities of commodities produced in each country should be produced with the minimum possible amount of labour. Since labour is assumed to be the only factor of production, the question of the " right " proportions of different factors does not arise.

Since the Ricardian construction does not provide for a determinate rate of exchange, we cannot deduce determinate quantities of commodities purchased and produced by each country. Thus, strictly speaking, it has not fulfilled our first condition. But it has progressed considerably towards the fulfilment of this condition by showing that divergences from the optimum can arise not only through differences in absolute labour costs but also through differences in the ratios of comparative labour costs. Although we do not have a determinate optimum, we at least have a more correct definition of the range of possible optimum positions.

It may appear pedantic to include the apportionment of " right " amounts of commodities among different individual consumers as one of our optimum conditions, since it cannot be attained without the marginal utility analysis. But the term " allocative efficiency " as we understand it nowadays, cannot be conceived without taking into account the satisfaction of given consumers' want. To re-define the term in a special way would be misleading. Therefore, it seems desirable to point out that the marginal utility equation is not fulfilled whenever the occasion calls for it.

The minimum labour cost condition is, of course, fulfilled. In the Ricardian system it is always presumed, not only in the theory of foreign trade but also in the theory of domestic trade. By means of this the conditions of the *technical* optimum of Production is fulfilled (cf. Chap. VII, secs. III and IV for distinction between the *technical* and the *subjective* optimum).

We now hope to show that although Ricardo did not formally provide for those optimum conditions relating to the consumers' market, in the theory of foreign trade, at least, he made a consistent attempt to show in general terms how the gains from the reduction of labour costs will diffuse throughout the economic system in the form of consumers' gains (assuming " the sum of enjoyments " to be proportionate to the quantity of physical products) (Ricardo, op. cit., pp. 77, 81). It is important to insist on this point, because otherwise an entirely different interpretation can be made of the theory of comparative costs in its practical application to the Corn Laws controversy. When we view the Corn Laws against the background of the Ricardian theory of Profits, we will see that Ricardo had a double motive for desiring the importation of cheap corn. Besides the strictly " allocative " advantages, which will be realised, to whatever class of society the gains from free trade may accrue, the importation of corn has the additional effect of lowering money wages and thus raising the rate of profits and stimulating general economic activity. At first sight, therefore, it is tempting to argue that Ricardo desired the importation of corn more for its effect on profits than for consumers' gains, more for the particular way in which the gain is distributed than for the amount of gain itself.

This fits in too well with the general Ricardian approach to the problem of economic prosperity to be entirely false. But, on a more careful examination of his arguments, it must be admitted that he seems to attach more importance to consumers' gains than to a rise in profits. Thus he wrote :

It is quite *as* important to the happiness of mankind that our enjoyments should be increased by the better distribution of labour, by each country producing those commodities for which by its situation, its climate, and other natural and artificial advantages, and by their exchanging them for commodities of other countries, *as* that they should be augmented by a rise in the rate of profit (op. cit., p. 80).

Further he took pains to distinguish between general gains to consumers and particular gains to profit earners.

The rate of profits is never increased by a better distribution of labour, by the invention of machinery, by the establishment of roads and canals, or by any means of abridging labour either in manufacture or in the conveyance of goods. These are causes which operate on price and never fail to be beneficial to consumers ; . . . but they have no effect whatever on profit. On the other hand, every diminution in the wages of labour raises profits, but produces no effect on the price of commodities. One is advantageous to all classes, for all classes are consumers ; the other is beneficial only to producers (ibid., p. 81).

The clearest proof that Ricardo was concerned more with general consumers' gains from the importation of cheap corn than with the gains of profit earners is shown by his following retort to Malthus.

But it may be said that the capitalist's income will not be increased ; that the million deducted from the landlord's rent will be paid in additional wages to labourers ! Be it so ; this will make no difference to the argument : the situation of society will be improved and they will be able to bear the same money burthens with greater facility than before ; it will only prove what is still more desirable, that the situation of another class, and by far the most important class in society, is the one which is chiefly benefited by the new distribution (ibid., Chap. XXXII, p. 289).

J. S. Mill's attempt to fix a definite rate of exchange between two commodities within the limits set by the comparative ratios of the two countries trading in them led him to the analysis of reciprocal demand, perhaps his only original contribution to economic theory. He dealt with the problem first in his *Essays on some Unsettled Questions of Political Economy*, Essay I, and repeated and developed it in Book III, Chap. XVIII of his *Principles*. He tried to show that the rate of exchange will

adjust itself to the inclinations and circumstances of consumers on both sides, in such manner that the quantities required by each country, of the articles which it imports from its neighbour, shall be exactly sufficient to pay for one another.

On the question of how the gains from exchange are shared between the two countries, he believed that

A country which desires few foreign productions, and only a limited quantity of them, while its own commodities are in great request in foreign countries, will obtain its limited imports at extremely small cost, that is, in exchange for the produce of a very small quantity of its labour and capital.

The implication of Mill's theory, if it had been followed up, would have opened up the whole vista of demand approach to the theory of value. But the Cost approach of the labour-theory outlook was too strong for such a follow-up. Further there was a peculiar accident which weighted down the classical analysis to the cost side, viz. the habit of studying the equilibrium of exchange between two countries trading in two commodities and presuming that the conclusion will hold for more general conditions. With two countries and two commodities, it is possible to tell, merely from an inspection of the comparative cost ratios, which commodity will be exported and which will be imported. As Edgeworth has pointed out, once we assume more than two commodities, the new assumption

brings into view an incident which is apt to be masked as long as we confine ourselves to two commodities . . . namely, that it is not in general possible to determine a priori from a mere observation of the costs of production in respective countries, which commodities will be imported and which produced at home. . . . [That] depends not only on the cost of production in each country, but also on the law of demand in each country for the different commodities (Edgeworth, *Papers*, Vol. II, p. 55).

A further influence of the theory of international trade on the development of classical analysis may be seen in Cairnes' idea of " non-competing " groups of labour within a nation. The only significant modification which Smith's model of free competition within the closed system received seems thus to be inspired by the theory of international trade.

CHAPTER V

THE WELFARE SIGNIFICANCE OF PRODUCTIVE LABOUR

THE steady tendency of the previous chapters has been to shift the focus of our attention from the economics of equilibrium to the economics of expansion. Our survey of the classical economists' general outlook towards the nature of the economic problem has brought out their deep-rooted belief that the economic welfare of society can be promoted in a more far-reaching manner by expanding the total volume of its economic activity than by accepting its available resources as given and by trying to allocate them more efficiently among different industries. Our further analysis has shown that, in accordance with this general standpoint, the classical economists looked upon their policy of free competition primarily as an auxiliary instrument of economic expansion opening up new markets and outlets for investment rather than as an instrument of allocative efficiency. If that is true, one conclusion clearly emerges. The doctrine of Productive Labour with its intimate connection with the " balance of production and consumption " which determines the total level of economic activity must be regarded as the key proposition of the classical welfare analysis, ousting the allocative concept of competition from the central position normally ascribed to it in current interpretations.

In the preceding chapters, to avoid overloading the argument, we have used productive labour in its broad sense, meaning by that the labour which produces " necessaries " or basic wage goods and durable capital goods, both of which can be used in the further reproduction of wealth. This has been sufficient to distinguish it in general terms from unproductive labour which produces " luxury" services catering for immediate consumption. Our above conclusion, however, calls for a more detailed examination of the various ideas underlying this distinction and a brief history of the doctrine in its later phase may be instructive.

As early as 1804, Lauderdale had put forward a criticism of this " extraordinary distinction " which few later economists have improved.

If exchangeable value is considered to be the basis of wealth—the practice of mankind in estimating these [unproductive] services, if we can judge from what is paid for them, bears sufficient testimony of its inaccuracy. If, on the other hand, wealth is regarded in its true light, as consisting of the abundance of objects of men's desire, it would be impossible to discern why that should not be considered wealth which tends to the satisfaction of men's immediate desire as that which is stocked and stored up for the satisfaction of the future desire (J. M. Lauderdale, *Inquiry into the Nature and Origin of Public Wealth*, pp. 151-2).

In this he was followed by J. B. Say, who, reacting against the materialist bias involved in the Physiocratic concept of the *Produit Net*, consistently expounded the view that " Production is the creation, not of matter, but of utility " (Say, *Traité*, Vol. I, p. 5, English Translation of the 4th ed.). But the doctrine continued to be the centre of interest up to the time of J. S. Mill, partly because the classical school was, as a rule, impervious to the influence of the early demand economists, and perhaps more importantly because the critics who rejected productive labour themselves subscribed to the view that the " balance of production and consumption " was the most important determinant of society's economic welfare. Thus Lauderdale attacked productive labour, not only because of its logical defects but also because of his fears that excessive saving might lead to a general depression (Lauderdale, op. cit., pp. 217–20). In spite of his demand approach, Say came to be regarded as the chief exponent of the law that saving and employment of productive labour can never fail to benefit the community (cf. Say, *Letters to Mr. Malthus*, Original English Translation, 1821, pp. 28–9, 42).

It was not until about the eighteen-nineties that the doctrine of productive labour fell to its present state of discredit [1] and was summarily dismissed from economic thought as an obvious crudity which caused " more trouble than its worth " (Marshall, *Economics of Industry*, p. 42 ; cf. Taussig, *Wages and Capital* for a notable exception to this general reaction against the doctrine). The apparent reason for this was, of course, the success of the marginal utility analysis which recognises no other criterion of productiveness except the satisfaction of given consumers' wants. But the real reason seems to rest not as much on the marginal utility theory as on the concept of general equilibrium of the economic system under conditions of Perfect Competition. As we have noted, this set up

---

[1] Recently the tide has turned. Cf. " A Policy for Wealth ", a pamphlet incorporating articles reprinted from *The Economist*, August to October 1944, p. 14, for a vigorous reiteration of the Productive Labour Doctrine in relation to capital formation in Great Britain, 1938.

the current fashion of interpreting the significance of the classical theory of competition purely in terms of allocative efficiency, which naturally led to the view that productive labour is a minor aberration from the norm which can be left out of classical economic thought without altering its central significance. Further, the theory of Perfect Competition, formulated within a stringent Static framework, implicitly favoured the idea that the allocation of society's resources between the satisfaction of its present and its future wants may be safely left to the time-preference of the individual savers and that any interference with this free choice will lead to a loss of satisfaction. Thus, summing up, it would appear that the doctrine of productive labour was to be rejected because (i) it failed to realise that all gainful labour is productive, (ii) it restricted the criterion of productiveness to the creation of material goods and (iii) it created a bias in favour of the satisfaction of future wants as against the satisfaction of present wants.

In what follows, we hope to show that although these objections are partly justified, they never really got to the root of matters as they failed to grasp the nature of the central economic problem as seen by the classical economists.

I

Smith opened his famous Chapter III, Book II, with the following passage :

There is one sort of labour which *adds to the value of* the subject upon which it is bestowed : there is another which has no such effect. The former, as it produces a value may be called productive ; the latter, unproductive labour.

This distinction is further elaborated as follows. Productive labour

fixes and realises itself in some particular subject or vendible commodity, which lasts for some time at least after that labour is past. It is, as it were, a certain quantity of labour *stocked and stored up* to be employed, if necessary, upon some other occasion. That subject, or what is the same thing, the price of the subject, can afterwards, if necessary, *put into motion a quantity of labour equal to that which had originally produced it.*

Unproductive labour on the other hand

does not fix and realise itself in some particular subject or vendible commodity. His services generally perish in the very instant of their performance, and seldom leave any trace or value behind them, for which an equal quantity of service could afterwards be procured (op. cit., Cannan ed., Vol. I, pp. 313–14).

Three salient points emerge from this definition :

   (i) Productive labour must not be perishable ; it must be capable of being " stocked and stored up " for future use. This may be called the " storage " version for short.

   (ii) After being stored up productive labour will be capable of reproducing at least itself. It may be noted that the reproduction is conceived not in terms of physical product but in terms of the " quantity of labour put into motion ".

   (iii) By means of these two processes productive labour is supposed to " add to the value " of the annual produce. We hope to show that " value " here means not money value, but value in terms of the quantity of labour " commanded " or " put into motion ". As distinct from (i) this may be called the " value " version of productive labour.

(i) The " storage " version systematically exalts the satisfaction of the future wants against the satisfaction of the present wants. It confines socially desirable things to durable commodities which can congeal or store up labour for future use. These include not only basic wage goods and durable capital goods, but also durable consumers' goods such as houses and furniture (ibid., pp. 328–31). It is worth noting, however, that the " storage " version is not based on an explicit recognition of the superior physical productivity of the roundabout process. This idea was implicit, but Smith classed the advantages of the roundabout process under the heading of the advantages of the division of labour, although he took care to emphasise that " the accumulation of stock, in the nature of things, must be previous to the division of labour ".

A weaver cannot apply himself entirely to his peculiar business, unless there is beforehand stored up somewhere, either in his own possession or in that of other persons, a stock sufficient to maintain him, and to supply him with materials or tools of his work, till he has not only completed but sold his web (ibid., pp. 258–9).

On the whole, however, Smith seemed to argue simply that accumulation is desirable because the more society saves up labour from present consumption, the more labour it will have for future use.

The bias for accumulation involves a materialist bias, because only material commodities can store up labour. But it should be noted that the material goods were desired not as ends in themselves, but merely as the means of conserving the resources of society for future use. The classical economists were working on the basis of an economic system where the bulk of material commodities consisted of " necessities " or basic wage goods, and where " luxuries " were mainly made up of the services of the menial and professional classes. Thus the bias in favour of material goods as against immaterial services roughly came to the same thing as the bias in favour of saving. Considered in this way, the frequent argument that it was unreasonable of Smith to regard the violinist as unproductive while on his own definition he should regard the maker of violins as productive, appears to be a perverse argument sticking at the letter and missing the real intention of Smith's distinction. Since the violin maker ultimately aims at satisfying unproductive consumption and since violins are not normally a component part of the basic wage goods which formed the bulk of " material " commodities in Smith's scheme of thought, both should be classed as unproductive. It must, of course, be admitted that the distinction between the solid furniture satisfying the honest needs of the productive labourer and the fancy violin cloying the extravagant wants of the prodigal cannot be very clear-cut.

(ii) The minimum clause stating that once a quantity of labour is stored up it will always be able to reproduce or " put into motion " at least an equivalent quantity of labour in future, is the extension of Smith's earlier proposition noted above, viz. while the quantity of labour " commanded " by a commodity may exceed, it can never fall short of the quantity of labour " embodied " in the production of that commodity (cf. above, Chap. II). As we have seen, the explanation given was that in a developed economy, while the " value " or the total quantity of labour " commanded " by a commodity is made up of rents, profits and wages, the quantity of labour " embodied " in its production merely accounts for a share of its total value represented by wages. Thus the minimum clause that the stored-up labour will always be able to reproduce at least its own equivalent, seems to be derived ultimately from the implicit idea that the capitalistic production characterising the developed economy creates a net addition (and not a deficit) of wealth, over and above wages, whether or not that is to be ascribed to capital. The significant point is that Smith preferred to calculate this net reproduction in terms of " value " or the quantity of labour " commanded " or " put into motion " rather than in terms of physical product. In this way he was able to reconcile the " storage " version of productive labour with his labour " commanded " measure of value and passed on from the " storage " version to the " value " version of productive labour. Thus he argued that society has nothing to lose by storing up labour because in the last resort it will always be able to command a quantity of labour not less than that which it has originally stored up.

(iii) Adam Smith's phrase that productive labour " adds to the value " is perhaps the most important and the least understood part of his argument. Critics have, naturally enough, assumed that " value " here means money value and have accordingly replied that all gainful labour will add to value whether embodied in a durable commodity or rendered directly. In this, however, they have been too hasty. Smith's long sermons on parsimony should have made it clear to them that far from denying that unproductive labour has money value, Smith's main thesis was that it had excessive money value ; that due to the willingness of prodigals to pay high prices for luxury services, too much of society's resources was diverted to consumption instead of being employed in the further reproduction of wealth.

Our study of Smith's measure of value suggests that " value " in the above context should be interpreted not as money value but value as measured by the quantity of labour " commanded ". This is clearly confirmed by the following passage which occurs later in the chapter on productive labour.

Parsimony, by increasing the fund which is destined for the maintenance of productive hands, tends to increase the number of those hands whose labour adds to the value of the subject upon which it is bestowed. It tends, therefore, to increase the exchangeable value of the annual produce of the land and labour of the country. *It puts into motion an additional quantity of labour which gives an additional value to the annual produce* (ibid., p. 320).

Hence, if properly interpreted, the phrase that productive labour " adds to the value " should mean that productive expenditure or investment " puts into motion an additional quantity of labour " and adds to the total volume of employment. This goes further than the " storage " version, for it implies not only that investment creates a physical net product but further that there will be enough effective demand generated to absorb the additional output in its stride. The statement that investment will subsequently create additional employment is merely another way of saying that there will be effective demand in terms of labour for the additional physical output it produces. Thus it would appear that Smith's " labour-commanded " measure of value at last broke away the admixture of Cost approach which fettered its development in his earlier chapters.

If our interpretation is correct, one main question arises, viz. why should productive expenditure create more employment than unproductive expenditure, since labour seems to be merely transferred from one use to another by it ? Here at the outset it should be noted that there were special contemporary circumstances which favoured Smith's contention. He was dealing with the pre-industrial age where it was likely that the community, particularly in the households of landlords and nobility, supported a large number of dependents who were at most only partly occupied and whose removal would not have appreciably reduced social output (cf. ibid., pp. 318–19). Thus it was plausible to argue that the attempt to attract these " unproductive " dependents to the regular and full-time occupations of trade and industry would not merely transfer labour from one use to another but would further add to the effective volume of employment by reducing partial and " disguised " unemployment.

Apart from this, Smith's specific reasons for holding that productive expenditure is likely to create a greater volume of employment than unproductive expenditure of the same amount, are already contained in his " storage " version of productive labour although they do not come out clearly unless taken in conjunction with the " value " version. The " storage " version contains the following two propositions. (i) Labour stored up in durable commodities and used in indirect production can subsequently command a quantity of labour greater, but never less than, itself (presumably due to superior physical productivity of the roundabout method of production), while labour rendering direct services for consumption can, so to speak, command only itself and no more. Thus, assuming constant real wages, the additional volume of employment which can be created will be proportional to the amount of the physical net product of the investment. (ii) Although unproductive expenditure may immediately create as much employment as the productive expenditure, it has " nothing to show for itself afterwards " and cannot, therefore, bring about a permanent addition to employment. Whereas productive expenditure " establishes, as it were, a perpetual fund for the maintenance of an equal number in all times to come ", like some " pious foundation consecrated to the maintenance of industry " (ibid., p. 321).

However, Smith's theory of employment reaches its climax only when we come to Book II, Chap. V, " Of the Different Employment of Capitals ", which begins with the following proposition.

Though all capitals are destined for the maintenance of productive labour only, yet the quantity of that labour which equal capitals are capable of putting into motion, varies extremely according to the diversity of their employment ; as does likewise the value which that employment adds to the annual produce of the land and labour of the country (ibid., p. 340).

Here Smith tabulated a hierarchy of industries arranged according to their capacity to create employment.

When the capital of any country is not sufficient for all these three purposes, in proportion as a greater share of it is employed in agriculture, the greater will be the quantity of productive labour which it puts into motion within the country; as will likewise be the value which its employment adds to the annual produce of the land and labour of the country. After agriculture, the capital employed in manufactures puts into motion the greatest value to the annual produce. That which is employed in the trade of exportation, has the least effect of the three (ibid., p. 346).

This argument, however, contains a noticeable kink. In the earlier part, agriculture and manufactures were supposed to create a greater volume of employment, simply because they were observed to employ a greater quantity of labour per unit of capital. In the latter part, Smith's attention was directed to the question whether capital " resides within the country " or not. In pursuing this line of thought Smith was led to certain ideas which, though fragmentary and inconsistent, are suggestive enough to entitle him as a forerunner of Malthus's theory of employment. Thus he argued that capital employed in foreign trade " will give but one-half the encouragement to the industry or productive labour " compared with other investments where capital " resides within the country ", since the purchasing power created by the production of exports will be counterbalanced by the purchasing power reduced by imports. Moreover, he estimated that the rate of turnover in domestic trade is twelve times as great as that in foreign trade. Thus

If two capitals are equal, the one will give four and twenty times more encouragement and support to the industry of the country than the other (ibid., p. 348).

This modern-sounding theory of " time-lags " would, Cannan pointed out, spoil his previous case for agriculture where the rate of turnover is only once a year. But, in spite of this, a far-reaching source of divergence between social and private interests is revealed.

The consideration of his own private profit, is the sole motive which determines the owner of any capital to employ it either in agriculture, in manufactures or in some particular branch of wholesale or retail trade. The different quantities of productive labour which it may put into motion, and the different values which it may add to the annual produce of the land and labour of the society, never enters into his thought (ibid., p. 354).

Thus, if the rate of profit is equal everywhere, there will be less than the optimum amount of investment in agriculture and manufacturing industries and more than the optimum amount of investment in foreign trade. The total volume of employment will be increased by redirecting investment from the latter to the former.

In the next chapter, " Of the Natural Progress of Opulence ", Smith tried to tone down this disturbing possibility by marshalling historical evidence to the effect that in " the natural course of things ", however, the capital of growing society is likely to be attached first to agriculture and manufactures, before it overflows to the other socially less-productive industries (ibid., Book III, Chap. I, p. 359). Even here he conceded that " this natural order of things " may be " entirely inverted " though he would attach the blame more to " retrograde " governmental interference than to the anti-social actions of private individuals.

However, taking it by and large, it is fair to say that the doctrine of productive labour does amount to a confession that in the particularly important sphere of saving and investment the free choice of individuals and the automatic working of the price system may not always result in the maximum possible expansion of economic activity ; and further that it may be possible to increase the economic welfare of society by stimulating saving and perhaps by redirecting investment into those industries like agriculture and manufactures where it can generate a greater volume of employment. Smith's willingness to consider the possibility of a legal control of the rate of interest has an added significance in this light (ibid., pp. 338–9).

The upshot of our argument is rather damaging to the " allocative " interpretation of Smith's theory of free competition. Whatever the defects in his theory of employment, Smith made one thing clear : viz. in judging the merits of an economic system we must not stop short at the consideration of its efficiency in allocating resources according to the given preferences of individuals within a Static framework ; we must further consider the more far-reaching Dynamic repercussions of individuals' actions on the total volume of employment and the rate of economic expansion. In this light Smith's " system of natural liberty " acquires a different significance. It does not appear to be an uncompromising insistence on the inviolable rights of individuals to exercise their own preferences, for Smith was quite willing to interfere with the given time-preferences of individuals when he thought they would clash with the maximum possible expansion of economic activity. The " natural order " should not therefore be interpreted merely as a free choice of individuals within a Static framework ; it should rather be treated as a normal pattern of economic development in which the unfettered economic system expands and evolves from the state of agriculture to manufactures and thence to foreign trade. After all, when we reflect that Smith was writing on the eve of the Industrial Revolution and had a broad sense of history, such a standpoint appears to be quite " natural " (cf. ibid., Book III, Chap. I).

II

The reader may have been struck by a parallelism between the two measures of value, viz. the " labour-embodied " and the " labour-commanded " measure, and the two versions of Smith's productive labour, viz. the " storage " and the " value " version. This is the manifestation of a deep-rooted cleavage between the Cost approach and the measurement of economic welfare in terms of the physical product on the one hand, and the Income approach and the measurement of economic welfare in terms of " value " (however quaintly defined) on the other.

Thus, Ricardo as the arch exponent of the Cost approach, concentrated on the pure " storage " version of productive labour which bears an obvious family resemblance to his " labour-embodied " measure of value. The Net Revenue or the physical magnitude of the net product from investment accordingly became the centre of his welfare system. Malthus, however, did not round off the symmetry by matching his " labour-commanded " measure with the " value " version of productive labour, because he could not accept Smith's fundamental proposition that *whatever may be the quantity of labour stored up*, it will always be able to command more, but never less, than its equivalent. Thus, while he agreed with Smith in regarding the quantity of labour commanded as the most significant measure of economic welfare, he insisted that it is the ideal balance of saving and consumption, rather than the way in which saving is invested, which determines the level of employment. Thus, if saving is carried beyond a certain critical point, the Effective Demand will collapse and the national dividend will command only a much lesser quantity of labour than that which has been stored up or " embodied " in its production, however carefully the type of investment may have been selected. If, on the other hand, care is taken that beyond the critical point the social income is not saved but spent on unproductive consumption, this condition in itself will be sufficient to ensure that there is sufficient Effective Demand to generate a high level of employment. Thus it served

Malthus's purpose of pointing out the dangers of over-saving to adopt productive labour in its purely " storage " sense and contrast it sharply with unproductive labour which renders direct and perishable services for immediate consumption.

Ricardo's views on productive labour do not require much elaboration after what we have said above (cf. Chap. II, sec. III, above). He started from the following two basic propositions : (i) The economic welfare of society depends on the size of its Net Revenue, i.e. the share of physical product left for profit and rents after wages have been paid off (Ricardo, op. cit., p. 235). (ii) The roundabout method of production is generally capable of creating a physical net product over and above the amount of the wage fund advanced to the labourers during the process (cf. Edelberg, *Economica*, 1931, pp. 55 et seq.). Whence it followed that productive labour is socially desirable so long as the roundabout method of production is capable of yielding a positive physical net product to add to the Net Revenue of society. Of course, due to the principle of diminishing returns, successive doses of investment would add to the Net Revenue only at a diminishing rate. But so long as it was capable of adding something, further investment was desirable since it meant that the physical product of the roundabout method of applying labour was greater than of direct labour. When we are concerned with economic welfare at the physical level, as Ricardo was, this is a sufficient criterion of desirability. Thus the stationary equilibrium with zero profit which wipes off further incentive to invest may be taken as the point of optimum investment which equates the physical product of indirect labour to that of direct labour. But since this extreme limit of the stationary equilibrium was not likely to occur in the immediate future, and might be postponed further by technical developments, Ricardo concluded that, as a rule, the employment of additional productive labour would always add to the Net Revenue and the economic welfare of society by the amount of the physical net product left after the wages had been paid off.

Of the two aspects of Smith's productive labour, viz. the process of storing up labour for future use and the process of redissolving this congealed labour into active employment, Malthus concentrated on the latter and tried to show that if saving is carried beyond a critical point, it will contract rather than expand the total volume of employment. This does not mean that he denied the importance of saving as the means of economic expansion. On the contrary, he took care to show that unless there is a favourable " balance of production over consumption " society cannot be in a " progressive " state (Malthus, op. cit., p. 41). Later he reiterated that capital accumulation is the necessary physical basis of economic progress and that if the entire net revenue were consumed unproductively, society would be at a standstill (ibid., p. 235). Besides he was not unsympathetic to the materialist bias contained in the " storage " version of productive labour. Thus he wrote :

> Some degree of duration and a consequent susceptibility of accumulation seems to be essential to our usual conceptions of wealth, not only because produce of this kind seems to be alone capable of forming those accumulations which tends so much to facilitate further production, but because they so essentially contribute to increase that store reserved for consumption, the possession of which is certainly one of the most distinguishing marks of riches compared with poverty. The characteristic of poverty seems to be to live from hand to mouth (ibid., pp. 45–6).

But while conceding the importance of saving, Malthus objected to Smith's and Ricardo's habit of regarding productive expenditure as a social virtue under all circumstances. He pointed out that storing up labour is merely a preliminary step ; the final effective addition to the wealth of society depends not on the quantity of labour stored up, but on the volume of employment and income which can be generated when the stored-up labour is set free at a future date. Therefore, it is not enough to rely on the superior physical productivity of the roundabout method and say with Ricardo and Smith that saving is beneficial to the community at any stage before the attainment of the stationary equilibrium. We must further consider the more important problem of how to redissolve the congealed labour represented by saving into active employment and circulate it back into the economic system. The solution of this latter problem, Malthus maintained, depends entirely on the Effective Demand for the social output, on the quantity of labour " commanded " by the physical output of the roundabout process. Here, as we have seen, he brought forward his Glut theory to show that if the community save up beyond a certain optimum point the Effective Demand will collapse, plunging the economic system into a state of general depression. When this happens the superior physical productivity of the roundabout process will merely serve to aggravate the Glut. Since there is no demand for the finished products, the labour energy locked up in the social output will run to waste instead of being released and circulated back into the economic system in the form of employment and income. Thus the vitamin pill of saving has proved too large and indigestible for the body politic and the social output will " command " a much

lesser quantity of labour than that which has been originally
" embodied " in its production (cf. above, Chap. III, sec. IV).
Therefore, Malthus concluded, in order to ensure a synchronisation
of the power of production and consumption, productive expenditure must be balanced by unproductive consumption and the amount
of saving must be prevented from exceeding the critical optimum
limit (op. cit., Book II, Chap. I, sec. ix).

Although Malthus did not subscribe to the " value " version
of Smith's productive labour, the overwhelming defeat of the Glut
theory was very damaging to the " value " version and speculations
concerning the dynamic repercussions of investment on the volume
employment received a fatal setback. By the time of J. S. Mill
nothing but the " storage " aspect was left of the productive labour
doctrine and Mill set out to systematise the technological and the
materialist bias contained in it. The first consequence of this
was the shift of emphasis from the flow of annual produce to the
stock of capital accumulation and the identification of the latter
with the wealth and the economic welfare of society.

It has been proposed to define wealth as signifying *instruments* : meaning not
tools and machinery alone, but the whole accumulation possessed by individuals
and communities, of means for the attainment of their ends (Mill, *Principles*,
Ashley ed., pp. 8–9).

This proposal to measure wealth in terms of capital rather than in
terms of income is the natural consequence of the view that the size
of income in physical terms follows as a determinate technological
function from a given stock of productive resources. Productive
expenditure is, therefore, desirable under all circumstances because
it directly adds to society's store of resources. Mill also believed
that for the purpose of finding out the exact magnitude of the net
addition which can be made to society's stock of resources, the
distinction between productive and unproductive *consumption* was
more reliable than that between productive and unproductive
labour. He argued that if the wages were above the minimum
requirements of the labourers, the exact amount of net saving will
depend not only on the quantities of productive and unproductive
labour employed but also on the decision of the labourers (both
productive and unproductive) to save or spend their surplus incomes
(ibid., p. 52). This may be a symptom of the growing importance
which the durable capital goods had assumed since the days of
Smith and Ricardo and the consequent realisation that saving may
take place in some other form besides the traditionally accepted

" advances to labour ". This conjecture seems to be supported by the fact that while Ricardo was content to calculate the Net Revenue by deducting wages from the Gross Revenue without making allowances for the depreciation of capital goods, Mill was already anticipating the Marshall-Pigou idea of " maintaining capital intact " (cf. above, Chap. III, sec. II).

> The net revenue of a country is whatever is annually produced beyond that which is necessary for maintaining the stock of materials and implements unimpaired, for keeping all the productive labourers alive and in condition for work, just keeping their numbers without increase (*Essays on Unsettled Questions of Political Economy*, p. 89).

Besides the allowance for depreciation, Mill's definition of the net produce differs from Ricardo's in that it is not confined to rents and profits only. It would also include all the surplus earnings of the labourers above the minimum wages which just keeps their number without increase. This clinches with Mill's earlier emphasis on the distinction between productive and unproductive consumption, for Mill seems to imply that all consumption on the part of labourers above that which is necessary to keep them " in condition for work " is unproductive consumption (cf. *Principles*, Book I, Chap. XI). We have directed the readers' attention to this distinction because later on we hope to point out a family resemblance between this and Marshall's distinction between the " standard of life " and the " standard of comfort ".

III

Our survey of the classical economic doctrines has been uncommonly like a tour round a dilapidated old building. As we picked our way through the winding passages, not without trapdoors, we have seen how many of the rooms have fallen down with disuse and how tangled growths obstruct some of the corridors connecting them. However, now that we have finished our tour and have seen the ground plan as a whole, we can reconstruct what the building might have looked like when it was newly built and for what purpose it was designed. Whatever our inaccuracies in filling in the ruined structure at minor points, one thing seems to be abundantly clear. The usual guide-books to this classical shrine have given too much attention to its façade (freshly repainted by each succeeding pilgrim) while the real high altar behind has so fallen down with disuse that no tourist ever thought it worth his while to explore its inner recesses.

In less literary language our conclusions may be summarised as follows :

(i) The classical economists have played such an historic part in the free trade controversy that we have been too inclined to concentrate on that aspect of their economic policy at its face value and have been too ready to assume that the " allocative efficiency " of the competitive market is the central theme of their whole system. On a closer examination this interpretation is unsatisfactory because it fails to account for a formidable array of things which each generation of the classical economists have reiterated as the integral part of their tradition, e.g. the technological view of production, the bias for capital accumulation and material wealth, the doctrine of productive labour, etc.   We have suggested that the root of the trouble here lies in the fact that the " allocative " interpretation has prejudged the issues by imputing the modern Scarcity concept of the economic problem to the classical economists, a concept alien to their mode of thinking.

(ii) The classical economists never started from the premise that the available quantity of resources is given once for all for the purpose of economic analysis and that the main function of economics is to try to get the maximum result out of these given resources by allocating them efficiently among competing uses.   On the contrary, they normally divided resources into two main groups, Land, the passive and non-augmentable factor, and Labour, the active and augmentable factor, the development of which is limited only by the progress of human civilisation.   Thus, the essence of the economic problem as seen by them consists in the struggle of man against nature and economic welfare may be measured by the degree of success which man attains in this perennial struggle.   Since Land is a passive factor, the economic destiny of a nation will depend on the potentialities of its labour, on the physical productivity of its labour and on the quantity of labour available to be pitted against nature.

(iii) Since the economic problem was conceived as the struggle of man against nature, it was natural to measure economic welfare in terms of the " measuring rod of labour ".   As we have seen, Smith suggested two methods of applying that measuring rod, each of them developed, respectively, by Ricardo and Malthus.   The first, known as the " labour-embodied " measure identified the economic welfare of society with its Net Physical Product, i.e. Gross Social Output minus the subsistence fund required to maintain the labour which produces that Output.   The second, known as the " labour-commanded " measure, roughly approximates to an attempt to measure economic welfare by the number of wage units contained in the national dividend. As developed by Malthus, however, the quantity of labour commanded was not merely a simple arithmetical magnitude obtained by dividing the national dividend by a given wage unit in physical terms ; it was meant to measure the total effective volume of employment. The Glut controversy, in fact, cannot be fully appreciated except in terms of the different measures of value adopted by Malthus and Ricardo.

(iv) We have said above in conclusion (ii) that in the classical scheme of thought the economic destiny of society depends on the potentialities of labour, on its physical productivity and on its quantity. In many ways the classical theory of free trade may be regarded as an offshoot from the basic theme of the physical productivity of labour. Physical productivity, to begin with, will depend on existing technique and this consideration gave a pervasive technical outlook to classical economics. But even with the given technical knowledge, productivity can be strikingly increased by a better division of labour. The scope of the division of labour is, however, limited by the extent of the market and the area within which free exchanges are possible. Thus it follows that, apart from technical progress, the most effective means of raising physical productivity is by promoting a greater freedom of exchange. By a detailed textual examination, we have shown that this desire to widen the area of the market seems to be a weightier consideration behind Smith's advocacy of free competition than the conventionally accepted aim of promoting the efficient allocation of resources within a given market framework. We have further shown that none of the succeeding classical economists ever tried to arrive at the concept of competitive optimum within a closed system and that, anyhow, the assumption of constant labour cost was not favourable to such a concept. It must, however, be admitted that the Ricardian theory of Comparative Costs was a notable exception to this general neglect of allocative considerations. Taking it by and large, however, it is fair to say that if we take Adam Smith as the authoritative exponent, the classical theory of free competition appears to be primarily, not a " tightening " process delving inwards into a given market framework to make finer readjustments of given resources to given wants, but a " widening " process expanding the area of the market to bring about a better division of labour.

(v) The second determinant of the economic welfare of society is the quantity of labour available to be pitted against nature. This entirely depends on the size of the subsistence fund with which to maintain labour, on the amount of savings. Apart from this obvious function, saving, however, has far-reaching effects on the physical productivity of labour. Without savings machinery " abridging labour " and raising its productivity cannot be installed and the opportunities of widening the area of the market offered by the removal of trade restrictions cannot be fully utilised. " The accumulation of stock must, in the nature of things, be previous to the division of labour." Thus, although greater freedom of trade and capital accumulation are complementary instruments of expansion, the latter must be regarded as the senior partner without whose assistance no appreciable addition can be made to the economic welfare of society. Here at last we have arrived at the high altar of the classical shrine.

(vi) From the above, the doctrine of productive labour with its intimate connection with the " balance of production and consumption " emerges as the key proposition to the classical welfare analysis as a whole. For it is nothing short of an attempt to discover the source of the motive power of the economic system and the method of controlling it to achieve the maximum possible expansion of economic activity. As we have seen, there were two versions of the productive labour doctrine parallel to the two measures of value. According to what we have called the " storage " version, labour is productive only when it is stored up in material goods to be used in the future reproduction of wealth. Ultimately this amounts to saying that labour is productive only if it adds to the net physical product of society. According to what we have called the " value " version, the criterion of " productiveness " was shifted from the creation of a net physical product to the transformation of that net product into an active volume of employment. We have seen that with the defeat of Malthus's Glut theory, the " value " version of productive labour was entirely superseded by the " storage " version. But before its downfall the " value " version had suggested a far-reaching proposition, viz. that the desirability of individual's actions should not be judged merely by their direct effects on physical output or even consumers' satisfaction ; we must further take into account the more far-reaching dynamic repercussions of these actions on the volume of employment and the level of economic activity. The " storage " version also has an important lesson to offer to us. It shows that even the Ricardian approach in its pure form judges the desirability of individual's action in terms of Production welfare economics by finding out whether or not they add to the net product of society after the cost of factors and the depreciation of equipment has been paid off. This should dispel the fashionable misconception (for which Ricardo himself was partly responsible) that while Malthus was concerned with the total volume of economic activity, Ricardo was concerned merely with the Distribution of the national dividend into relative shares. We have shown that Ricardo was concerned not merely with the proportions of the dividend shared between various groups of factors, but also with the absolute size of the Net Revenue, on which, according to him, the economic welfare of society depends. Thus both Ricardo and Malthus were concerned with increasing economic welfare by expanding economic activity, although they might differ in the methods of measuring and achieving it.

(vii) We are now ready for the final synthesis. The nature and significance of the classical welfare analysis cannot be fully appreciated except by considering it against its proper background of the man-against-nature conception of the central economic problem. Once we have obtained this correct focus, the various classical doctrines fall in with each other into a unified whole which exhibits a design and structure widely differing from those generally taken for granted in the conventional interpretations of classical economics. It now becomes clear that the principal welfare objective of classical economics is to attain a continuous state of economic expansion, rather than to " tighten " up the equilibrium allocation of resources within a given Static framework. This of course follows from the view that the welfare of society, as measured by the measuring rod of labour, may be regarded as being roughly proportional to the volume of output and economic activity. The allocative approach accepts given labour supply, capital equipment and technique as data and tries to make the best of them to satisfy given consumers' preferences. The classical economists, on the other hand, accepted Land as given ; they believed that instead of accepting the rest of the data as given, far-reaching additions to the welfare of society can be made by changing these data into component parts of an expanding framework, even if it entails interfering with the given time preferences of individuals. Even Malthus, with his emphasis on Demand, was not concerned primarily with the satisfaction of particular consumers' demand for individual commodities. He emphasised demand in so far as it helps to synchronise the expanding volume of output with expanding volume of total consumption. We have, however, seen that since labour depends on the wage fund, the only independent variable of the whole system is the amount of saving.   Hence the entire classical economic policy was primarily directed towards the attainment of the ideal " balance of production and consumption ".

If our interpretation is correct, we are not really justified in invoking the ghosts of the classical economists to support our present-day preoccupation with the allocative properties of the competitive system.   On the contrary, it would be truer to say that the allocative problem has survived in spite of the classical economists, because since their times the non-institutional imperfections in competition have grown to such dimensions as to raise serious problems of mal-distribution of resources.   However far they may have sub-scribed to their rather vulgarised social philosophy of laissez-faire, they have clearly implied that once the legal restrictions to trade are removed, the central economic problem would rest mainly on the savings-investment equation and its repercussions on the expansion of output and economic activity.   The allocative problem would look after itself.

PART II

SUBJECTIVE LEVEL

CHAPTER VI

MARGINAL REVOLUTION AND THE SCARCITY APPROACH

LOOKING back on the " marginal revolution " of the eighteen-seventies, one is now tempted to say that the application of the principle of marginal utility to the theory of prices was perhaps the least interesting of its results. This will not sound so paradoxical when we reflect how little the marginal utility theory helps us to explain the determination of prices in real life and what a great number of ordinary problems of " price-economics " may still be dealt with by the traditional demand and supply analysis without using the marginal apparatus (cf., for example, K. E. Boulding, *Economic Analysis*, Part I). If that is true, then the undoubtedly far-reaching significance of the marginal revolution should be sought elsewhere. It should be sought in the realm of welfare economics as distinct from price-economics.

From the point of view of welfare economics, the marginal revolution did two things : (i) It extended welfare analysis from the physical to the subjective level and substituted the principle of diminishing marginal utility in the place of the classical economists' first approximating assumption that quantities of consumers' satisfaction were proportional to quantities of physical products. Thus welfare propositions could now attain a second degree of approximation. (ii) Further, it offered an alternative to the labour-theory outlook : viz. the *Scarcity* approach to the economic problem.

Of these two results of the marginal revolution, the second was perhaps even more far-reaching than the first. For it was the scarcity approach to the economic problem, and not the marginal utility theory as such, which led to the new concept of " pure " economics as contrasted with the classical Political Economy. In particular, the scarcity concept shifted the focus of attention from the classical theory of Economic Expansion to the theory of the General Equilibrium within a given Static framework.

This will become clearer when we consider why welfare economics developed on different lines in England and on the Continent in spite of the fact that Jevons, Walras and Menger published their discovery of the marginal utility theory almost simultaneously in their respective countries. The development of Continental welfare economics was typified by a systematic search for the *formal* and *ideal* conditions of the Optimum allocation of given resources from the viewpoint of the economic system as a whole. This development culminated in Pareto's stringent formulation of the conditions of the General Optimum. On the other hand, the development of English welfare economics was typified by a search for *ad hoc* and *concrete* cases where the free play of economic forces lead in practice to Deviations from the Optimum in particular sectors of the economic system. This can be seen in Sidgwick's cases of divergences between Social and Private interests and Marshall's use of the Consumers' Surplus analysis to show the desirability of subsidising industries working under increasing returns. In this light Prof. Pigou's *Economics of Welfare* attains an added significance as the fusion point of the two different trends of thought ; Prof. Pigou has worked the *ad hoc* cases of divergences between the Social and Private products into the framework of the General Optimum.

The apparent reason for the different development of welfare economics in England and on the Continent is the English economists' neglect of the General Equilibrium. Jevons evaded it by using his clumsy device of the " trading bodies " ; and Marshall, who lacked none of Walras's technical equipment, deliberately eschewed the " heroic abstraction " of the General Equilibrium of the Static State under Perfect Competition in favour of a more realistic Partial Analysis, taking into account the process of equilibrium adjustments in different periods of time.

But there is also a much deeper reason. While the " pure " marginal utility economists of the continental schools immediately took to the scarcity concept of the economic problem, the English economists dominated by Marshall were not willing to give up the classical labour-theory outlook completely. They preferred to retain a link with the classical thought via the Real Cost theory.

Admittedly there were differences among the two groups of Continental economists themselves. Thus while the Austrians, with their greater awareness of methodological difficulties, were chary of making explicit welfare propositions, the Lausanne school had always been interested in the welfare implications of the General

Equilibrium, starting from Walras's unsuccessful attempt to deduce the principle of Maximum Satisfaction from equilibrium under Perfect Competition. Again, while the Austrian economists, particularly Wieser, made a sharp break with the labour theory by adopting the Opportunity Cost, Walras left room for the Real Cost theory by exhibiting the supplies of factors of production as functions of their prices. But these differences seem to be immaterial, since the Austrian economists themselves implied some concept of an optimum when they criticised Collectivist economic planning and since the Real Cost function dropped out unobtrusively from the writings of Walras's disciples. Thus Pareto's curves of " complete transformation " are nothing but Opportunity Cost curves based on the assumption of a given quantity of resources, while Barone started from a given stock of productive resources (including land) which he called " capital " in Prof. Fisher's inclusive sense (cf. Pareto, *Manuel d'economie politique*, Chaps. V and VI ; E. Barone, *Ministry of Production* in *Collectivist Economic Planning*, Hayek ed., p. 245 n.).

But what really made the Lausanne and the Austrian schools similar was their common use of the following three concepts : (i) the Static State, (ii) Perfect Competition and (iii) the General Equilibrium. The Static State neatly circumscribed analysis within a framework of given preferences, technique and resources while the General Equilibrium of Perfect Competition, by rigorously bringing out the mutual interrelations between the different elements of the economic system, stressed the essential unity of the formal means-ends relationship of the scarcity problem. Given this common approach, the common central welfare economic problem emerged as the choice between alternative uses of *given* resources to obtain the maximum satisfaction of *given* individuals' preferences.

On the other hand, few English economists completely accepted these three adjuncts of the new " pure " economics as contrasted with the Classical Political Economy.

(i) Marshall's distrust of the Static State is well known (cf. Letter to J. B. Clark, *Memorials of Alfred Marshall*, p. 415). Further, instead of regarding changes in the supplies of factors as the " exogenous changes in data " as the Austrian economists would have done, Marshall was concerned with tracing out the long-term mutual repercussions between the supplies of factors and the equilibrium process through the slow but steady working of the Real Cost. Besides this, the English economists had inherited from J. S. Mill the deep-rooted classical belief that the economic welfare of society depends, not only on the efficient allocation of *given* resources, but also on the " dynamic " laws of changes in capital accumulation and population (cf. Mill, *Principles*, Book IV, Chaps. I–III). This comes out very clearly in the theory of Optimum Population developed by Sidgwick and Cannan.

(ii) Again the full-fledged concept of Perfect Competition with its formidable array of assumption concerning perfect mobility, divisibility and knowledge was too unrealistic for the English economists. They were not interested in the purely academic question of how Optimum would be attained under idealised conditions ; they were concerned with testing how efficiently the free play of economic forces in real life work to promote economic welfare. Thus they adopted a more realistic model of Free Competition which assumes free entry to industry but is compatible with a certain amount of friction and divergence from the Optimum.

(iii) Given their interest in concrete cases of exceptions to the general principle of laissez-faire, the English economists found it more convenient to use a method of Partial Analysis rather than the General Equilibrium. It was not that the leaders of English economics were unaware of the General Equilibrium implications ; it was merely that they believed that more useful results could be obtained by selecting a few relations which have a quantitatively significant bearing on a concrete problem at hand, rather than by making a complete but unwieldy catalogue of all the theoretically possible relations between the different elements of the economic system.

Besides all these, what really distinguished the English welfare economics from the Continental approach was its implicit acceptance of the labour-theory outlook which conceives the economic problem as the struggle of man against his environment. As we have seen, once the economic problem was conceived in this way, welfare analysis was inevitably focused as man's net gain from his efforts on the Social Surplus which is equal to Gross Social Output minus the Outlay required to produce it. Thus the Marshall-Pigou definition of the national dividend as the net annual product after " maintaining capital intact " is nothing but a more refined concept of Ricardo's physical Net Revenue [1] multiplied by appropriate money prices. Further, the introduction of the Marginal Utility analysis did not alter the basic structure of the problem : it merely turned Ricardo's physical surplus into a subjective surplus which for

[1] With wages added back to it.

society as a whole is equal to the sum of Total Utilities from all the goods and services minus the sum of Total Disutilities in producing them. Thus Edgeworth constructed elaborate equations purporting to represent this Aggregate Subjective Surplus while even Marshall toyed with this unwieldy concept before he turned to a more workable Partial analysis of the Consumers' and Producers' surpluses from particular commodities (cf. Edgeworth, *Mathematical Psychics*, pp. 67 et seq. ; Marshall, *Principles*, Mathematical Appendix, note xiv, p. 851). Later on we shall see that Marshall's Partial Surplus analysis is usable whether or not we accept the labour-theory outlook ; nevertheless, it is useful to know its historical antecedents.

This then is the general view of the various theories of welfare economics at the subjective level which we are going to study in Part II of this book. Since they represent more or less parallel developments it will be unpractical to arrange them in their exact chronological order. We therefore propose to adopt the following arrangement which, though arbitrary, has certain advantages.

In Chapter VII which follows we will consider " The Theory of the General Optimum ", representing the development of welfare economics in Continental schools. Since this will be used as a general map of reference, we shall incorporate the modern economists' interpretation and extension of the theory wherever necessary. In Chapter VIII we will pick up the thread of the development of the English thought and consider the transition from the classical to the modern English welfare analysis under the heading of " The Characteristics of the Neo-Classical Welfare Economics ". In Chapter IX we shall consider " The Marshallian Surplus Analysis " as one of the most important fruits of the English approach to welfare economics. We will conclude Part II of this book by a study of Prof. Pigou's *Economics of Welfare* as the fusion point between the English and the Continental approach to welfare economics.

CHAPTER VII

THE THEORY OF THE GENERAL OPTIMUM

THE development of the theory of optimum by the marginal utility economists can be best appreciated by recapitulating where the classical economists had left off in their analysis of the competitive equilibrium. We have seen that the central problem of the classical economists was the problem of economic expansion and not the problem of allocative efficiency but that nevertheless they also possessed a rough workable theory of the competitive optimum (cf. Chap. IV above).

The *locus classicus* of this is Chapters VII and X in Book I of the *Wealth of Nations*. There Smith had established two general propositions. Firstly, that free competition in the consumers' market would equate the price of each commodity to its cost of production and that this would ensure that the " right " quantity of each commodity was produced. Secondly, that free competition in the producers' market would equalise the Net Advantages of the factors of production in all industries and that this would ensure that the " right " amount of resources was allocated to each industry. These two conditions were quite sufficient for the classical economists' purpose of considering the problem of allocative efficiency as a subsidiary problem. When, however, we want to consider the problem of allocative efficiency as the central problem a more stringent formulation of the optimum becomes necessary ; for the classical formulation leaves at least three main gaps to be filled :

(i) Smith had shown how the " right " total quantities of different commodities would be produced, but he had not shown how these " right " total quantities would be parcelled out in " right " amounts and in " right " combinations among each of the individual consumers.

(ii) Similarly, Smith had shown how the " right " total quantities of resources would be allocated to different industries, but he had not shown how the different factors of production would be combined in " right " proportions and how each of the individual producers would be producing the " right " output. Here, however, the gap left behind by the classical economists is not so clear-cut since they had always implicitly assumed that each producer would be producing at the minimum average cost. This assumption does imply the two further conditions although these were not brought out clearly by the labour-theory approach. The problem of the " right " proportions of different factors was obscured due to the habit of treating labour as the only factor and of subsuming capital under the heading of stored-up labour. The problem of the " right " output for each firm was pushed to the background since all industries, except agriculture, was supposed to be working under constant returns to scale. It will be remembered that in the Ricardian system, diminishing returns from land, by raising money wages and costs all round, merely served to limit the expansion of the total volume of economic activity and not the expansion of a particular industry. A particular industry could expand at constant costs, so long as the additional labour required for its expansion was released by other industries, leaving the margin of cultivation for society as a whole unchanged. This in effect meant that once the technically most efficient method of production was adopted the producer attained the position of minimum cost and that the size of his output did not matter.

(iii) 'Finally, none of the major English classical economists from Smith downwards ever clearly understood the proposition that the relative demand for factors by different industries was derived from the relative consumers' demand for the respective products of these industries. Thus although it was stated that the price of a commodity was made up of " natural " rates of rewards of the factors, a systematic relation between the equilibrium in the consumers' market and the equilibrium in the producers' market was not worked out.

The task of this chapter is now clear. In section I we will show how the sharper edge of the theory of Diminishing Marginal Utility or rather Marginal Rate of Substitution enables us to fill up the first gap and to arrive at a rigorous formulation of the optimum in the consumers' market. In section II we will show how the Marginal Productivity theory and the concept of the Opportunity Cost enables us to fill up the second gap and to arrive at a stringent formulation of the optimum in the producers' market. In section III we will co-ordinate the optima in the consumers' and the producers' market to arrive at the General Optimum of the whole economic system, thus filling up the third gap left behind by the classical economists.

This plan easily fits into our fundamental classification in terms of the different levels of analysis. The optimum in the consumers' market may be regarded as the optimum at the purely subjective level if we concentrate on the maximisation of consumers' wants on the basis of the given quantities of the commodities brought to the market (postponing the question whether or not the commodities have been produced in the technically most efficient way). Again the optimum in the producers' market may be regarded as the optimum at the physical or technical level by a reverse process of abstraction. Strictly speaking, of course, the optimum in the consumers' market cannot really be separated from the optimum in the producers' market since they are merely the different facets of the General Equilibrium process, and the maximum economic welfare for society will not be achieved in a complete sense unless the subjective and the physical optima are attained simultaneously. It is, however, instructive to study the individual properties of each optimum separately, isolating it from the web of the General Equilibrium process so long as we remember that it is an extremely artificial expository device.

I

The logical scaffolding necessary for a stringent formulation of the optimum in the consumers' market is the theory of the determinateness of the equilibrium of exchange under free competition. The main problems involved here may be stated as follows in their logical order. Given the quantities of various commodities brought to the market by the individuals and given their tastes and propensities to trade : (i) How are the equilibrium prices of these commodities established ? (ii) What determine the quantities of the commodities purchased by each of these individuals at these equilibrium prices ? (iii) In what precise sense can we say that these equilibrium prices and quantities purchased under free competition maximise the satisfaction of the consumers in the market ? It should be noted that for the solution of all these problems, we accept the quantities of commodities brought to the market as given, without inquiring further whether they are produced in the most efficient way. We are here interested only in the optimum at the subjective level ; the latter question belongs to the optimum at the physical level which will be considered in the next section.

(i) The equilibrium set of prices are those prices which equate the total demand for each commodity (including withheld supply) with the total quantity brought to the market. From the point of view of the individual, prices in the market are given, but, from the point of view of society as a whole, market prices are merely the result of the various individual exchanges.   The question is, how can the combined actions of the various individuals each possessing only a fragmentary knowledge of the facts of the market result in the correct equilibrium prices which will clear the market? If at the beginning of the market some individual makes exchanges at wrong prices, might not the final prices diverge from the equilibrium prices?   How can we establish a determinate set of equilibrium prices independently of the incidental disturbances of the trial and error method?   Marshall, Walras and Edgeworth each suggested a method of getting out of this difficulty.

Marshall's method was to concentrate on a particular market and to show that the marginal utility of money from the point of view of that market may be considered constant, since the individuals spend only a small proportion of their total incomes on each of the commodities.   He was then able to establish that the final rate of exchange would be independent of the path followed to reach it (*Principles*, Book V, Chap. II).   This solution is all right for a partial analysis, but when we consider the market for all commodities simultaneously, the incidental losses and gains from exchanging at wrong prices may be far from being negligible.

Walras and Edgeworth put forward solutions which are available for the General Equilibrium but which appear artificial compared with Marshall's solution.   Walras, with Gallic exuberance, pictured the equilibrium as being reached by " crying " the prices in the market, while Edgeworth preferred to have his individuals whisper " recontracts " to each other like gentlemen (cf. Walras, *Éléments*, Édition définitive, p. 44 ; Edgeworth, *Mathematical Psychics*, p. 19). In either case, the solution seems to depend on the condition that individuals acquire the requisite knowledge of the market by preliminary skirmishes and that no real exchanges take place until the correct equilibrium prices are arrived at.   This is unsatisfactory because it is merely a roundabout method of assuming that perfect knowledge exists in the market.   Without belittling the importance of the General Equilibrium, it seems fair to say that the Walrasian system of equations relating to the total demand and supply of commodities " hardly amounts to more than an assurance that things will work themselves out somehow, though it is not very clear how they will work themselves out " (cf. J. R. Hicks, *Value and Capital*, pp. 60–1).   We should, however, remember a basic condition which favours a determinate solution, viz. the assumption that, in a competitive market, the amount of commodity demanded and supplied by each individual is such a small proportion of the total demand and supply of the market as to have no palpable effect on the price. This eliminates all those complicated reactions of the activities of one individual on those of the others which make the determination of the equilibrium in an oligopolistic market so much more difficult.

(ii) Let us, however, follow Walras and Edgeworth and assume that a determinate set of equilibrium prices has been established somehow or other before actual exchanges take place. These prices determine the distribution of income among the individuals according to the quantities of different commodities each of them respectively possesses. It is now possible to determine the relative quantities of different commodities which each individual will acquire at these given prices on the basis of his given tastes and preferences. The principle of Diminishing Marginal Utility makes it clear that the individual will maximise his satisfaction by acquiring each commodity up to the point where its marginal utility is equal to its price. Thus the individual attains equilibrium when his marginal utilities of the commodities are proportional to their prices, for at that point he can no longer increase his satisfaction by re-allocating expenditure and has therefore no incentive for further exchanges. This solution was severally arrived at by most of the Marginal Utility economists and was perhaps most clearly expressed in terms of the General Equilibrium by Walras.

The fact that each individual tries to make his marginal utilities proportional to the given prices is, however, not peculiar to the competitive market. Individual buyers would behave in exactly the same way even if the prices were monopoly prices or discriminated prices. What really distinguishes the competitive market from other types of market is that no individual buyer or seller (or groups of them) can influence the prevailing market price and that a uniform price is charged to everyone in the market. Only when these two further conditions are fulfilled, a significant result emerges. Then, since every individual is trying to make his marginal utilities proportional to the same set of prices, the ratio of marginal utilities of any pair of commodities must be the same for all individuals when equilibrium of the market is attained. From the point of view of welfare analysis, this, and not the mere fact that each individual makes his marginal utilities proportional to given prices, is the most important characteristic of the competitive equilibrium.

However, to be able to define the competitive equilibrium in this way, the classical concept of free entry into the market is not sufficient by itself. We need a more elaborate concept of Perfect Competition which further assumes that there is perfect mobility in the market and that commodities are capable of being bought and sold in small amounts (cf. Chap. IV above for a fuller distinction between the concepts of Free Competition and Perfect Competition). This new concept of " atomistic " competition came naturally to all mathematical economists and may be traced to the pioneer work of Cournot (*Researches*, Chap. VIII). Like the Static State it may be regarded as a logical device to formulate the optimum under the most favourable conditions and was therefore more popular with the Continental economists than with the English economists who, with the exception of Edgeworth, preferred to use the more realistic concept of Free Competition (cf. Edgeworth, *Mathematical Psychics*, p. 18 ; Marshall, *Principles*, pp. 8–13).

(iii) In order to find out in what precise sense we can say that the equilibrium of exchange under Perfect Competition maximises the satisfaction of the consumers, we need to follow Pareto in his refinement of the Utility theory. These refinements are now so familiar to the modern students that we can go on directly to consider their influence on welfare economics (cf. J. R. Hicks, *Value and Capital*, Chap. I for a standard exposition of Pareto's Utility theory and its relation to the theory of Value). Given the older conception of Utility as the measurable function of the quantity of a given commodity, it was natural to look upon an individual's satisfaction as a definite magnitude equal to the sum of total utilities derived from the commodities he consumed. Similarly, the satisfaction of society as a whole was regarded as the sum of the quantities of individuals' satisfaction, which implied that the satisfaction of different individuals could be compared and added up.

Pareto profoundly changed the approach to the subjective optimum by introducing the concept of the " index of ophélimité " or the individual's position of preference as determined by the alternative combinations of different commodities at his choice. By means of this he was able to generalise the utility analysis to the case of related commodities and to define the optimum without using the question-begging concept of measurable utility and without entering into interpersonal comparisons of utility. Without postulating the sum of different individuals' satisfaction, he simply defined the optimum as a situation where no single individual can move to a more preferred position without pushing the others to less preferred positions. So long as this condition is not fulfilled there would be no optimum since then some individuals would be able to improve their positions while leaving the others as well off as before (cf. Pareto, *Manuel*, Chaps. IV and VI).

Pareto's concept of the subjective optimum can be best illustrated in terms of Edgeworth's Indifference Curve technique, although strangely enough Edgeworth reverted to the concept of measurable utility when he came to the section on Utilitarian Calculus (Edgeworth, op. cit., pp. 21–2 ; 59–60). In Fig. 1, below, measuring the quantities of two commodities X and Y along the co-ordinates OX and OY, let us draw the familiar indifference

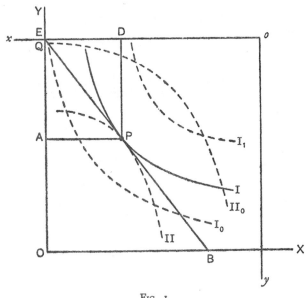

FIG. 1.

curve I for a given individual, representing the various combinations of X and Y, the choice between which leaves him indifferent, i.e. they represent the same total utility to him. The indifference curve is convex towards the origin O, since as we move down along the curve the increase in X diminishes his marginal utility of X in relation to Y (cf., however, Hicks, op. cit., for a more stringent formulation). On the same principle we can draw a family of indifference curves for this individual : curves like I_0 on the diagram which lies below and to the left of I representing less preferred positions, while curves like I_1, which lies above and to the right of I, representing more preferred positions. Let our individual come to the market with OQ of commodity Y and no X. Let the rate of exchange given by the competitive market be OQ of Y for OB of X. He is then on the indifference curve I_0 and can increase his satisfaction by exchanging Y for X. After he has given up QA of Y and acquired AP of X, he will stop exchanging, since at that point the price line QB is tangential to his indifference curve I. P represents the most favourable position he can attain with his initial income OQ and the prevailing price opportunity represented by QB. At that point the ratio of his marginal utilities or his marginal rate of substitution between X and Y is equal to the ratio of their prices ; or in the old terminology his marginal utilities are proportional to the prices.

Similarly, we can construct another family of indifference curves (II and II_0 on the diagram) for a second individual, measuring the quantities of X and Y along ox and oy. Let us assume that the second individual comes to the market with oE of X and no Y. The same price line QB is given to him by the market. Keeping OX parallel to ox and OY parallel to oy we can superimpose the two sets of co-ordinates in such a way that the point E coincides with Q. By a similar argument it can be shown that the second individual will attain the most favourable position opened to him when he has exchanged ED of X for DP of Y and when his indifference curve II is tangential to the price line QB at P. Fig. 1 now clearly illustrates the important characteristic of the competitive equilibrium we have pointed out above. At the equilibrium point P, the marginal rate of substitution between X and Y for the first individual is equal to the ratio of prices of X and Y which is in turn equal to the marginal rate of substitution between X and Y for the second individual. Thus the marginal rate of substitution between X and Y is the same for both individuals and this condition is shown by the tangency of their two indifference curves I and II at P.

The tangency of the two individuals' indifference curves is a very powerful device to illustrate the properties of the subjective optimum. In Fig. 2, let us draw a family of indifference curves I_0, I_1, I_2, I_3, for the first individual and another family of indifference curves II_0, II_1, II_2, II_3, for the second individual, both in an ascending order of preference. Let us assume as before that the first individual comes to the market with OQ of Y and no X and the second, oE of X and no Y. As before these two indifference maps can be superimposed so that Q which coincides with E is the common starting-point for both individuals. Joining the locus of points at which the curves Is are tangential to the curves IIs we have what

Edgeworth calls the Contract Curve, CC in Fig. 2. Now, at least two far-reaching propositions can be deduced from the contract curve.

The first is that through the equilibrium process we have described above, exchange in a competitive market must always land both individuals on a point on the contract curve, e.g. P on the diagram, and that once the individuals are on the contract

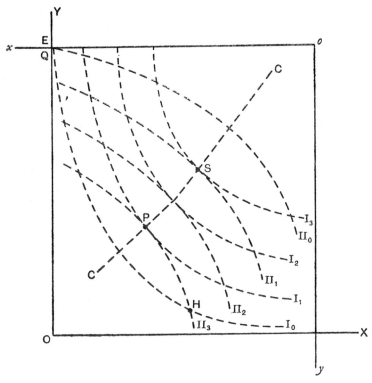

FIG. 2.

curve neither can move to a more preferred position without pushing the other to a less preferred position. On the other hand, if the individuals are at some point H away from the contract curve, it can be seen that the first individual can move up from H to P, which lies on a higher indifference curve I_1, while leaving the second individual on the same indifference curve II_3 as before. If one of the individuals is a monopolist, exchange will take place outside the contract curve since the monopolist will obtain maximum profit by forcing exchange to the point where the offer curve of the buyer is tangential to his highest indifference curve. Thus the monopoly equilibrium will not fulfil the optimum condition of equal marginal rate of substitution for all individuals (cf. N. Kaldor, " A Note on Tariffs and the Terms of Trade ", *Economica*, Nov. 1940, p. 379, for an illustration of this point).

The second proposition concerns the relation between the subjective optimum and the sum of individuals' satisfaction and the distribution of incomes among them. Let us take the equilibrium point P on the diagram. It merely states that with the initial quantities of X and Y brought to the market by the two individuals and the distribution of income among them determined by the price line QP, each individual is at the most favourable position opened to him. It does not go on to state further that the sum of the first individual's satisfaction represented by I_1, and the second individual's satisfaction represented by II_3, is the maximum sum of satisfaction which can be obtained for both individuals. On the contrary, different points on the contract curve will represent different aggregate satisfactions for both individuals and the subjective optimum defined in the Paretian way has nothing to do with the maximum sum of satisfaction of both individuals. Thus the point S in Fig. 2 which redistributes income in favour of the individual who exchanges Y for X has as much right to represent an optimum position as the original equilibrium point P. Thus the subjective optimum is a purely relative optimum defined on the basis of given prices and a given distribution of income however unequal that distribution may be.

Wicksell in criticising Walras and Pareto had argued that the method of deducing the condition of maximum satisfaction from the proportionality of the marginal utilities tends to obscure the existing inequalities of incomes, and that the position of maximum satisfaction in the full sense of the term is not attained until the absolute marginal utilities and not the ratio of marginal utilities is equal between all individuals. Abstracting from peculiarities in tastes, this in effect means that maximum satisfaction will not be attained without equal incomes (Wicksell, *Lectures*, Vol. I, pp. 72–83, p. 4). Wicksell's criticism, motivated as it was by his magnificent social sympathies, does not seem to be justifiable, at least with regard to Pareto. The Paretian formulation abstracts from unequal distribution of incomes simply because it is not possible to formulate a scientific concept of subjective optimum which does not involve interpersonal comparisons of utility except on the basis of a given income distribution.[1] This does not at all mean that the given distribution of income which is accepted for the purpose of analysis is socially desirable and should not prevent the economist from pursuing equalitarian principles if he desires. Thus Pareto and Barone postulated " an ethically desirable distribution of income " when they considered the ideal working of a collective economy (Pareto, *Manuel*, French ed., 1909, pp. 362–3 ; Barone, *Ministry of Production*, Hayek ed., p. 246). Even Walras who, on self-admission, set out to counter the attacks of the Saint Simonite, Lambert Bay, advocated that unearned incomes should be abolished by the state ownership of land. Finally, Marshall, whom no one could accuse of being unaware of the inequalities of incomes, accepted that the equilibrium of demand and supply will bring about a position of maximum satisfaction in the limited sense we have defined above (Marshall, *Principles*, pp. 470–1).

II

So far we have been concerned with the optimum at the subjective level which is defined on the basis of given quantities of finished products. We have now to inquire whether these given products are themselves produced in the most efficient manner and to find out the conditions of optimum production at the physical level. Before we do that it will be helpful to sketch briefly the development of the marginal productivity theory in its relation to the General Equilibrium analysis.

The connecting link Smith provided between the equilibrium of the consumers' market and that of the producers' market was that the price of a commodity which equates its market demand and supply gravitates towards its " natural " price ; and this natural price is equal to its cost of production at the " natural " rates of earnings of the factors employed. Nevertheless, the concept of the " natural " price is not determinate. Although it was stated that in equilibrium the earnings of the factors of production would be equal in all industries, there was no attempt to explain what determined the rate of earnings themselves. The " natural " rates merely seem to be the long-term average of the prevailing market rates.

---

[1] Modern economists have now developed a method of " compensation " by which it is possible to find out whether society as a whole is better off or worse off by a given change even if this change involves changes in the distribution of income. For the full treatment see Scitovsky's " Note on Welfare Propositions", *Review of Economic Studies*, Nov. 1941.

Ricardo made a great stride forward when he explained that the rate of profit on capital was determined by the physical product of labour at the margin of cultivation minus its wages : i.e. the rate of profit would be determined by the marginal net product of the capitalistic process of production (cf. Dr. Edelberg's reconstruction of the Ricardian theory of Profit, *Economica*, 1931). However, Ricardo's theory falls short on two points. Firstly, the marginal product approach was confined to the application of capital only ; thus the rate of wages was supposed to be determined, not by the marginal product of labour, but by the minimum subsistence level determined by habits and customs ; secondly, the essential connecting link between the consumers' and the producers' market, i.e. the fact that the producers' demand for factors is derived from the consumers' demand for the products, was not recognised.

Ricardo's first shortcoming was decisively remedied by Thünen, who has a high claim to be recognised as the founder of the marginal productivity theory. In the first part of his *Der Isolierte Staat*, he generalised the Ricardian theory of rent in terms of the distance from the market. However, it is only when we come to the second part of his book (published some twenty-six years later in 1850) that we have the marginal productivity theory in its modern form. On the analogy of the distance from the market which determines the " margin of cultivation ", Thünen argued that the successive application of labour " must be continued up to the point at which the extra yield obtained through the last labourer employed equals in value the wage he receives ". " And the wage which the last employed labourer receives must form the norm for all labourers of the same skill and ability ; since for the same services it is impossible to pay unequal wages." Similarly, the earnings of capital " is determined by the yield of the last particle of capital employed " (J. H. v. Thünen, *Der Isolierte Staat*, Waentig's ed., 1930, pp. 415, 577 and 498).

The second shortcoming of Ricardo's theory, i.e. its failure to connect the demand for factors with the demand for products, was made good by J. B. Say who was brought up in the utility tradition of Condillac. In an interesting passage in the 4th edition of his *Traité*, Say maintained that—

The current value of productive exertion is founded upon the value of an infinity of products compared one with another ; that the value of the product is not founded upon that of productive agency as some authors have erroneously affirmed ; and that, since the desire of an object, and consequently its value, originates in its utility, it is the ability to create utility wherein originates that desire, that gives value to productive agency ; which value is proportionate to the importance of its co-operation in the business of production, and forms, in respect to each product individually, what is called the cost of its production (op. cit., Prinsep's translation of 4th ed., p. 8).

This passage was omitted from the 6th edition, but the same idea was reiterated when Say pointed out that entrepreneurs are the " intermediaries who demand the productive services required for any product in relation to the demand for the product " (op. cit., 6th ed., 1841, p. 349).

Before we follow the development of the marginal productivity theory proper, let us consider Walras's approach to the General Equilibrium of Production which bypasses the marginal productivity theory and at the same time reconciles the Austrian Opportunity Cost with the English Real Cost concept. Walras did this by considering the problem of the pricing of factors assuming " the coefficients of production " to be fixed.

> With fixed coefficients, and with perfect competition, the equilibrium prices of the products must depend on the prices of the factors ; thus, given the prices of the factors, the whole price-system [of products and factors] can be derived by simple process of addition. But, given this whole price-system, the demands for the products and the supply of the factors can be determined from the tastes and abilities of the individuals composing the economy. Again, once the demands for the products are determined, the demands for the factors can be technically deduced. We can thus write both the demands for the factors and the supplies of the factors as functions of the set of factor-prices ; and determine equilibrium in the factor markets as before. The equilibrium prices in the factor markets now determine the equilibrium prices of the products (J. R. Hicks, " Leon Walras ", *Econometrica*, 1934, pp. 343-4).

As is well known, Walras's proposition that in equilibrium prices of the products are equal to their costs so that entrepreneurs make " neither profit nor loss " is merely the method of reckoning the " normal " profits into costs.

For our purpose, Walras's construction is remarkable because it offers a short-cut method of deriving the General Optimum of Production and Exchange from Adam Smith's simple conditions of equilibrium in the consumers' market. Once the demands and supplies of the various products are equated at their equilibrium prices, optimum production is ensured because (a) the " right " proportions in which the different factors should be combined with each other are given by technical conditions and (b) all the scarce factors will be used up. Thus let us suppose that the total demand for a particular factor (which can be technically deduced from consumers' demand for various products at existing prices) is less than its total available supply. Its price will fall and this will expand the output of those products the production of which requires more of this factor relatively to other factors, and contract the output of those the production of which requires relatively less of this factor until its entire supply is absorbed. If the technical conditions and consumers' tastes are such that the surplus factor cannot be absorbed in this way, then it becomes a free good and does not raise any economic problem of its utilisation. Thus in the Walrasian scheme of thought the equilibrium in consumers' market implies the optimum both at the subjective and the physical level. It may also be noted that the assumption of fixed coefficients of production which cannot be modified by the substitution of one factor for another brings out the technical obstacles facing the physical process of production more prominently than the assumption of variable coefficients and thus paves the way for the concept of optimum production at the physical level. In contrast, if we follow the Austrian economists and assume that the technical rigidities of production can be eliminated to a large extent by human choice, it is natural to push the objective determinants of production to the background and concentrate only on the subjective level of analysis (cf. W. L. Valk, *The Principles of Wages*, Chap. XII, pp. 113–14).

The marginal productivity theory proper was developed by a distinguished series of economists. Menger and his followers put forward the method of imputing the reward of a factor according to the loss in value of the product caused by its withdrawal from production and Wieser introduced the concept of the Opportunity Cost which defines cost in terms of foregone opportunities of creating utilities and not in terms of the disutility of effort (Menger, *Grundsatze*, p. 124, L.S.E. Reprint ; Wieser, *Natural Value*, Smart's English ed.). Marshall, independently of his contemporaries but basing his work on that of Thünen, arrived at both the Principle of Substitution similar to the Austrian theory and the concept of the Marginal Net Product which can be applied to Walras's case of fixed technical coefficients (Marshall, *Principles*, pp. 355–9 ; ibid., 1st ed., p. 548). J. B. Clark's *Distribution of Wealth* and Wicksell's formulation of the marginal productivity theory in his *Lectures*, Vol. I, deserve special mention. Wicksell's treatment is more compact and more satisfactory on some points than Clark's, but both authors have the merit of enabling us to see very clearly the marginal productivity theory, not merely as a theory of the pricing of the factors but further as the means of integrating the social process of production with exchange. As Clark succinctly puts it : " Production, a synthesis ; Distribution, an analysis " (*Essentials of Economic Theory*, Chap. V).

The final version of the General Equilibrium of Production which has emerged from the works of these and the succeeding authors is very similar in structure to the General Equilibrium of Exchange, and the main problems we have to solve may be arranged in a similar way.

(i) First of all there is the pricing of the factors. Just as in the product market, the equilibrium prices are those prices which equate the demand and supply of each factor at those prices. Given the price of a factor, total demand for it can be derived from its physical productivity at given technique (assuming either fixed or variable coefficients of production) and by the market values of the products it helps to produce. On the supply side, however, there is a complication which does not arise in the product market except in particular cases when the income effects on the sellers cannot be neglected. In the factor market, however, since each owner of the factors normally obtains the bulk of his income from the sale of his factors, the price which can be got for them in the market will exert a considerable influence on the amount he is willing to supply. Thus he may decide to withhold a part of his supply, not only when the price offered has fallen too low to be worthwhile, but also when the price offered has risen enough to give him the same income as before by selling a smaller quantity. Marshall pointed out the importance óf the elasticity of supply in the analysis of the factor market and we should bear this complication in mind when we assume a " given " stock of resources (Marshall, *Principles*, p. 523 ; also Robbins, " Note on the Elasticity of Demand for Income in Terms of Effort ", *Economica*, 1930).

(ii) The next problem is how each producer should combine the different types of factors in " right " proportions. As before, from the point of view of the market as a whole, the prices of both the products and the factors are determined by the result of individuals' transactions ; but from the point of view of an individual producer (assuming perfect competition in the factor and product markets) the prices of both the factors and the products are given to him by the market. In the same way as an individual consumer maximises his gains from exchange by making his marginal utilities of the products proportional to their prices, an individual producer will maximise his gains from production by making the value of the marginal products of the factors proportional to their prices.

But there is a further difficulty here which does not arise in the consumers' market. The total quantity of products which a consumer buys is normally limited by his given income, but, on the other hand, the total quantity of factors which a producer may buy is not so limited beforehand ; so long as he is making " abnormal profits " it will pay him to borrow and expand his scale of production. Thus the equilibrium of the firm requires a further condition, viz. its total receipts from the sale of the product should be exhausted by payments to the factors employed according to their marginal products. Treating " normal profits " as the marginal product of the entrepreneurial factor and reckoning it in factor costs, this means that the firm should have " zero profits ". The mathematical condition required by this equality of the total product to the sum of the marginal products of the factors employed is that the firm should be working under conditions of constant returns to scale and at first it looked as though we should have to confine our analysis to this highly restricted case. However, Wicksell came to the rescue and showed that what was really required by the equilibrium condition of the firm was not that it should be working under constant cost for the entire range of its scale of output but merely that it should conform to the law of constant returns at a given point. It then turned out that this required condition of constant returns was nothing but the classical presumption that under competition each firm should somehow be working at minimum average cost, for, at the point of minimum cost, the cost curve of the firm, which, after sloping down is about to curl upwards, is horizontal (Wicksell, *Lectures*, Vol. I, p. 129 ; also Walras's " Note sur le réfutation de la Théorie anglaise du fermage de M. Wicksteed ", appendix to the 3rd ed. of the *Éléments*, 1896). The minimum cost condition further implies that the price of the output should be equal to its marginal cost since the marginal cost curve cuts the average cost curve at the minimum point. Thus the gaps left behind by the classical theory, viz. the problem of how the factors should be combined with each other in " right " proportions and the problem of the " right " output for each producer, are now filled by the marginal productivity theory.

(iii) We now come to the final problem of finding out how the General Equilibrium of Production under Free Competition leads to the optimum production at the physical level. In deriving the subjective optimum from the General Equilibrium of exchange, we started from the equilibrium condition that each consumer makes his marginal utilities of the products proportional to their prices. But, since the same set of product-prices are given to all consumers, we were able to eliminate the price ratios and arrive at the definition of optimum in purely subjective terms : viz. the marginal subjective rate of substitution between any pair of products must be the same for all consumers. Exactly the same process can now be applied to the producers' market. Since the same sets of factor-prices and product-prices are given to all producers, we will be able to eliminate the price ratios and arrive at the definition of optimum production in purely physical terms : viz. the marginal technical rate of substitution between any factor and any product, any pair of two factors and any pair of two products, must be the same for all producers. These conditions can be worked out by taking three type cases :

(*a*) In the case where each producer produces a single type of product with a single type of factor,[1] to equate his marginal cost to price, he must make the marginal rate of transformation between the factor and product equal to their price ratio. Since, however, all producers buy the factor and sell the product at the uniform market price, it follows that the marginal (technical) rate of transformation between the factor and product must be the same for all producers.

(*b*) Next take the case where each producer produces a single type of product with many types of factors. We have said that in equilibrium each producer will make the values of the marginal products of the factors proportional to their prices. Since, however, we are assuming a single product, we can eliminate the value of the product. Thus each producer will make the ratio of the marginal physical productivity of any pair of factors, or the marginal technical rate of substitution between these factors, equal to their price ratio. Since, however, the same set of factor-prices are given to all producers, it follows that the marginal technical rate of substitution between any pair of factors must be the same for all producers.[2] Wicksell was one of the first to give a clear formulation

---

[1] If " a single type of factor " is strictly interpreted, constant returns to scale would necessarily prevail and thus diminishing marginal rate of transformation implies the existence of a third factor.

[2] This proposition can be illustrated by using the geometry of the indifference curves in Fig. 1 above. If we measure along the X and Y axes, the quantities of two factors, the indifference curve can be turned into an " isoquant " curve, indicating the constant quantity of the product which can be produced by various combinations of the two factors. Given the principle of diminishing marginal productivity, the isoquant curve will be convex towards the origin and its slope will measure the ratio of the marginal physical products, or the technical rate of substitution between the two factors. In equilibrium, each producer will make his isoquant curve tangential to the price ratio

of this condition of optimum production in purely technical terms and to distinguish between the optimum at the physical level and the optimum at the subjective level (Wicksell, *Lectures*, Vol. I, pp. 133–44).

(*c*) The most interesting case for our argument is where each producer produces many products with a single type of factor or " resources in general ", for this serves as a convenient basis for the co-ordination of the physical with the subjective optimum.   The proposition that the marginal rate of substitution between any pair of products must be the same for all producers follows from the condition that each producer equates the price of each product to its marginal cost and that therefore the price ratio of any pair of products must be equal to the ratio of their marginal costs for him. Since, however, the same set of product-prices are given to all producers, it follows that the ratio of marginal costs must be the same for all producers.

The technical aspect of optimum production in this case can, however, be more vividly illustrated by using the Substitution Curves of the Comparative Cost theory (Haberler, *Theory of International Trade*, p. 176).   The ancestry of the modern Substitution Curve may be traced to Wieser's theory of Opportunity Cost which defines the cost of a product as the foregone utility of another product which might have been produced with the same resources and also to Pareto's " line of complete transformation " in the celebrated example of wine and vinegar (Wieser, *Natural Value* ;   Pareto, *Manuel*, Chaps. IV and VI).   The modern Substitution Curve differs from Wieser's concept in that the cost of a product is calculated in terms of foregone physical quantities of other products rather than in terms of foregone amounts of satisfaction (cf. Robbins, " Certain Aspects of the Theory of Cost ", *Economic Journal*, 1934). It further takes into account diminishing returns so that instead of Pareto's *lines* of transformation we have curves of transformation.

The Substitution Curve technique is based on a given distribution of resources among different regions, ruling out the migration of factors between one region or another.   In adapting that technique to the condition of optimum production [1] for producers within a single economy, there is no compelling reason why we should base

---

of the factors and since the same price ratio is given to all producers, the isoquant curves of all producers must therefore have the same slope.   Cf. Hicks, *Value and Capital*, p. 91, diagram 21.

[1] The argument and diagrams in the remainder of this section are adapted from J.R. Hicks's " Foundations of Welfare Economics ", *Economic Journal*, 1939, pp. 701–6.

our analysis on a given distribution of resources among the producers. It will be remembered that we have accepted a given distribution of incomes among the consumers for the purpose of the subjective optimum. But that was because we could not make interpersonal comparisons of utility. On the other hand, comparisons of productivity between different producing units is perfectly legitimate and therefore we will have to face the question whether it is not possible to increase the total social product by transferring the outlay of resources from one producing unit to another, i.e. by changing scale of output of the individual producing units. In real life this question will lead us to a number of highly interesting and complex questions ; but for our simplified model of perfect competition with perfect divisibility of factors, we may rule out the potential increase in productivity from "rationalisation" schemes. We may then accept Wicksell's condition of the equilibrium of the firm as a sufficient condition ensuring the optimum distribution of resources among the producing units.

If our method of getting over the difficulty of defining the optimum distribution of resources among producing units is accepted, then the problem of optimum production in our case (c) is reduced to the " right " combinations of the products which each producer should produce. Assuming that there are only two products in the economy, the technical potentialities facing each producer can be shown by a substitution curve. The abscissa of each point on this curve represents a certain quantity of one product, and the corresponding ordinate represents the maximum amount of the other whose production is consistent with that amount of the first. The slope of the curve at each point measures the marginal technical rate of substitution or the ratio of marginal costs of the two products for the producer. Thus assuming that each product is produced under conditions of diminishing returns, the curve will be concave towards the origin. We have seen that in equilibrium the ratio of marginal costs or the marginal rate of substitution between the two products must be the same for all producers. In geometrical terms, this condition can be vividly shown by compounding or " sitting " the production substitution curve of one producer with origin O_2 in an obversed way on the substitution curve of another with origin O_1, keeping the axes parallel (Fig. 3). The equality of the marginal rate of substitution between the products for both producers means that their substitution curves must be tangential to each other at some point P on the diagram, and if both curves are concave towards their respective origins, the tangency condition ensures that the two curves are just touching each other without overlapping. Once this condition is fulfilled, the total output of the two producers $O_1N + O_2n$ of the first product and $PN + Pn$ of the second product conforms to the condition of the technical optimum ; that is to say, the combined output of the first product cannot be increased without reducing the combined output of the second and vice versa.

If on the other hand we start from a situation Q in the diagram, where the marginal rate of substitution between the products is different for two producers, their production substitution curves will overlap when one is superimposed on the other in an obverse way (Fig. 4). Starting from this situation it will then be possible to

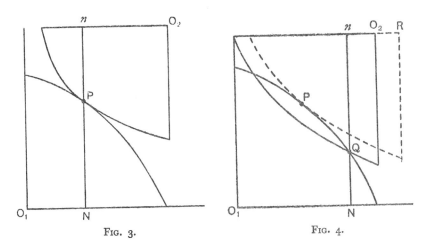

FIG. 3.   FIG. 4.

increase the total output of any one or both of the products by " tightening up " production and moving about the substitution curves until they are tangential to each other. Thus in Fig. 4, keeping the total output of the second product $QN + Qn$ constant, the total output of the first product can be increased from $O_1N + O_2n$ to $O_1N + nR$, i.e. by O_2R. The same " tightening up " process can be repeated by keeping the total output of the first product $O_1N + O_2n$ constant, in which case there must be a net increase in the total output of the second product. Alternatively, we can increase the total output of both products within the limits set by the maximum possible net increase of each product.

So far we have been assuming that diminishing returns prevailing throughout the productive range of each producer, i.e. each substitution curve is concave towards its origin without points of inflexion.   If this assumption is relaxed, we may have queer production substitution curves which may overlap with each other although they are tangential to each other at a certain point (Hicks, " Foundations ", Fig. 4, loc. cit., p. 705).   This means that the equality of the *marginal* rate of substitution or the tangency condition is not sufficient to ensure optimum production.   We must further take into account the " total conditions " which require that there is no overlap between the two curves.   In this case, optimum production will not be attained until the production of one product is abandoned by one of the producers and complete specialisation of production takes place (cf. Hicks, ibid., for another queer case where one producer is producing both products at increasing returns).   This condition, although plausible for a big economic unit as a country, is extremely unlikely for a private producer.

Thus in all our type cases (*a*), (*b*) and (*c*) we are able to define optimum production in purely physical terms, free from the subjective elements contained in price ratios.

III

We are now able to synthesise the optimum at the subjective level and the optimum at the physical level which we have been analysing separately in the last two sections.   The co-ordination of these two optima can be most effectively done by adopting Pareto's method of looking on the economic problem as the opposition of " tastes " and " obstacles ", each individual trying to satisfy his tastes as far as is possible in view of the obstacles to satisfaction which confront him.

Our analysis of the subjective optimum was done on a basis of a given quantity of finished products ; this means we abstract from technical obstacles of production assuming that they have been overcome in a given way.   On this basis the " obstacles " to satisfaction facing each individual are the " tastes " of other individuals and the given distribution of incomes.   The subjective optimum is therefore concerned with resolving the conflicting plans of various individuals to satisfy their tastes in the given circumstances. These individuals' plans are adapted to each other in the most efficient possible way when, with given tastes and incomes, it is not possible for any individual to move to a more preferred position without pushing the others to less preferred positions.   Similarly our analysis of the physical optimum was done by temporarily abstracting from the conflicting tastes of the individuals.   We assume that the conflicting tastes have been resolved in a certain way and, as the result, a certain system of product-prices and factor-prices has been established. Now these given prices may well be entirely arbitrary (i.e. not conforming to the requirements of the subjective optimum). But so long as the uniform set of prices are given to all producers, we can find out the conditions which must be fulfilled before the technical obstacles facing social production as a whole can be most efficiently overcome. As we have seen, with given sets of factor- and product-prices, the technical obstacles facing the society are most efficiently overcome when it is no longer possible to increase the physical output of a given producer or a given product without reducing the output of other products or other producers. The General Optimum of Production Welfare Economics [1] is the integration of these two partially constructed optima.

The concept of the General Optimum of Production and Exchange can be most clearly realised by using the geometrical device of the Indifference Curves and the Substitution Curves. Let us return to the theory of Comparative Cost and consider an isolated community producing two products. From the tastes of its members (and their income distribution) we can derive the community's indifference maps for these two products. From its resources and technique we can derive its production substitution curve measuring the first product along OX axis and the second along OY axis (Fig. 5). In the isolated state the community will attain the optimum by producing AP of the first product and OA of the second product, for at the point P its indifference curve I_0 is tangential to its substitution curve and therefore its subjective rate of substitution between the two products will be equal to its technical rate of substitution between them. Let us now suppose that this isolated community comes into contact with outside market where AP of the first product can be exchanged for AC of the second. Now the given price-line CP is not tangential to its indifference curve I_0 and its substitution curve at P. Even if it continues to produce

---

[1] Pareto's *Manuel*, Chap. VI, may be regarded as the *locus classicus* of the concept of the General Optimum in our sense. Unfortunately Pareto's *Manuel*, like Barone's *Ministry of Production*, is written in a crabbed way and marred by numerous slips and loose statements. Therefore in order to obtain a complete picture of the Paretian optimum we are obliged to resort to later authors' interpretation and development of the Paretian scheme, particularly J. R. Hicks's works, typified by his " Foundations of Welfare Economics",*Economic Journal,*1939. Cf. also Abraham Burke,"Alternative formulations of Welfare Economics", *Quarterly Journal of Economics*, 1937, and O. Lange, " Foundations of Welfare Economics ", *Econometrica*, 1942.

AP of the first product and *OA* of the second as before, the community can move to *Q* on a higher indifference curve *I* by exchange. It will, however, not maximise its gains until its production substitution curve is tangential to the price-line *ET* (parallel to *CP*) at *T*. Then it can move by exchange to *R* which lies on the highest possible indifference curve *I₂* which is open to it. At the point *R* optimum is attained, because its subjective rate of substitution between the two products is again equalised to its technical rate of substitution between the two, since both rates of substitution are

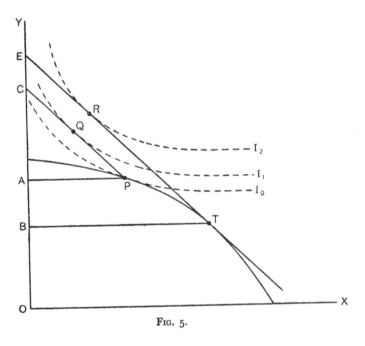

FIG. 5.

equal to the slope of the price-line *ET*. Now the price-line *ET* is given to other communities participating in exchange and thus in equilibrium (which under perfect competition brings about the optimum) the marginal subjective rate of substitution between the two products must be the same for all the participants in exchange ; the marginal technical rate of substitution between the two products must be the same for all participants in exchange : and both rates of substitution must be equal to given price ratio and therefore must be equal to each other.

This result can be adapted to state the condition of General Optimum for consumers and producers within a single economy.

In Optimum, the marginal subjective rate of substitution between any pair of products must be the same for all consumers ; the marginal technical rate of substitution between any pair of products must be the same for all producers : and since the ratio of prices between any pair of products is equal to the ratio of their marginal costs, the marginal rate of substitution between any pair of products both in the subjective and the technical sense must be the same for every one within the economic system.

IV

In judging the usefulness of the Paretian theory of the Optimum we should avoid two extreme attitudes. We should not follow the stick-in-the-mud " practical men " and dismiss the whole thing as a theoretical toy based on ideal conditions which can never be fully realised in practice. On the other hand, we should not be seduced by its formal elegance and symmetry and get ourselves lost among its theoretical refinements and ideal marginal adjustments which are not likely to involve significant quantities of economic welfare in real life.

In spite of the drastic simplifications involved in assuming Perfect Competition and the Static State, it has been a great achievement of the Paretian theory to build up a coherent system of general principles of economic efficiency which are applicable to all types of economic systems. The Optimum conditions are valid as much in a Collectivist economy as in a Private Enterprise economy, although at the moment their chief interest lies in providing a basis of criticism of the latter.

Further, there are many far-reaching questions of principle which can be best settled by referring to the Paretian scheme of thought. The two traditional bugbears of welfare analysis have been interpersonal comparisons of utility and normative value judgments. We have seen how the Paretian reformation of the Utility theory and the Indifference Map technique has overcome the first difficulty. With regard to the second also, the Paretian definition of the economic problem as the opposition of given tastes and obstacles is very helpful in clearing up our minds. Once that definition is accepted, it will be seen that the economist cannot be content with the mere description of how the economic system works ; by the very definition of his problem, he is obliged to consider the further question how efficiently the economic system fulfils its function of adjusting the means to *given* ends.

We are not like geologists, comparing rocks laid down by natural forces ; we are like archæologists, comparing flint instruments made by man for a purpose, one of whose functions must be to compare the relative efficiency of these implements (J. R. Hicks, loc. cit., p. 699).

Again, once we have grasped the concept of a welfare economics which studies the purely mechanical efficiency of the economic system in satisfying *given* individuals' wants, it will be seen that it need not involve any normative value judgments.   So long as we take the individuals' wants as given and constant and confine ourselves to the purely subjective level of welfare analysis we can still be ethically neutral.   An archæologist who shows that a given flint spearhead is an effective weapon of hunting need not necessarily approve of the slaughter of animals.   Similarly, when we have demonstrated that a given method of allocating the resources will satisfy the given wants better than another, it is not a categorical imperative that this particular method *ought* to be chosen.   In order to translate our proposition into actual policy, we need a further premise, viz. all these given wants of the same quality of ethical goodness.   It is true that some welfare economists are frequently inclined to assume this premise implicitly ; but there is a distinct scope for studying the purely mechanical efficiency of the economic system in satisfying given individuals' wants without accepting the utilitarian ethics.   We shall follow this discipline strictly throughout Part II of this book.

Taking into account all these points, it is perhaps not too much to say that the Paretian theory of the Optimum lays the foundations and clearly defines the limits of a scientific welfare economics whose propositions are logically as stringent as those of price economics.

On the other hand, the fact that the Optimum theory is merely a beginning and is very inadequate taken by itself will become clear as we trace the development of English welfare economic thought in the succeeding chapters, although even there we shall have to use the Optimum theory as a general reference map by means of which we can fit the different types of welfare analysis into their proper places.

The limitations of the Optimum theory are obvious.   Since the ideal conditions of Perfect Competition and the Static State are not obtained in real life, the normal feature in any actual economic system would be, not the attainment of the Optimum but Deviations from the Optimum.   It is therefore not enough to state the formal conditions of Optimum or even to advocate " structural planning " to make the economic system more competitive and hope for the best. We must study the actual technique of preventing these Deviations. Further, the most considerable gains or losses of welfare involved in the deviations from the Optimum are on the whole too large to be effectively tackled by *marginal* adjustments on which the bulk of the Optimum analysis is based. We must therefore take into account what Prof. Hicks has called the " Total Conditions " which can be most suitably studied in terms of the Marshallian Surplus analysis. For instance, the Optimum analysis in this chapter has been conducted on a given list of commodities. We have still to find out whether this list itself is an ideal list or whether on the basis of given and latent consumers' tastes, the economic welfare of society (calculated in terms of Consumers' and Producers' Surpluses) may not be increased by stopping the production of an existing commodity or by introducing a new commodity (cf. J. R. Hicks, " Rehabilitation of Consumers' Surplus ", *Review of Economic Studies*, 1941, pp. 112 et seq.). On the technical side also, the " Total Conditions " might be very important in Prof. Pigou's cases of " lumpy investments " and those far-reaching technical complimentarities and external economies which form the basis of the Increasing Returns (Pigou, *Economics of Welfare*, Book II, Chap. XVII).

Finally, the assumption of ideally Perfect Competition has virtually assumed away those rigidities and interrelations which give rise to those uncompensated services and disservices. These divergences between the Social and Private Products can be studied more conveniently in the more realistic models of economic system adopted by the Neo-classical economists like Sidgwick and Pigou.

CHAPTER VIII

CHARACTERISTICS OF NEO-CLASSICAL WELFARE ECONOMICS

THE term " Neo-classical " is used here in a literal and pre-Keynesian sense, meaning a new compound of thought which emerged from the mixture between the Classical economic ideas and those of the Marginal Utility school. This mixture, fused with the native common-sense pragmatism, gave the English economic thought between the eighteen-nineties and the nineteen-twenties a distinctive character of its own, different both from the pure Classicism of J. S. Mill and from the pure Marginal Utility approach as typified by Jevons, Walras, Menger and J. B. Clark.

I

As we have seen, from the standpoint of welfare economics, the impact of the marginal revolution on the classical tradition centred around three main issues :

(i) While the classical economists used a physical or materialistic concept of wealth, the utility school insisted that wealth should be conceived at the subjective level, as consisting in the satisfaction of consumers' wants.

(ii) The classical theory of production was based on the proposition that the wealth of society could be regarded as a determinate technical function of the available resources. Thus it was concerned mainly with raising the physical productivity and with the " Dynamic " laws of changes in population and capital accumulation. On the other hand, the " pure " utility economists of the Continental schools were inclined to reject such an approach as a confusion between the " technical " and the " economic " problem of production. They believed that economics could not usefully concern itself with the changes in the supply of factors and technique since these changes partook of the character of broader social and institutional forces operating outside the framework of the equilibrium process of the market. They proposed, therefore, to accept these as " exogenous changes in data " and to concentrate on the purely formal aspect of the problem of allocating *given* resources among given alternative uses.

(iii) Although the utility economists seemed to share the classical belief in the beneficial effects of competition, this agreement was more apparent than real ; for their concept of " competition " was rather different from the classical concept. To the classical economists, " competition " meant freedom of private enterprise which would prevail in real life if there were no State interference. " Free Competition " in this sense was meant to promote dynamic expansion of economic activity, (*a*) by giving free rein to individual initiative and incentive to save and invest and (*b*) by " widening " the area of the market and the division of labour, thus absorbing new resources and technical possibilities into the economic system. On the other hand, the concept of " Perfect Competition " as used by the utility economists was not meant to describe any realistic condition of free enterprise ; it was a purely theoretical (and frequently mathematical) model of the general equilibrium of the economic system as it would work under ideal conditions. Thus even if all restrictions to the free entry to industry were removed, " Perfect Competition " was not likely to be attained in real life since it required a further set of idealising assumptions such as perfect mobility and divisibility of factors and perfect knowledge. Again, its function was not to promote the dynamic expansion of economic activity, but to define the necessary logical conditions which would automatically lead to the optimum allocation of *given* resources within a given static framework. Thus as contrasted with the classical " Free Competition " it was not an instrument of " widening " the framework of economic relationships ; it was an instrument of " tightening " up the allocative adjustments within the same framework. The difference between these two meanings of competition can be best seen by contrasting the classical view of competition as it has ossified into a rule-of-thumb precept in the hands of J. S. Mill and Cairnes with the extremely abstract and elaborate concept of " atomistic " competition formulated by Cournot and Walras.

The group of economists whom we have described as the " neo-classical " economists entered into this affray as a third party having definite ideas of their own. The keynote of their whole approach was common-sense pragmatism : they wanted to build up a " workable " economic theory designed for practical use and not for formal elegance and logical stringency. In so far as it suited this purpose they were willing to absorb the contributions of both the opposing schools. Thus while they took over the marginal utility analysis they also retained the classical labour-theory approach to the "concrete content" of the economic problem. Beyond this point, however, they developed a new type of analysis of their own, concentrating *ad hoc* on concrete cases of exception to the general principle of competition advocated both by the classical and the utility economists.

The characteristics which gave a peculiar strength and weakness to the neo-classical economists may be best appreciated by summarising their views on the three issues raised by the marginal revolution described above :

(i) On the definition of wealth and economic welfare the neo-classical economists compromised between the classical materialism and the utility approach. Thus while accepting the marginal utility theory they would not carry it to the logical conclusion and define economic welfare as consisting in the satisfaction of *any given* consumers' wants. They normally qualified these wants as those belonging to the " material " aspects of life, capable of being brought into relation with the " measuring rod of money ". They were of course quite aware that this distinction between the economic and the non-economic welfare was not logically watertight. But for their purpose it was quite sufficient that it could be used for the ordinary purposes of economic analysis without great errors (cf. Cannan, *Wealth*, pp. 17–18 ; *Economist's Outlook*, p. 271, for a vigorous statement of this " common-sense " view).

(ii) The neo-classical economists agreed with the utility economists that " the obvious and uncontroverted aim of all rational effort—private or public—is, other things being equal, to produce as much as possible in proportion to the cost " (Henry Sidgwick, *Principles of Political Economy* p. 25). Marshall himself expounded this fundamental principle of economic calculus in terms of the " principle of substitution ". But at the same time they believed that this formal approach to production would be sterile if it were divorced from the " real content " of the problem. They were of opinion that the wealth of society was determined as much by institutional forces governing the supply of labour and capital and the state of technique as by the efficiency of the market forces in allocating given resources. Thus instead of accepting the former group of elements as data given by " exogenous " forces, they extended their interests to the technical aspects of production and to the problems of the ideal supply of labour and capital required in a given state of society. It was this trend of thought which led to the Sidgwick-Cannan theory of " Optimum Population " and to Marshall's fundamental belief that changes in the modes of production and their influence on human character were more important determinants of economic welfare than the mechanical efficiency in allocating given resources to satisfy given wants within a static framework (cf. *Principles*, p. 90).

(iii) The real mettle of the neo-classical economists was perhaps shown to its best advantage in their reaction against the general principle of free competition favoured both by the classical and the utility schools. Here they effectively breached the classical presumption of general economic harmony by pointing out concrete cases of exception where laissez-faire would lead to a conflict between social and private interests and consequently to a loss in economic welfare. Then, carrying their attack to the camp of the utility economists, they pointed out that the " heroic abstraction " of the Walras-Clark Static State was sterile since it succeeded in depicting the working of the general equilibrium only at the cost of diluting economic theory beyond the dictates of practical usefulness. Thus, rather than search for the General conditions of Optimum Production by postulating a pale ghost of the economic system which arrives at the ideal competitive equilibrium by simultaneous and automatic adjustments, they preferred to come to grips with full-blooded and intractable economic reality bit by bit. It was by this method of Partial analysis that Marshall forged his powerful instrument, the Consumers' Surplus analysis, which culminated in his celebrated case for subsidising industries working under increasing returns. The Partial analysis method, with its emphasis on selection and concentration of concrete details of particular sectors of the economic system, is a typical outcome of the neo-classical approach. It is based on the belief that the compilation of a systematic catalogue of all the theoretically possible interrelations between the different elements of the economic system *à la Walras* is both fruitless and unmanageable, and that the economist can serve a more practical purpose by selecting particular sectors of the economic system for a detailed study and by concentrating only on those key links between the selected sectors and the rest of the economic system which are likely to involve significant quantities of economic welfare. When the facts of a particular situation do not indicate the existence of any such key links, then the assumption of *ceteris paribus* is brought into full play and the selected sectors can be studied in " isolation " from the rest of the economic system for certain well-defined purposes. It cannot be denied that such a short-cut method may lead to serious errors in unskilled hands, but, as Marshall has pointed out, the economist can acquire an intimate knowledge of the concrete details of the sectors on which he is concentrating, so that " each source of possible error is pushed into prominence " (*Principles*, Mathematical Appendix, note xiv, pp. 851–2).

These then are the broad characteristics of the neo-classical approach which influenced most of the English economists for about four decades from the eighteen-eighties. Neo-classicism, as we have defined it, was inevitably dominated by the towering figure of Marshall, but it was a much wider influence than the Marshallian tradition in a strict sense. Thus it may be traced back to that frequently neglected economist, Henry Sidgwick, a senior contemporary rather than a disciple of Marshall. Again it should include many eminent economists of the " older generation " who are not necessarily Marshallian, such as : Nicholson, who rejected Marshall's concept of the Consumers' Surplus ; Edwin Cannan, a vigorous critic of the " Cambridge Bible of Economics " ; and other figures like Taussig and Allyn Young. Prof. Pigou's *Economics of Welfare* may again be treated as a landmark, representing both a culminating point of, and a departure from, the neo-classical tradition of welfare economics. Perhaps the famous debate between Prof. Clapham and Prof. Pigou on the " Empty Economic Boxes " may be taken as symptomatic of the latter's departure from the strict concrete neo-classical approach in favour of a more elaborate and formal analysis.

In what follows we shall select the two great representatives of the neo-classical approach, Sidgwick and Marshall, to point out the distinctive marks which that tradition has left on English economic thinking.[1]

---

[1] Edwin Cannan, who might perhaps be regarded as the third notable neo-classical economist rather stands apart from the two we have chosen. In many ways Cannan was not as much neo-classical as a reversion to the Smithian classicism disguised with a thin layer of later Marginal Productivity economics. Yet with his characteristic vigour he brought out the peculiar strength and weakness of neo-classicism in the sharpest relief. Cannan carried the neo-classical insistence on bluff common sense and distrust of abstract analysis almost to a point of caricature. Thus the consumers' surplus to him was nothing but an optical illusion possible because one draws demand and supply curves on the blackboard ! (cf. *Economica*, Old Series, No. 10, p. 21). Yet it is to him that we owe the most vigorous exposition and defence of the " materialistic " concept of wealth (cf. *Wealth*, pp. 17–18). His theory of the " Optimum Population " reveals the unsatisfactoriness of a " simple economics " ; yet nevertheless it clearly brings out the basic belief which links up the neo-classical with the classical tradition, viz. the wealth of a nation depends to a large extent on those techno-institutional factors outside the equilibrium process. In his *Wealth* and again in his *Review of Economic Theory* he has given us a very succinct statement of the view that Population, Co-operation and Accumulation of Knowledge and Equipment are the most influential determinants of Physical Productivity per head, on which the economic welfare of society ultimately depends.

II

Henry Sidgwick should be accorded an important place in the history of welfare economics for two reasons. Firstly, he was perhaps the most clear-headed representative of that early transition stage, when, under the impact of the " marginal revolution ", economic thought started moving away from the classical materialistic level to the modern subjective level of analysis. Thus Sidgwick's *Principles of Political Economy*, first published in 1883, is an epitome of the formative period. In it, we can find a striking co-existence of the two levels of economic thought, the materialistic level predominating in Book I on " Production " and the subjective level predominating in Book III on the " Art of Political Economy ". Sidgwick himself was converted to the subjective approach, but he loyally started by giving a very tolerant reformulation of the traditional approach and incidentally arrived at a new proposition at the materialistic level, viz. the concept of " Optimum Population ", which later came to be associated with Cannan.

Secondly, besides being an important historical link, Sidgwick's own contributions to welfare economic thought are very considerable. He was the first to stress that far-reaching distinction between the Production and the Distribution Welfare Economics. He also initiated the neo-classical method of concentrating on concrete exceptions to the general principle of free competition. Thus most of Prof. Pigou's famous cases of divergences between the social and the private net products may be paralleled in Book III of Sidgwick's *Principles*.

Sidgwick's attempt to adjust the two layers of thought can be best appreciated against the background of J. S. Mill's *Principles*. As we have seen, by the time of J. S. Mill, wealth came to be identified not only with tangible material products but also with the Capital stock of society ; the Net Income of society was supposed to follow as a determinate technical function of the stock of resources previously accumulated after " maintaining capital intact " in a purely physical sense. On the other hand, Sidgwick pointed out that

The stock of wealth requires not only continual expenditure of labour in care and repairs, and continual additions to take the place of what is slowly consumed, but also *continual adaptation to the changing tastes*—and sometimes changing needs —*of successive consumers*. . . . We thus fix our attention on the " real income " of a community as distinguished from its resources (op. cit., 3rd ed., pp. 87–8).

Sidgwick also quietly poked fun at the theoretical stock-in-trade of the old-fashioned nineteenth-century economists which later provoked less kindly criticisms, viz. the familiar discussions on the " gains from the Division of Labour " and " counterbalancing drawbacks ", the " advantages of the ' grande ' and the ' petite ' culture in farming ", " kinds of business adapted to management by joint-stock companies ", etc. (op. cit. p. 26 ; cf. Robbins, *Nature and Significance of Economic Science*, p. 65). But, in spite of this, Sidgwick did not favour the abstract formal analysis on the other extreme. He retained the classical viewpoint that technical and institutional factors exerted a very significant influence on the welfare of a country and pointed out that in practice " it does not seem possible to draw a sharp distinction between the ' technical ' and the ' economic ' aspects of these questions ". He, however, very neatly reconciled the formal logical distinction between the " technical " and the " economic " problem with the classical labour-theory outlook when he wrote :

. . . it is important to notice that the use of a more efficient machinery would not always result in the efficiency of labour as a whole ; since the better instrument might require more labour to make and to keep in repair, and it is possible that this extra labour might be more productive if applied in some other way. Thus an invention *technically* successful may fail *economically* (op. cit., pp. 124–5).

Following J. S. Mill's *Principles*, Sidgwick concluded his Book I on " Production " by a chapter on the " Laws " of variation in the supply of the factors of production on the " amount of produce ". Here he expounded the idea of " Optimum Population ".

The " Laws of Diminishing Returns ", then, affirms that the productiveness of labour does tend to diminish, as the proportion of labourers to land increases, after a certain degree of density in population—much below what would be on other grounds insanitary—has been reached. The degree of density, it should be observed, varies with the industrial arts, and the accumulation of capital ; and it tends to be continually advanced by the progress of invention, provided that through the accumulation of capital, the improvement of processes which invention renders possible is actually realised (op. cit., pp. 150–1).

It may be noted that this concept of " Optimum Population ", although not popularised until the nineteen-twenties by Prof. Cannan, is clearly a return to pure Classicism. It is a natural logical step from the man-against-nature view of the economic problem which characterises the productive situation as the application of the variable factor, labour, to the constant factor, land. With given technical conditions, the Optimum is supposed to be attained when a further increase in population no longer raises but lowers the *physical* output per head. The concept of " Optimum Population " has turned out to be rather disappointing, but it is to the credit of Sidgwick that it has remained essentially the same as when he originally formulated it.

However, it is not until we come to Book III of Sidgwick's *Principles* that we find his most important contributions. Here he turned his attention to a critical examination of the classical doctrine of the " System of Natural Liberty ". The first point which struck Sidgwick was the incongruity between the classical materialistic concept of wealth and the proposition that a competitive market will lead to the maximum satisfaction of consumers' wants.

> . . . the argument for *laisser-faire* does not tend to show that the spontaneous combination of individuals pursuing their private interests will lead to the production of a maximum of *material* wealth, except so far as the individuals in question prefer material wealth to utilities not embodied in matter (op. cit., p. 403).

This anomaly had always been present in classical economics ever since the time Smith introduced the doctrine of Productive labour side by side with his demand analysis of the competitive market. The older generation of the classicals had a good excuse for overlooking it, since, as we have seen, they conceived free competition primarily as the means of widening the area of the market and the division of labour, which would in fact increase the production of wealth even at the physical level (cf. Chap. IV above). The same cannot, however, be said for the later classicals like Mill and Cairnes. Living in a later stage of industrial development, they had lost most of their predecessors' fresh enthusiasm for industrial expansion and never fully appreciated the older expansionist view of free competition. In contrast, they were inclined to look upon laissez-faire as a " safe practical rule " and if they attempted to introduce a dash of belief in the allocative efficiency of the free market they did not realise that it would not mix well with their materialistic concept of wealth (cf. Cairnes on " Laissez-faire " in his *Essays on Political Economy, Theoretical and Applied*). Sidgwick's rebuke may also be extended to those Marginal Utility economists who endorsed the classical theory of free competition without realising that the classicals were working on a different level of analysis from theirs, and were advocating free competition for a different reason, or at least with a very different emphasis on the importance of allocative efficiency.

Sidgwick next pointed out that the doctrine of " Natural

Liberty " as put forward by reputable classical economists claimed to bring about only the most economic production of wealth and not the most economic or equitable distribution of wealth.

Many, at any rate, of those, who in England have held most strongly that it is expedient for government to interfere as little as possible with the distribution of wealth resulting from free competition, have not maintained this on the ground that the existing inequalities are satisfactory ; but rather in the belief that any such interference must tend to impair aggregate production more than it could increase the utility of the produce by a better distribution (op. cit. p. 400).

He was aware of the methodological gap which separates considerations concerning the ideal production from those concerning the ideal distribution of wealth. " The latter inquiry," he wrote, " takes us beyond the limits of the properly separate Political Economy to the more comprehensive and more difficult art of general Politics " ; " we can no longer use the comparatively exact measurements of economic science, but only those vague and uncertain balancings of different quantities of happiness " (ibid., p. 397). This, however, did not prevent him from pointing out that—

we have to assume that utilities valued highly by the rich are useful to the community in proportion either to their market price, or to the pecuniary gain foregone in order to obtain them. . . . It is only by this strained extension of the idea of social utility that production of such utility under the system of natural liberty can be said to have even a general tendency to reach the maximum production possible (ibid., p. 404).

Thus he favoured the view that " a more equal distribution of wealth tends *prima facie* to increase happiness ", not neglecting the possible reduction in the aggregate production of wealth which may be caused by the redistribution (op. cit., Book III, Chap. VII).

Having thus got the considerations concerning the ideal distribution of wealth out of the way, Sidgwick next expounded the method of judging the Productive efficiency of a given economic system, temporarily abstracting from the Distributional effects. He admitted that this is an abstraction, for the distribution of wealth is bound to affect the types of commodities produced, and via its effects on economic incentives even the total amount of wealth produced (op. cit., p. 55).

None the less does it seem desirable that we should practise ourselves in contemplating the process of production from the point of view of a society as a whole, abstracting as far as possible from the "adjustment of the terms of co-operation" among producers ; so that the total gain or loss in wealth resulting from any given change to the aggregate of human beings concerned, may be habitually distinguished from those gains and losses by individuals and classes which do not involve changes in the wealth of the society as a whole. Normally, no doubt, what is productive of wealth to an individual tends to increase the wealth of the community of which he is a part ; but this is not always the case, for example, a man may make money by promoting a joint-stock company that fails ; and even when the two effects are combined, they may be combined in indefinitely varying proportions. And to confound the effect of any cause on the wealth of a portion of society with its effect on the whole wealth of the society is one of the commonest forms of error in popular economic discussion (op. cit., p. 56).

Here it can be seen that Sidgwick had succeeded in laying down the foundations of the modern approach to welfare economics in its essential form. His beautifully worked out distinction between the Production and the Distribution welfare economics led him directly to consider the possible divergences between the private and the social net products.

The enterprising nature of Sidgwick's analysis of these divergences cannot be fully appreciated except with reference to the general belief in laissez-faire prevalent among his contemporaries both of the classical and the marginal utility schools. Thus, while Cairnes and Mill were reiterating the policy of non-interference, the marginal utility economists like Walras and J. B. Clark were trying to deduce the principle of maximum satisfaction from a general competitive equilibrium of the Static State. The general tendency was to divide the economic system into two rigid conventional divisions, viz. (i) where private enterprise should function without any restraint, and (ii) extreme cases, where, with the sanction of Adam Smith, the State may interfere. Thus J. S. Mill's *Principles* in spite of its alleged " applications to social philosophy ", mentioned only the obvious cases of limitations to the laissez-faire policy, e.g. cases of minors and lunatics where the individuals are admittedly incapable of looking after their own interests (cf. Mill, op. cit., Book V, Chap. XI). Sidgwick refused to accept this easy conventional partition and tried to show that conflicts between the private and the social interests may occur, even where there are no obvious monopolies, and even when the individuals concerned are competent adults and grave reasons of national defence are not involved. He tried to show that instead of a clear-cut boundary line there is an extensive " no-man's " land between the zones of private enterprise and state interference and that it should be reduced into order by weighing up the social gains and losses involved in interference with given individual cases on their specific merits.

It does not of course follow that wherever laissez-faire falls short, Government interference is expedient ; since the inevitable drawbacks and disadvantages of the latter may, in any *particular* case, be worse than the shortcomings of private enterprise (ibid., p. 414).

Sidgwick's analysis of the divergences between the private and the social net products is based on this fundamental consideration, viz. whether there is any guarantee that under conditions of free competition the individual will always be able to appropriate an amount of wealth neither more nor less than the whole of his net contribution to the wealth of society.

Sidgwick started with the cases where socially desirable goods and services are not produced, because, due to technical peculiarities, the private producer cannot collect his reward. This category includes the famous cases of the lighthouse, afforestation, promotion of scientific research, etc. (ibid., pp. 406–7). The principle involved here is not different from that of a " new " commodity which is not produced although the total consumers' surplus it yields is greater than its total cost of production, because in a competitive market the private producer cannot obtain sufficient revenue to cover his costs.

Sidgwick next considered those cases where the entrepreneur appropriates " not less but more than the whole net gain to the community of his enterprise ". These may be divided into two classes : (i) Cases of social wastes when the " economic " exploitation of the natural resources cannot be achieved without State action, e.g. fishing and hunting during the " closed " seasons. Here the State's function is merely to impose an " economic " rent on the use of these resources (Sidgwick, op. cit., p. 410). (ii) Cases of social wastes due to the interlocking of immobile factors like land sites leading on to the problems of industrial location and town planning. The actual example Sidgwick gave, viz. the construction of a new railway line where an older one already exists, is perhaps arguable. But the underlying idea is clear enough and we have it later on in Prof. Pigou's famous case of the smoky chimneys (Sidgwick, op. cit., p. 408).

Lastly, Sidgwick considered the possibility of long-term social wastes arising out of a conflict between the interests of the present and the future generations. He argued :

an outlay which would be on the whole advantageous, if the interests of future generations are considered as much as those of the present, may not be profitable for any individual at the current rate at which wealth could be commercially borrowed. . . . I do not see how it can be argued from the point of view of the community that the current interest, the current price that individuals have to be paid for postponing consumption, is the exact condition that has to be fulfilled to make a postponement desirable ; though of course it is a condition inevitably exacted in a society of economic men organised on a purely individualistic basis (op. cit., pp. 412–13).

It may be pointed out that this last case of divergence between the social and the private interests is on a different logical footing from that of the previous cases. The existence of the previous types of social wastes can be demonstrated by using ordinary economic analysis without postulating the arguable concept of " Social Mind ". Thus it can be shown that the money cost of the smoke-reducing equipment is less than the money cost of damages done to society by excessive smoke, although admittedly such damages as bad health cannot be adequately expressed in terms of money. Although in practice we should be inclined to accept Sidgwick's argument that society should make a greater provision for the future than a private individual, if only for the fact that it has a longer life, it is rather hard to demonstrate the correctness of the argument in a stringent way. The fundamental difficulty is that there is no objective method by which we can compare the interest of the present generation determined by the existing system of preferences with the interest of the future generations who will have entirely different systems of wants. Perhaps, at the level of basic consumption goods, we may be able to anticipate the wants of the future generations with a tolerable accuracy. Thus, given stable population trends, we may be able to estimate the number (but not the types) of houses, schools and hospitals likely to be required by the future generation. We may also try to reduce the risk of burdening the later generations with unwanted capital goods by concentrating on the construction of non-specific durable goods like plants for generating electricity, etc., although even these are liable to obsolescence due to technical changes. But our estimates of the wants of the future generation will become increasingly wide of the mark the longer the period we take and the higher up the level of consumption we go, so that when we come to " tertiary " goods like wireless sets and books, it will be quite impossible to anticipate the state of future demand. Ultimately, the problem of comparisons between the interests of the present and the future generations can be solved only by introducing ethical values in the place of given consumers' wants. This point is worth noting for we shall have to say more about the " third " level of welfare analysis which follows after the physical and subjective levels. We will also find that concern with these ultimate ethical values is a notable trait of the neo-classicals, some of whom like

Sidgwick and Marshall had the makings of evangelical reformers. Thus, characteristically enough, Sidgwick concluded his *Principles* by a chapter on " Political Economy and Private Morality " (op. cit., Book II, Chap. IX).

III

Marshall is too great an economist to be neatly pigeon-holed in a textbook classification. From one point of view, Marshallian economics is Marshallian economics and needs no other label. But from an historical point of view, it will perhaps help us to appreciate the continuity of economic thought if we look upon Marshall's writings as the mature expression and development of the neo-classical characteristics described above. Allowing for the imprint of his powerful mind, the essential pattern of the neo-classical thought is easily recognisable.

Thus Marshall's celebrated case for subsidising Increasing Returns industries is merely a particular instance of the neo-classical method of concentrating on cases of exception to the general principle of free competition. Marshall's well-known preference of the " concrete realism " of the Partial analysis to the abstract symmetry of the General Equilibrium analysis is a direct expression of the neo-classical pragmatism. Equally well known is his insistence on the fact that economic processes take place over a period of time and that therefore the " timeless " Static State should be discarded in favour of the long-term normal equilibrium analysis (cf. Letter to J. B. Clark, *Memorials of Alfred Marshall*, p. 415 ; *Principles*, pp. 850–1). This substitution of the Flow or rather the process analysis in the place of the Stock analysis carries us beyond the assumption of " given resources " ; and then via the real cost theory we are led to consider the long-run repercussions of the equilibrium process of the rate of flow of the factors of production, in a way rather reminiscent of the older economists' search for the " laws " of changes in the supply of factors. Perhaps Marshall's famous analogy of the upper and lower blades of the scissors is a crowning symbol of the neo-classical approach. It also expresses his deep-seated belief that the process of economic Development (and not merely economic Equilibrium) is determined as much by the technical and institutional factors governing the Cost side of the equation as by the " given consumers' wants " governing the Demand side. Indeed, as we shall see, in Marshall's view it is rather superficial to concentrate merely on the mechanical satisfaction of " given " wants, since human wants are never given once for all but are themselves determined by the environment of production ; the aim of human activity is thus not merely to satisfy given wants, but also to cultivate and develop successive cycles of new wants generated by and adjusted to corresponding cycles of activities. Postponing a detailed study of Marshall's Surplus analysis to the next chapter, let us now consider how the different elements of the neo-classical thought found a congenial framework in Marshall's outlook on the problem of human welfare.

Marshall has been frequently criticised for his excessive ancestor-worship of the classical economists, particularly of Ricardo. It is therefore well to point out that his general outlook on the economic problem is fundamentally similar to theirs. Thus he wrote :

> In a sense there are only two agents of production, nature and man. Capital and organisation are the result of the work of man aided by nature, and directed by his power of forecasting the future and his willingness to make provision for it. *If the power of nature and man be given, the growth of wealth and knowledge and organisation follows from them as effect from cause* (*Principles*, p. 139).

This reiteration of the man-against-nature view of the economic problem will also remind us of the family relationship between the classical measuring rod of labour and Marshall's measuring rod of money. Of course, Marshall's application of the measuring rod is much more sophisticated ; he carefully pointed out that money could measure economic incentive at the margin only and that the " real " or subjective costs influence the money expenses only indirectly and in the long run. But the kinship between the two measuring rods is clearly seen from the following passage :

> A point of view was conquered for us by Adam Smith, from which a commodity is regarded as the embodiment of measurable efforts and sacrifices. . . . Proceeding from its new point of view, Political Economy has analysed the efforts and sacrifices that are required for the production of a commodity for a given market at a given time ; she has found a measure for them in their cost to the person who will buy them (*Memorials of Alfred Marshall*, p. 126).

It may be noted that in thinking of Real Cost in terms of the subjective disutility of effort Marshall was more akin to Smith, Senior and Malthus than to Ricardo. As we have seen, Ricardo would have measured Cost objectively, in terms of the quantity of labour required to overcome the given technical obstacles of production (cf. Chaps. II and III, above). But, apart from this, however, Marshall had a fundamental affinity with Ricardo based on the common acceptance of the man-against-nature view of the economic problem (cf. G. F. Shove, " The Place of Marshall's

Principles in Economic Theory ", *Economic Journal*, 1942, pp. 296 et seq.). Thus rebutting Jevons's attack on Ricardo he wrote :

the reaction against the comparative neglect of wants by Ricardo and his followers shows signs of being carried to the opposite extreme. It is still important to assert the great truth on which they dwelt somewhat too exclusively ; viz. while wants are the rulers of life among lower animals, it is to changes in the forms of efforts and activities that we must turn when in search for the keynotes in the history of mankind (*Principles*, p. 85 ; also p. 90 and Appendix I).

However, Marshall's speculations soon carried him beyond the physical level of analysis of the classical economists and indeed even beyond the purely subjective level of utility analysis into the realm of ethical values. The departure took place in the following way. The Ricardians, concerned as they were with the quantity of physical output, had been content to regard it as being determined by the " laws " of changes in the size of population, accumulation and technique. Marshall, looking deeper, came to the conclusion that these changes in data themselves may be ultimately traced to the changes in human character and to the changing pattern of interaction between human character and environment. " Capital and organisation are the result of the work of man aided by nature " and " if the power of nature and man be given, the growth of wealth and knowledge and organisation follows them as effect from cause " (*Principles*, p. 139). This being so, changes in the quantity of physical output are merely the manifestation of the potentialities of human character. If the human character were " rightly " developed, the rest would follow. This basic idea that a large part of the problem of economic progress is the development of human character is apparent from Marshall's preliminary definition of economics as

on the one side the study of wealth, and on the other, and more important side, a part of the study of man. For man's character has been moulded by his everyday work, and the material resources which he thereby procures, more than by any other influence, unless it be that of his religious ideals (op. cit. p. 1).

Since " man is the centre of the problem of production as well as consumption ", the study of the development of his character should include not only his productive activities but also the relations between these activities and his wants.[1] This led Marshall to divide human wants into three broad classes :

(i) " Man's wants in the earliest stages of his development which give rise to activities." These may be regarded as biological needs.

---

[1] Cf. Talcott Parsons, *Structure of Social Action*, Chap. IV.

(ii) " Wants adjusted to activities ", the satisfaction of which " affords strength " and increases efficiency. Here wants are not regarded as giving rise to activities in one way causation. " Each new step upwards is to be regarded as giving rise to new wants," presumably of a more refined type. This class of wants Marshall approved of as being " natural ".

(iii) " A mere increase in artificial wants among which the grosser may predominate." Marshall regarded this type of wants merely as arbitrary whims with no permanent value for lie, " evil dominion of wanton vagaries of fashion " and " sensual cravings ".

(Op. cit., p. 89 ; also Book VI, Chap. XIII.)

This classification of wants is the basis of Marshall's distinction between " the standard of life " and " the standard of comfort ". A rise in the standard of life means an increased satisfaction of wants belonging to categories (i) and (ii). It is supposed to result in " an increase in intelligence and energy and self-respect ; leading to more care and judgment in expenditure and to an avoidance of food and drink that gratify the appetite but afford no strength and ways of living that are unwholesome physically and morally " (ibid., p. 690). A rise in the standard of comfort, on the other hand, means a mere multiplication of effete wants belonging to category (iii) which fritter away the income without leaving a corresponding increase in efficiency.

As we have pointed out above, Marshall's distinction between " the standard of life " and " the standard of comfort " is rather similar to the classical distinction between the " productive " and the " unproductive " consumption (cf. Chap. V, sec. VI, above). Marshall, too, believed that " Any increase in consumption that is strictly necessary for efficiency pays its own way and adds to, as much as it draws from, the national dividend " (ibid., p. 530). However, while the classical economists adopted the simple minimum subsistence level, Marshall further made allowances for improvement in efficiency :

But it is still true even in England today that much the greater part of the consumption of the main body of population conduces to sustain life and vigour ; not perhaps in the most economical manner, but yet without great waste. Doubtless some indulgences are positively harmful ; but these are diminishing relatively to the rest, the chief exception perhaps being gambling. Most of that expenditure which is not strictly economical as a means towards efficiency, yet helps to form habits of ready resourceful enterprise, and gives that variety to life without which men become dull and stagnant, and achieve little though they may plod much (ibid., p. 531).

The classical economists, concerned only with the physical quantity of social output, had advocated that all the surplus above

" productive " consumption should be saved and added to the capital accumulation of society. Marshall, concerned with the development of human character, wanted a part of the surplus income invested in human beings instead of in durable capital goods ; he, so to speak, preferred to bank on their character.

> The older economists took little account of the fact that human faculties are as important as a means of production as any other kind of capital. . . . A slight and temporary check to the accumulation of material wealth need not necessarily be an evil, even from a purely economic point of view, if, being made quietly and without disturbance, it provided better opportunities for the great mass of people, increased their efficiency and developed in them such habits of self-respect as to result in the growth of a much more efficient race of producers in the next generation (ibid., pp. 229–30).

We can now understand why Marshall insisted on adding " Organisation " as a separate agent of production to the classical triology.

It will be seen that Marshall's views on the progressive nature of man were bound to lead him not only beyond the classical material level of analysis but also beyond the " pure " subjective level based on the assumption of *given* wants. Given his concept of human progress as the successive development of new wants, generated by, and adjusted to new activities, it was superficial to approach the problem of human welfare in terms of the Utilitarian Calculus alone. " The gratification of a want or desire is merely a step to some new pursuits ", and activities are directed not merely towards satisfying given wants but also towards inventing and cultivating new wants and activities (cf. ibid., pp. 89–90). Therefore Marshall maintained that beyond the purely mechanical problem of allocating given resources so as to obtain the maximum satisfaction of given wants, there was a further and more important " biological " study of the development of human character. This might of course merely lead to a " genetic " study of development of wants ; but to Marshall, the reformer, the " eugenics " of wants was inseparable from the " genetic " approach.

Thus the problem of bringing out the full potentialities of human character led Marshall into the realm of ethical values, or what we have called the " third " level of discourse. A fair sample of Marshall's value judgments can already be seen from his classification of wants above. The general moral principle behind these judgments was, however, not clearly stated. In some places Marshall seems to adopt a sort of glorified Utilitarianism ; thus the improvement in man's character is desirable because it enables him to enjoy deeply and permanently by helping him to reject the harmful and transient pleasures which might impair his long-run capacity to enjoy and produce (cf. ibid., pp. 65–6, 310). In other places, Marshall speaks of " finer sensibilities and nobler aspirations ", although, as we shall see, his concept of the " higher wants " is not untinged with Victorian morality and a puritanical concept of virtue (cf. ibid., pp. 228–9).

As might be expected, Marshall stressed the character-forming effect of work. He pointed out that in spite of the principle of increasing marginal disutility of labour, a certain minimum amount of work may yield a positive utility, and quoted Jevons approvingly on the " pains of idleness " (ibid., p. 65 n.). In contrast to his usual sombre understatements he wrote : " work in its best sense, the healthy exercise of faculties, is the aim of life, is life itself " (*Memorials*, p. 115). Marshall's substitution of the term " waiting " for " abstinence " is another instance where he pushed the disutility function to the background to bring out the importance of character. Thus we are told that the supply of savings " is dependent on man's *prospectiveness* ; that is, his faculty of realising the future " (ibid., p. 233). While Marshall attached no virtue to saving at high established income levels, there is no doubt that his heart warmed towards the self-made men " brought up upon narrow means to stern hard work, who have retained their simple habits in spite of success in business " (ibid., p. 229). Perhaps Marshall's opinions on what ought to be the right behaviour comes out most clearly when he is discussing the elasticity of supply of labour.

No universal rule can be laid down ; but experience seems to show that the more ignorant and phlegmatic of races and individuals, especially if they live in a southern clime, will stay at work a shorter time, and will exert themselves less while at it, if the rate of pay rises so as to give them their accustomed enjoyments in return for less work than before. But those whose mental horizon is wider, and who have more firmness and elasticity of character, will work the harder and longer, the higher the rate of pay which is open to them ; unless, indeed, they prefer to divert their activities to higher aims than work for material gain (ibid., pp. 528–9).

In the light of Marshall's emphasis on the evolutionary nature of human character it is not difficult to understand why he was dissatisfied with the Continental type of Optimum theory based on the Static General Equilibrium analysis of Walras and J. B. Clark. These economists had depicted the economic system purely as a mechanical model made up of atomistic individuals making simultaneous equilibrium adjustments in the allocation of their given resources to satisfy their given wants.   Marshall was quite familiar with the mechanics of such a type of analysis (cf. ibid., pp. 470–1, and Mathematical Appendix, note xii).   But he preferred to look upon society as a biological organism composed of individual cells which, either growing or declining, are being continually moulded by the reaction of the long-term equilibrium process on their environment.   Since human character would be moulded by numerous social and institutional factors outside the equilibrium process of the market, Marshall concluded that it was clearly unprofitable merely to formulate abstract conditions of the General Equilibrium and the Optimum on the basis of " given data ".

> For the progressive nature of man is one whole.   It is only temporarily and provisionally that we can with profit isolate for study the economic side of his life ; and we ought to be careful to take together in one view the whole of this side (ibid., p. 85).

In this connection it is interesting to consider Marshall's attitude towards free competition.   Although he made his most interesting contributions trying to point out the exceptions to the doctrine of Maximum Satisfaction even when accepting the Static limitations of the Optimum theory, Marshall nevertheless firmly believed in the beneficial effects of free enterprise.   To him it was the best school to form and develop those qualities in man's character he most admired.   Thus his concept of free enterprise is characterised by a predominance of rather small firms, each under the guidance of a resourceful " captain of industry " who at his own risk continually experiments with new combinations of productive factors and with new commodities (*Memorials*, p. 307).   Marshall believed that it would develop the virtues of " energy, initiative, rationality, frugality, industry and honourable dealing " while it would discourage " stagnation, sluggish slavery to customs and habits and lack of ambition ".   In the earlier editions of his *Principles* Marshall had looked upon the tendency towards monopoly merely as a " little more than eddies which flutter over the surface of progress " and that " now as ever the main body of movement depends on the deep silent strong stream of normal (competitive) distribution and exchange " (ibid., p. 628).   The turn of the century probably robbed Marshall of much of his earlier optimism, although there seems to be much justice still in J. M. Keynes's remark :

> The solution of the economic problem was for Marshall not an application of the Hedonist Calculus, but a prior condition for the exercise of men's higher faculty, irrespective almost of what we mean by the " higher " (*Memorials*, p. 9).

Marshall's excursions beyond the assumption of " given and constant wants " (shared to some extent by Prof. Pigou) have caused many misunderstandings. Victorian morality in itself is irritating enough for the later generations, but the introduction of moral values whatever their brand creates very far-reaching methodological problems. If welfare economics is to be placed on the same scientific footing as " price " economics, it should be confined to the purely subjective level on the basis of given wants. For we cannot definitely say whether the individuals' wants are more efficiently satisfied in one situation compared with another unless we have the common basis of an unchanged system of wants for the two situations compared. And welfare analysis is nothing but such relative comparisons of individuals' positions. Indeed, as Prof. Hicks has suggested, the assumption of constant wants seems to offer the only logically satisfactory distinction between the " economic " and the " general " welfare. So long as we are considering the problem of satisfying given wants we are discussing economic welfare, whether or not these wants belong to the " material " side of life or are capable of being brought into relation with the measuring rod of money. Once we move beyond the assumption of constant wants, however, we are stepping into the realm of general welfare where the economist *qua* economist cannot make any authoritative pronouncements (cf. J. R. Hicks, " The Valuation of Social Income ", *Economica*, May 1940, p. 107).

These are very weighty considerations and it has been interesting to consider Marshall's general attitude towards the problem of welfare and the jumps he had taken from the " first " materialistic level of analysis to the " second " subjective level and thence to the " third " ethical level of discourse. When, however, we have cleared up the logical untidiness affected by the Anglo-Saxon mind we shall see that Marshall's particular philosophical judgments can be separated from his technical contributions to welfare analysis. In the next chapter it will be shown that his most important contribution, viz. the Surplus analysis, can be reduced to the purely subjective level of discourse and can be used as a very powerful tool of welfare analysis without accepting either the labour-theory outlook or the Utilitarian philosophy with which it is mixed up in Marshall's original exposition.

And further, there is still a very arguable point whether the natural morality of the great neo-classical economists like Sidgwick and Marshall might not after all be supported by the methodologically more sophisticated investigations of later writers like

F. H. Knight and J. M. Clark (cf. Knight, *Ethics of Competition*, pp. 20–3 ; J. M. Clark, " The Socialising of Theoretical Economics ", *The Trend of Economics*, pp. 73–102 ; reprinted in his *Preface to Social Economics*). In a world of changing wants where, as Clark has put it, " in a single business establishment, one department furnishes the desire which the other departments are to satisfy ", is it not very selective to restrict ourselves to the assumption of given and constant wants ? Are we not really following the line of least resistance under the guise of methodological purity when we concentrate only on those aspects of economic reality which are capable of being formulated into elegant logical propositions ? Is such a method of selection compatible with true scientific comprehensiveness and is there any guarantee that the significance of the selected elements is proportionate to the degree of their malleability into logically stringent propositions ? These later heart-searching questions are a far cry from Victorian morality and yet we have not progressed very far beyond Marshall's warning against " a tendency towards assigning wrong proportions to economic forces ; those elements being most emphasised which lend themselves most easily to analytical methods " (*Principles*, p. 850). And, finally, we have to face the fact that economic propositions, however carefully they may have been distilled according to the canons of logical purity, will have to be transformed into economic policy and in the practical execution of policy *somebody* must face the final necessity of making ethical judgments. We might palm that responsibility on to the hypothetical " economic planner " or the " statesman ". But so long as economic policy cannot be made " foolproof " like a motor-car which can be run without any profound knowledge of motor-mechanics, that " statesman " must to some degree be either an economist or advised by economists. " The progressive nature of man is one whole," said Marshall ; and to be a satisfactory practitioner of his science the economist can least of all avoid making ethical judgments.

Such considerations do not bridge the gap between positive welfare propositions based on " given " wants and normative judgments concerning the quality of these wants. But they do serve to shake the feeling of self-sufficiency of positive economics and an almost automatic fear of value judgments. The case against making value judgments is surely not directed against value judgments as such (since everyone in a free society should make value judgments and be tolerant about other people's judgments), but against untidily mixing them with positive propositions. There is no evidence that economists as a class are less capable of making acceptable value judgments than other people. We may provisionally restrict ourselves to the " second " or purely subjective level of analysis and explore the possibilities of the Utilitarian Calculus, so long as we realise and are content with making propositions on an intermediate level which are in some ways as inconclusive as propositions pertaining to the purely physical level of analysis. On the same token, so long as we clearly state what we are doing, we may equally confine ourselves to the material level of analysis or venture into the " third " level of ethical values without being accused of a " materialistic bias " or " philosophical preconceptions ". The complete solution of the problem of human welfare must embrace all three levels of analysis ; a study of Marshall's attitude towards the nature of the economic problem is a salubrious antidote to the exclusive exaltation of the subjective level of analysis as the essence of " scientific economics ".

CHAPTER IX

THE MARSHALLIAN SURPLUS ANALYSIS

SINCE its inception in the first edition of the *Principles* in 1890, Marshall's doctrine of the surpluses, particularly his concept of the consumers' surplus, has been a perennial source of controversy. The nature of this controversy cannot be fully appreciated unless it is kept in mind that Marshall's doctrine in its original form has two aspects. The first consists in his broader views on the nature of economic activity and its relation to the *surpluses in general*. The second consists in his practical applications of the surplus analysis in its *partial* form.

Marshall's broader views on the subject may be found in various passages scattered throughout the *Principles* and in a compact form in the Appendix K. To critics sensitive to methodological purity, these passages seem to contain overtones of a particular philosophical point of view. Thus the objections to the surplus doctrine put forward by such leading critics as Profs. Knight and Robbins have been, on the whole, of a severely methodological character. Having, as they thought, found the " fountainhead of errors " in Marshall's Utilitarian philosophy and the labour-theory outlook, they were inclined to dismiss the entire surplus theory as being tainted at the source (cf. Knight, *Risk, Uncertainty and Profit,* pp. 69–73).

From this, it is instructive to turn to the recent developments in the surplus analysis. These developments have no doubt been stimulated by the application of the Indifference Curve technique ; but they are also partly due to a reversal in the direction of approach. The new champions of the surplus doctrine, notably Prof. Hicks, seem to have started from a study of Marshall's partial surplus analysis in action, in its actual applications to practical problems. Having thus found it to be a powerful instrument of analysis, designed to deal with those problems which are intractable to the ordinary marginal analysis, they have then proceeded to show us how it can be used without committing ourselves to Marshall's " philosophical preconceptions " real or imaginary (J. R. Hicks, " Rehabilitation of Consumers' Surplus ", *Review of Economic Studies,* Feb. 1941, pp. 108–16).

In view of this it seems desirable to sort out Marshall's broader and more controversial opinions on the surpluses from his practical applications of the surplus analysis in its partial form. In this way we shall be able to locate the " kink " which diverted Marshall's attention to the partial method of analysis and shall be able to show how this actually freed his analysis from many of the methodological criticisms directed towards the " absolute " concept of surplus. We shall not attempt to give a detailed account of the recent reformulations of the surplus analysis, but we shall try to clear up a more limited but interesting question relating to the history of thought ; viz. to what extent can we consider these reformulations [1] as being made up of the original elements of Marshall's analysis.

I

We have seen in Chapter VIII, section III, above, that Marshall had a deep-rooted sympathy with the classical man-against-nature view of the economic problem and it is therefore reasonable to expect that his general conception of the surpluses would be coloured by this outlook (*Principles*, p. 139 ; *Memorials of Alfred Marshall*, p. 126). It is thus interesting to find Marshall regarding the surpluses as " the benefit which the individual derives from his *opportunities* or from his *environment* ; or to recur to a word that was in common use a few generations ago, from his *conjuncture* ". Marshall's use of the term " conjuncture " is, however, rather loose. He first introduced it in the sense used by the German economists, particularly Wagner, viz. as " the sum total of technical, economic, social and legal conditions " (*Principles*, p. 125, also n.). If this means that the benefit accrues from a given institutional framework *as it stands*, the surpluses would be in the nature of absolute magnitudes. A little later on, however, Marshall extended the term " conjuncture " and used it simply as the opportunity to buy a particular commodity at a given price (ibid., p. 127). Here, since the price or the quantity of a given commodity is more liable to change than the sum total of the individual's environment, Marshall could pass on to the relative concept of surplus as the loss or gain experienced by the individual due to a *movement* from one price-quantity situation to another.

Let us pursue this matter to the Appendix K, where Marshall

---

[1] Besides the article cited, see J. R. Hicks, " Consumers' Surplus and Index Numbers", *Review of Economic Studies*, summer, 1942 ; " The Four Consumers' Surpluses ", *R.E.S.*, winter, 1943 ; A. Henderson, " Consumers' Surplus and Compensating Variations ", *R.E.S.*, June 1941 ; also Hotelling, " The General Welfare in Relation to the Problems of Taxation and of Railway and Utility Rates ", *Econometrica*, July 1938.

set down his general view of the nature of economic activity and its relation to different types of surpluses.   Here we find a mixture of the relative and the absolute conception of the surpluses.   There is a passage which describes the consumer's surplus in the relative sense, as

> a true benefit which he as a consumer derives from the facilities offered to him by his surroundings or conjuncture.   He would lose the surplus if his surroundings were so altered as to prevent him from obtaining any supplies of that commodity and to compel him to divert the means which he spends on that to other commodities (one of which might be increased leisure) of which at present he does not care to have further supplies at their respective prices (op. cit., p. 830).

But there are other passages which suggest a return to the labour-theory outlook and the absolute concept of the surplus.   We have seen that the man-against-nature view focuses attention on man's net gain from economic activity which in subjective terms is equal to his total utility from the consumption of wealth minus his total disutility from the production of wealth.   It is the major theme of the Appendix K to show the essential unity of man's net gain from his efforts in spite of the fact that in an economy with division of labour and exchange, money transactions intervene between the acts of production and consumption.   " While the national income or dividend is completely absorbed in remunerating the owner of each agent of production at its marginal rate, it yet generally yields him a surplus which has two distinct, though not independent sides."   As a consumer, he obtains a consumer's surplus, since for all parts of his purchases except the " marginal unit " he would have been willing to pay a higher price than that at which he obtains them.   " Another side of the surplus which a man derives from his surroundings is better seen when he is regarded as producer."   As a worker, he derives a " worker's surplus " and as " owner of accumulated wealth in any form " he derives a " saver's surplus ", since for all parts of his services except the " marginal unit " he would have been content with a lesser rate of remuneration than that which he actually gets for them (op. cit., p. 830).

> These two sets of surpluses are not independent ; and it would be easy to reckon them up so as to count the same thing twice.   For when we have reckoned the producer's surplus at the value of the general purchasing power he derives from his labour or saving, we have reckoned implicitly his consumer's surplus, too, provided his character and the circumstances of his environment are given.

Perhaps the absolute concept of the surplus latent in Marshall's reiteration of the labour-theory outlook comes out most clearly when, after pointing out " the intimate connection " between the producer's and the consumer's surplus, he concluded that

in estimating the weal and woe in the life of a Robinson Crusoe, it would be simplest to reckon his producer's surpluses on such a plan as to include the whole of his consumer's surplus (ibid., p. 831).

Here, clearly, the surpluses are calculated with reference to a given situation *as it stands* and not with reference to a movement from one situation to another. The Appendix K is not an isolated instance where Marshall's conception of the surpluses is influenced by the labour-theory outlook. There is evidence to show that, at some stage in the development of his thought, Marshall toyed with the idea of calculating the subjective net gain of the community as a whole on the plan suggested by the labour theory. Marshall freely admitted the failure of this experiment and as a matter of fact ended by using it as a foil to his partial surplus analysis. But the steps by which he came to abandon the idea are of considerable interest from an historical point of view.

The labour-theory approach to the economic welfare of the community had no difficulties for the classical economists since they were concerned with the materialistic level of analysis. Thus Ricardo found it easy enough to measure the economic welfare of the community by its Net Revenue, which is a clear-cut physical magnitude : the total social output minus the subsistence fund for the quantity of labour required to produce that output. When, on the other hand, Marshall essayed a parallel approach and sought for a subjective counterpart of Ricardo's Net Revenue, he arrived at what he called the " net aggregate for the community ". This is denoted by his symbols $H-V$, where H is defined as " the sum of satisfactions, and V, as the sum of dissatisfactions (efforts, sacrifices, etc.) which accrue to the community from economic causes " (op. cit., Mathematical Appendix, note xiv ; cf. Edgeworth, *Mathematical Psychics*, pp. 67 et seq.).

Now in fairness to Marshall it should be observed that he was too much of a realist to be comfortable measuring the balance of weal and woe from human life in a cut-and-dried fashion. He pointed out that the problem is " as much philosophical as economic " and is complicated by the fact that " man's activities are ends in themselves as well as means of production " (op. cit., p. 831 ; also above, Chap. VIII, sec. III). But it should be noted that the concept of the Aggregate Surplus if seriously upheld repudiates the relative concept of surplus due to a change in the price of a *particular* commodity in one situation compared with another. However, what made Marshall abandon this concept was neither the philosophical doubts nor the methodological difficulties involved in adding up the absolute amounts of surpluses accruing to the community in a given situation. It was simply that Marshall did not think it *practically* possible to arrive at a reasonably accurate estimate of the constituent terms, the H and the V.

H is defined as the sum of total utilities of the commodities consumed by the community. The total utility of a given commodity is calculated with reference to the market demand curve for it (making suitable corrections when changes in consumers' incomes cannot be neglected). Now the demand curve for a given commodity is calculated on a partial plan ; it is a schedule of the different quantities of that commodity which would be purchased at different prices, assuming the prices of other commodities to be constant. Thus, if we try to add the total utilities from different commodities, each of which is calculated on this partial plan, we shall be guilty of treating the prices of the commodities both as constants and as variables at the same time. Thus Marshall confessed that

the task of adding together the total utilities of all commodities so as to obtain the aggregate of the total utility of all wealth is beyond the range of any but the most complicated mathematical formulæ. An attempt to treat it by them some years ago convinced the present writer that even if the task were theoretically feasible, the result would be encumbered by so many hypotheses as to be practically useless (op. cit., p. 131 n. ; cf. Pigou, *Economics of Welfare*, 4th ed., p. 57).

He was even more doubtful about calculating the V, the sum of efforts and sacrifices incurred in producing the commodities.

The forces of supply are especially heterogeneous and complex : they include an infinite variety of efforts and sacrifices, direct and indirect, on the part of people in all varieties of industrial grades : and if there were no other hindrance to giving a concrete interpretation to the doctrine, a fatal obstacle would be found in its latent assumption that the cost of rearing children and preparing them for their work can be measured in the same way as the cost of erecting a machine (op. cit., p. 852).

In view of these formidable difficulties of measuring the Aggregate Surplus for the community there were two alternatives which did not involve a sharp break with the traditional classical approach. The one to be chosen later by Prof. Pigou was to avoid using the surpluses whenever possible and to measure the economic welfare of the community indirectly by measuring the physical national dividend (which is not very different from Ricardo's Net

Revenue plus wages) valued at appropriate prices (cf., however, *Economics of Welfare*, Book II, Chap. XVII, also sec. IV, below). The other chosen by Marshall was to reduce the difficulties of measuring surpluses to manageable dimensions by concentrating on the *changes* in the surpluses from particular commodities, assuming the surpluses from other commodities to be constant.

Here then we have arrived at the " kink " at which Marshall glided off from his broader philosophical ideas concerning surpluses in general to the practical application of the surpluses in their Partial form. The Partial surplus analysis is not concerned with the economic welfare of the community as it stands in a given situation ; it is concerned with the *net changes* in economic welfare due to given changes in particular sectors of the economic system, *the rest of the system being assumed to be constant.* Thus from the very way in which the problem is formulated we are concerned only with the surpluses in the *relative* sense. We are concerned with the gain or loss to individuals due to a *movement* from one situation where they can buy or sell a particular commodity (or service) at a given price to another situation where they can only buy or sell it at a different price or may be deprived of the opportunity of buying or selling it altogether.

The fact that the surpluses depend on a given opportunity to buy or sell a particular thing on particular terms and would be wiped off if that opportunity was withdrawn suggests a further aspect to them which is very helpful in the study of Producers' surplus. It will be seen that when we are concerned with the gain or loss to owners of certain factors of production due to a movement from one occupation to another, the relevant concept of Producers' surplus is the *differential* rent arising out of special adaptability and specificness and not the scarcity rent based on the principle of diminishing marginal productivity. It is only when certain units of a given type of factor are more adapted to a particular use than other similar units that they would receive an excess of earnings over the normal marginal reward of that type of factor and it is only when they are relatively specific that they would lose a part of surplus earnings when shifted to their next best use. If the given units of factors were homogeneous and perfectly versatile, they would not receive any Producers' surplus in the sense relevant to Partial welfare analysis even if they should be earning high scarcity rent. For then they would not lose any part of their earnings by being shifted from one use to another ; their earnings here depend purely on the degree of their general scarcity in relation to the demand of the economic system as a whole and not on their special adaptability to a particular use.

When we come to Consumers' surplus, however, it is not possible to have a clear-cut separation between elements of " scarcity " rent due to the principle of diminishing marginal utility and elements of " differential " rent due to the fact that a particular commodity is better adapted to given consumers' tastes than other substitutes. From the point of view of the consumer who is the substitutor (as distinguished from that of the owner of the factor which is substituted) diminishing returns and imperfect substitutability are merely the two facets of the same thing. Thus it might be argued that Consumers' surplus is in the nature of " differential " rent since if all products were perfectly substitutable with each other, the demand curve for each would be perfectly elastic and there would not then be any Consumers' surplus on any particular product. But since a " commodity " can only be defined by its very fact of non-substitutability with others, these perfectly substitutable products cease to be separate " commodities " ; further, the assumption that the marginal rate of substitution between any pair of these products is constant is merely another way of saying that the principle of diminishing marginal utility does not operate. Thus, however much we try we cannot hope to get rid of " scarcity " rent elements in Consumers' surplus. There is a further point of asymmetry arising from the fact that the consumer is a substitutor whereas a factor (as distinct from the entrepreneur) is substituted. A given unit of factor is normally indivisible and draws its entire income from one source. Thus when the factor has chosen its most preferred employment, it is *not* in its next best use, even if it might still retain *a part*[1] of its differential advantage over the marginal factor when transferred there. On the other hand, the consumer's expenditure is highly divisible and he does not purchase his most preferred commodity to a point of absolute satiety to the exclusion of less-preferred commodities. Thus the withdrawal of *any* commodity (even if it stands low in his budget priorities) must cause some loss of surplus simply from the fact that he has already equated the ratios of marginal utilities of more-preferred commodities to their relative prices ; so that the expenditure which was yielding him some surplus on the commodity withdrawn must inevitably be frittered away in the marginal and non-surplus-

---

[1] If it retains *all* its differential advantage over the marginal factor, then it is an all-round superior factor which earns pure scarcity rent and no producer's surplus in our sense.

yielding purchases of other commodities which he has already bought to the point of relative satiety. The fact that the diverted unit of factor does not necessarily become a marginal factor in its next best use, whereas the consumers' expenditure on any given commodity if diverted does necessarily become marginal expenditure, blurs the distinction between the " differential " and the " scarcity " rent elements in Consumers' surplus. As we shall see, it also brings out a flaw in the usual method of treating the Consumers' surplus and the Producers' surplus triangles as if they were the exact counterparts of each other (cf. sec. III, below).

Without going any further into refinements, one thing now clearly emerges from our preview of the Partial surpluses : Marshall's change-over from the concept of the Aggregate Surplus for the community to Partial surpluses from particular commodities does not merely reduce the size of the problem ; it alters the fundamental nature of the problem. It involves a change-over from the absolute to the relative concept of the surpluses. And this seems to be the explanation of the apparently puzzling fact why recent champions like Prof. Hicks have been able to put the Partial surplus analysis on a methodologically secure footing, while there is some evidence to justify the Knight-Robbins contention that Marshall's *general* conception of the surpluses involves a particular philosophical outlook and the absolute concept of utility.

II

Let us now turn to a closer examination of Marshall's concept of the consumers' surplus on a given commodity and find out what refinements have been added to it in its recent rehabilitation. In the *locus classicus*, Book III, Chapter VI, Marshall started from the surplus of an individual consumer and defined it as " the excess of the price which he would be willing to pay rather than go without the thing, over that which he actually does pay " (*Principles*, p. 125). His meaning will become clearer if we compare this with the alternative definition in Appendix K, where the consumer's surplus is regarded as the benefit he would lose " if his surroundings were so altered as to prevent him from obtaining any supplies of that commodity and to compel him to divert the means which he spends on that to other commodities of which at present he does not care to have further supplies at their respective prices " (op. cit., p. 830). The second definition makes it clear that when we are estimating the consumer's surplus on a given commodity, we should assume that he is in an equilibrium position with regard to other commodities ; i.e. their marginal utilities to him are proportional to their prices. This means that the amount of money which the consumer pays for the given commodity is not capable of yielding any surplus satisfaction if diverted to alternative uses where it would only be frittered away as small increments in marginal expenditure all round.

Let us now follow up Marshall's famous illustration of the concept :

> Let us take the case of a man, who, if the price of tea were 20s. a pound, would just be induced to buy one pound annually ; who would just be induced to buy two pounds if the price were 14s., three pounds if the price were 10s., four pounds if the price were 6s., five pounds if the price were 4s., six pounds if the price were 3s., and who, the price being actually 2s. does purchase seven pounds (op. cit., p. 125).

The seven pounds of tea, Marshall observed, " are severally worth to him not less than 20, 14, 10, 6, 4, 3 and 2s. or 59s. in all. The sum measures their total utility to him and his consumer's surplus is at least the excess of this sum over the 14s. he actually does pay for them, i.e. 45s.".

The first thing to note about this definition is its concreteness. As Prof. Hicks has put it, " it involves nothing more introspective or subjective than the demand curve itself ". Thus if we draw the individual's demand curve for tea from the schedule given by Marshall, 45s. will be represented by the area under the demand curve after the consumer's outlay of 14s. has been deducted, which is a curvilinear triangle.[1]

The second thing to note is the relative element in Marshall's definition. This will become clear if we ask how exactly the consumer's surplus of 45s. is arrived at. It is arrived at by *hypothetically varying* the price of tea, assuming the consumer's tastes, his income and the prices of other commodities to be constant. We may start this process of *movement* either from the situation at which the price of tea is 20s. per pound and work downwards, or from the situation at which it is 2s. per pound and work upwards.[2]

To start from the situation where the consumer is just induced to buy one pound of tea at 20s. When the price is lowered to 14s. per pound, he would buy two pounds and obtain for 28s. what is at least worth to him 20s. plus 14s. ; i.e. 34s. Thus in the situation

---

[1] Subject to the assumption of " constant marginal utility of money " discussed below.

[2] For convenient exposition we have chosen a wide range of variation in price. Marshall is usually concerned with changes in consumer's surplus due to small variations around the existing price (cf. op. cit., pp. 132–3).

at which the price of tea is 14s. compared with the previous situation at which it is 20s., the consumer has gained a surplus of 6s. When the price is lowered to 10s. per pound, he would buy three pounds and obtain for 30s. what is at least worth to him 20s. plus 14s. plus 10s. ; i.e. 44s. Thus in the situation at which the price is 10s. compared with the initial situation at which it is 20s. the consumer has gained a surplus of 14s. We can carry on this process until the price is finally lowered to 2s. per pound, at which the consumer has gained a surplus of 45s. *compared with* the initial situation at which the price is 20s.

Alternatively, we may start from the situation where the consumer is buying seven pounds of tea at 2s. per pound. When the price is raised to 3s. per pound, he would cut down his purchase to six pounds and would have to pay 1s. extra on each pound. Thus in the situation at which the price is 3s. compared with the situation at which it is 2s., the consumer has lost a surplus of 6s. When the price is again raised to 4s. per pound, the consumer would cut down his purchase to five pounds and would have to pay another 1s. extra on each pound. Thus in the situation where the price is 4s. compared with the initial situation where it is 2s., he would have lost a surplus of 6s. in the first instance and another 5s. later ; altogether 11s. We can carry on this process until the price is finally raised to 20s. at which situation the consumer has lost a surplus of 45s. *compared with* the initial situation at which the price is 2s.

Strictly speaking, however, the consumer's gain in surplus due to a lowering of price from 20s. to 2s. will not be the same in terms of money as his loss in surplus due to a rise of price from 2s. to 20s., unless we assume with Marshall that his " marginal utility of money " is constant. Otherwise, a fall in price of tea (other things being equal) will increase the spending power of the consumer and usually makes him willing to buy more tea than before and a rise in the price of tea will have precisely the opposite effect. To adopt Prof. Hicks's terminology, the movement along Marshall's demand curve shows us only the " substitution effect " ; if we take into account the " income effect ", both the amount of money required to offset the consumer's gain due to the fall of price from 20s. to 2s., and the amount of money required to offset the consumer's loss due to a rise of price from 2s. to 20s. will be different from Marshall's consumer's surplus triangle. But, as Prof. Hicks himself has pointed out, the assumption of " constant marginal utility of money " used in the construction of Marshall's demand curves is a normally acceptable simplification and does not involve the utilitarian background it seems to suggest at first sight. To satisfy the conditions of constancy of marginal utility of money, we need merely assume that the consumer is spending only a small proportion of his total income on a particular commodity so that changes in its price would have a negligible effect on his total income (cf. J. R. Hicks, *Value and Capital*, Chap. I, p. 32 ; " Consumers' Surplus and Index Numbers," cited above ; and " Rehabilitation of Consumers' Surplus ", loc. cit., p. 109).

After showing that the individual consumer's surplus from tea is equal to the triangle under his demand curve for it, Marshall proceeded to equate the collective consumers' surplus from tea with the triangle under the collective demand curve in the tea market. The market demand curve is constructed on the same principles as the individual's demand curve ; that is to say, we start from a situation at which the price of tea is so much and then hypothetically vary the price and compile the schedule of different quantities of tea demanded by the market as a whole at various prices. As before we assume that the consumers' incomes and prices of other commodities are constant and that consumers as a body spend only a small proportion of their total incomes on tea. It will be seen that the total consumers' surplus on a given commodity, like the individual consumer's surplus, is a relative and not an absolute concept. To illustrate : in Fig. 6, let *DD'* be the market demand

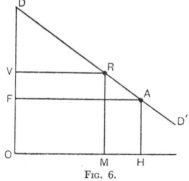

FIG. 6.

curve for tea ; let the quantity *OH* be bought at the price *OF* in a given situation. When the price is raised to *OV*, the quantity bought will be reduced to *OM*. The area *VRAF* measures the loss of the consumers due to a movement from *A* to *R*. Similarly, the total consumers' surplus triangle *DAF* may be looked upon as the measure of what the consumers would have lost when the price of tea is

raised beyond the highest point on the demand curve *OD*, which amounts to a complete withdrawal of tea from the market. Thus the calculation of the total consumers' surplus involves a comparison between two situations : one at which the commodity is available at a given price *OF* and the other at which it has disappeared from the market.[1] However, as Marshall has warned us,

Our list of demand prices is highly conjectural except in the neighbour-hood of the customary price ; and the best estimates we can form of the whole amount of utility of anything is liable to a large error (op. cit., pp. 132–3).

The market is, however, made up of many consumers with different tastes and incomes. Thus the change in the consumers' surplus merely shows the collective gain or loss of the consumers as a group, without telling us how this gain or loss is distributed amongst each of the individuals. This does not, however, appreci-ably affect the usefulness of the concept if we are concerned with an " isolated " market, the rest of the economic system being assumed to be optimally organised. In such a case, an increase in the consumers' surplus in the given market, other things being equal, should represent a gain from the point of view of the com-munity as a whole. Each of the individual consumers in this market would have gained, though they may not have gained equally, without making the consumers in other markets worse off.

In practice, however, more frequently than not we will have to face a change which increases the consumers' surplus in one market (say due to a subsidy) and decreases the consumers' surplus (say due to a tax). How then can we compare the loss and gain in surpluses of different groups of consumers ? Marshall's method of getting out of this difficulty was to assume that

by far the greater number of events with which economics deal, affect in equal proportions the different classes of society ; so that if the money measure of happiness caused by events are equal, there is not in general any great difference between the amounts of happiness in the two cases (op. cit., p. 131).

This assumption that quantities of money are proportionate to quantities of satisfaction amounts to abstracting from differences of incomes among individuals belonging to each group and also from the differences of incomes among different groups of individuals. It should, however, be noted that in the actual applications of the consumers' surplus analysis, Marshall was well aware of the poss-ible errors from this generalisation. Thus in the Mathematical Appendix, note xiv, he wrote :

We note that a few commodities are consumed mainly by the rich ; and that in consequence their real total utilities are less than is suggested by the money measures of those utilities. But we assume, with the rest of the world, that as

---

[1] So that the consumers' outlay on tea *FOHA* is diverted to marginal purchases of other commodities.

a rule, and in the absence of special causes to the contrary, the real total utilities of two commodities that are mainly consumed by the rich stand to one another in about the same relation as their money measures do ; and that the same is true of the commodities the consumption of which is divided out among the rich and middle classes and poor in similar proportions. Such estimates are but rough approximations, but each particular difficulty, each possible source of error, is pushed into prominence by the definiteness of our phrases (op. cit., p. 851).

Recent developments in analysis have, however, shown us a method of dealing with the gain and loss of different groups of individuals without assuming that quantities of money are proportionate to the quantities of satisfaction and without entering into interpersonal comparisons of utility. This method is the principle of compensation. In essence, it may be described as the extension of the proposition which is already latent in Marshall's concept of the consumers' surplus ; viz. it is the gain or loss to the consumers of a given commodity due to a change in its price (hypothetical or actual) in one situation compared with another. By using the Indifference Curve technique, the exponents of the compensation principle have been able to put a sharper edge to this idea. Thus, in order to banish the erroneous notion that consumers' surplus is an absolute amount of benefit which the consumers obtain just because they are buying so much of a given commodity at such a price, they propose to redefine it as the sum of money which will just offset the gain or loss to the consumers due to a given movement from one price-quantity situation to another. If, for the moment, we assume constant marginal utility of money and ignore " income effects ", this offsetting sum will be equal to Marshall's measure of the consumers' surplus. Granted this more pointedly relative concept of the consumers' surplus, the method of assessing the net result of a change which causes a gain to one group of individuals while it inflicts a loss to another group (assuming it leaves the rest of the community unaffected) may be stated as follows : We first ask what will be the sum of money which will just offset the gain of the first group of individuals and leave them no better off than they were before. We next ask what will be the sum of money which will just offset the loss of the second group of individuals and leave them no worse off than they were before. If the first offsetting sum of money is greater than the second, we conclude that the change has been an improvement from the viewpoint of the community as a whole ; if the two offsetting sums are equal, we should refrain from drawing conclusions ; and if the first offsetting sum is smaller than the second, we conclude that the change has resulted in a net loss to the community.[1]

To show that this method of offsetting or compensating does not involve interpersonal comparisons of utility, let us take a concrete example. Suppose that a change from one situation to another causes a gain to one group of individuals which can be offset by the sum of £120 and that it also causes a loss to another group of individuals which can be offset by the sum of £100. According to our criterion, we should conclude that the change has been an improvement from the point of view of the community. The reason for this conclusion, however, is not that we consider the £120's worth of gain enjoyed by the first group to represent a proportionately greater quantity of satisfaction than the £100's worth of loss suffered by the second group. It may be that while the first group which has gained is composed of rich individuals the second group which has lost is composed of poor individuals. Thus for all we know the £100's worth of loss in our illustration (if left uncompensated) may even represent a greater loss of satisfaction than the £120's worth of gain. But even accepting this, it is possible to show that the change has been an improvement ; for, after the loss of the poor group (whatever it may be in terms of real satisfaction) has been fully made good by a compensation of £100 taken out of the income of the rich group, the rich group will still be left with £20's worth of net again. Our concrete illustration makes it clear that the £20's worth of net gain has a precise quantitative significance only in relation to the tastes and incomes of the individuals in the rich group to which it accrues. If, for example, this sum of money was taxed and redistributed to the community at large, the real net gain in satisfaction might well be different, depending on the tastes and incomes of those who receive it. A priori, we may say that if a change results in a net gain of £40 instead of one of £20 to the same group, it should represent a greater improvement ; but since these sums of money are purely relative measures, we cannot by any means say that the community has gained twice as much when the sum of money left after compensation is £40 as when it is only £20.

So far we have neglected " income effects " and have not bothered to distinguish between the sum of money which will offset, let us say, the gain due to a movement from situation I to II and the sum of money which will offset the loss due to the reverse

---

[1] See, besides the articles of Prof. Hicks cited above, N. Kaldor " Welfare Propositions and Interpersonal Comparisons of Utility ", *Economic Journal*, 1939, pp. 549–52.

movement from situation II to I. If " income effects " are taken into account these two sums of money will be different. And similarly for the case where a movement from situation I to II causes a loss and the reverse movement causes a gain. Thus when a given change has a small net effect, it may happen that the balance of positive and negative offsetting sums of money from the point of view of the movement from situation I to II is positive, while it is negative or zero from the point of view of the reverse movement from situation II to I. It is this consideration which led Prof. Hicks to distinguish between the " Compensating Variation " and the " Equivalent Variation " in income and which led Mr. Scitovsky to propose a double criterion of improvement.

Firstly, we must see whether it is possible in the new situation so to redistribute incomes as to make everybody better off than he was in the initial situation. Secondly, we must see whether starting from the initial situation it is not possible, by a mere redistribution of income, to reach a position superior to the new situation again from everybody's point of view. If the first is possible and the second impossible, we shall conclude that the new situation is better than the old was. If the first is impossible and the second possible, the new situation is worse. Whereas if both are possible or impossible, we shall refrain from making a welfare proposition (Scitovsky, " Note on Welfare Propositions ", *Review of Economic Studies*, Nov. 1941, pp. 87–8).

These refinements are of great theoretical importance for it makes the principle of compensation neutral as between different patterns of income distribution which exists in situations I and II. We can tell which situation is to be preferred without accepting that the income distribution which prevails in one situation or the other is inviolable. They are, however, likely to be of little practical use. In practice we will have to confine the application of the surplus analysis to those " glaring " cases where the size of the gain or loss involved is big enough to remain substantially unaffected, whatever the point of view from which we may choose to consider it (cf. J. R. Hicks, " The Four Consumers' Surpluses ", loc. cit., pp. 40–1).

We may now summarise our findings as regards the question how far Marshall's original concept of the consumers' surplus has been reinterpreted in its recent rehabilitation.

(i) The beginning of the fundamental idea that consumers' surplus should be regarded as a relative and not as an absolute concept may be claimed for Marshall. Although his concept of the Aggregate Surplus for the community admits of absolute utility interpretation, Marshall was concerned with the changes in the size of the surpluses rather than with the size of surpluses as they stand when he came to apply the surplus analysis in the Partial form. The new definition of consumers' surplus as the sum of money which will offset the gain or loss due to a movement from one situation to another has more pointedly brought out the relativeness of the concept. But Marshall too had clearly stated that

the chief applications of the doctrine of consumers' surplus are concerned with such *changes* in it as would accompany *changes* in the price of the commodity in question in the neighbourhood of the customary price (op. cit., p. 133).

In the celebrated Chapter XIII, Book V, he had amply demonstrated that it is so. For there the whole structure of the argument rests on comparisons between changes in the consumers' surplus in industries with different laws of returns after a tax or a subsidy as the case may be.

(ii) The Indifference Curve technique has provided us with a more refined analysis of the " income effects " which Marshall had deliberately ignored as he did not consider them to be quantitatively important. Recent investigations by Prof. Hicks, Mr. Henderson and others have shown us that when we introduce these refinements the consumers' surplus is not one concept, but many concepts. But these investigations have also confirmed Marshall's judgment that while these distinctions are interesting from a theoretical point of view, they are not likely to be of much practical significance.

(iii) Where the recent formulations have taken a significant departure from Marshall's original theory is in the principle of compensation. This method has enabled us to avoid the traditional bugbear of welfare analysis, viz. interpersonal comparison of utility. It has enabled us to dispense with the doubtful assumption Marshall was obliged to use, viz. that quantities of money are proportionate to quantities of satisfaction.

Perhaps the most striking achievement of the principle of compensation is that it has brought the surplus analysis in line with the General Theory of Optimum which we have studied in Chapter VI above. We have defined the optimum as a state of affairs starting from which it is not possible to make any single individual better off while leaving other individuals as well off as before. Similarly, the optimum via the surplus analysis may be defined as a state of affairs starting from which it is not possible to make any group of individuals better off while leaving other groups of individuals as well off as before. That is to say, a given situation is not an optimum so long as there are possibilities of improvement in the sense defined above ; optimum is attained only when all such possibilities are exhausted.

The change-over from the " atomistic " analysis of the position of the individuals to the classical analysis of the position of groups merely reflects the fact that in practice the type of information we can obtain relates to prices and quantities for the market as a whole and not for individuals. As we have seen, however, we can be reasonably sure that if the group as a whole is better off or worse off, everybody in it will be similarly affected, irrespective of the way in which the collective gain or loss is divided amongst each of the individuals. Besides, we now attain a greater concreteness. The General Theory of Optimum states that if the basic condition of the proportionality of marginal utilities to marginal costs is not fulfilled, *some* individuals can be made better off without making others worse off. In the surplus analysis, by concentrating on the demand and cost curves of particular commodities, we know *which* groups of individuals will be affected by the proposed reorganisation and by *how much*. (Cf. sec. IV below for a further account of the advantages of the surplus analysis over the marginal optimum analysis.)

III

It is now time to turn to the Producers' surplus which has been frequently crowded out by the Consumers' surplus both in Marshall's original exposition and in subsequent discussions. Two main types of producers' surpluses can be found in Marshall's argument : (i) The worker's and saver's surplus based on the principle of increasing marginal disutility of effort and saving, and (ii) Rent and quasi-rent, which is the excess of the " abnormal " earnings of special instruments of production in particular uses over the " normal " earnings of the " marginal " instruments of the same class (cf. *Principles*, Appendix K, pp. 830–2).

In Book IV, Chapter I, immediately after the definition of the consumers' surplus, Marshall introduced the first type of the producers' surplus and pointed out the analogy between the two.

If a person makes the whole of his purchases at the price which he would be just willing to pay for his last purchases, then he gains a surplus of satisfaction on his earlier purchases, since he would get them for less than he would have paid rather than go without them. On the other hand, if the price paid to him for doing any work is an adequate reward for that part which he does most unwillingly ; and if, as generally happens, the same payment is given for that part of work which he does less unwillingly and at less real cost to himself ; then from that part he obtains a producer's surplus (op. cit., pp. 140–2 n.).

In short, the producer's surplus in this sense is the excess of his actual earnings from a given quantity of work or saving over that sum of money which he would accept rather than refuse his services altogether. The interesting thing about this concept is that Marshall introduced it obliquely in the footnote quoted and then dropped it out of his argument until we come to the Appendix K. In the celebrated Chapter XIII, Book V, which contains Marshall's standard applications of the surplus analysis, there is only one reference to the producers' surplus, and that in a footnote on p. 473, which refers us to Appendix H.   When we follow this up, we find that producers' surplus has been redefined in the meantime and that it now emerges as the " Producers' Surplus triangle " drawn on the basis of the " Particular Expenses " curve, which may be regarded as the marginal cost curve for the industry for a *given output*, excluding general economies of production due to changes in the scale of output (op. cit., p. 811).

This second concept of producers' surplus differs from the first in two ways. (i) It is not the money measure of producers' surplus satisfaction, but the actual excess sums of money obtained by the more favourably placed firms compared with the earnings of the marginal firm. (ii) It has nothing to do with the principle of increasing marginal disutility of effort. The differential advantages of the surplus-earning firms are simply due to the fact that they have access to special land or instruments of production which are better adapted to the production of the commodity in question than the marginal instruments of production. Assuming that all firms in the industry receive only " normal profits ", then all the abnormal receipts of the non-marginal firms must pass into the hands of the landlords and the owners of the special instruments of production in the form of rent or quasi-rent.

How can we explain this change in definition and Marshall's neglect of the workers' and savers' surpluses in his producers' surplus triangle ?   It can be accounted for only if we assume that ordinary factors such as unskilled labour or free or floating capital may be moved about at the margin from one industry to another without making an appreciable difference to their producers' surpluses. This amounts to saying that the general " worker's surplus " of an unskilled labourer may be regarded as his gain in satisfaction in possessing a job as compared with being unemployed and that, there-fore, so long as the general level of employment is constant, the total workers' surplus of the community may be left out of the argument as an unspecified constant which is unaffected by the distribution of the labour supply among different industries.   It is not clear how far Marshall would have subscribed to this argument in its explicit form, but, in any case, it needs modification. It is true that the money earnings of the ordinary factors, i.e. normal wages and interest, will remain appreciably unaffected by their transfer from one industry to another ; but if we allow for their owners' preferences between one occupation and another their Net Advantages are bound to be affected. It would therefore be rash to " direct " resources from one industry to another without making adequate allowances for loss of satisfaction due to interference with producers' preferences. Much would, however, depend on the degree of knowledge concerning occupational opportunities and what appears as " inertia " may turn out to be an expression of genuine preferences and vice versa.

Let us now turn to the second type of producers' surplus which we are used to regarding as *the* producers' surplus when thinking in terms of Marshallian triangles. Marshall pointed out that this is a special surplus as contrasted with, and in addition to, the general worker's and saver's surplus a producer enjoys. The general producers' surplus will arise even when each agent of production is rewarded at the marginal rate and when this rate has settled down at the " normal " level at which there is no incentive for the supply of factors either to expand or to contract. On the other hand, the special producers' surplus can arise only when the agent of production in question enjoys either rent or quasi-rent. Marshall developed this idea at length in Book V, Chapters VIII–XI ; but for a more pointed exposition we may turn to the Appendix K.

All appliances of production, whether machinery, or factories with the land on which they are built, or farms, are all alike in yielding large surpluses over the prime costs of *particular* acts of production to a man who owns and works them : also in yielding him normally no special surplus in the long run above what is required to remunerate him for his trouble and sacrifice and outlay in purchasing and working them (no *special* surpluses, as contrasted with the general worker's and waiter's surplus). But there is this difference between land and other agents of production, that from a social point of view land yields a permanent surplus while perishable things made by man do not. The more nearly it is true that the earnings of any agent of production are required to keep up the supply of it, the more closely will its supply so vary that the share which it is able to draw from the national dividend conforms to the cost of maintaining the supply : and land in an old country stands in an exceptional position, because its earnings are not affected by this cause (op. cit., p. 832).

From this, it will be seen that there are two separable causes of producers' surplus in this sense.[1] The first is that the supply of

[1] For a more systematic analysis of this problem the reader is referred to Mrs. J. Robinson's brilliant Digression on Rent, *Economics of Imperfect Competition*, Chap. VIII.

the factors of production in question does not respond, immediately
in the case of man-made instruments of production and not at all
in the case of land, to the " abnormal " earnings they are receiving.
The second is that the pieces of land or concrete instruments of
production in question are better adapted than the ordinary or
" marginal " instruments of similar types to the requirements of
a particular line of production. That is to say, they enjoy
differential advantages in this *particular* use. Marshall did not
favour a sharp distinction between the " scarcity " and the " differential " rent and pointed out that " in a sense, all rents are scarcity
rents, and all rents are differential rents " (op. cit., pp. 422–3).
While much may be said for this dictum, it will be seen that the
concept of producers' surplus relevant to the Partial Welfare analysis
is the differential rent and not the scarcity rent, although in any
given industry it will be a mixture of both elements. This is so,
because in the applications of the surplus analysis we are concerned
with a detailed analysis of the gain and loss of particular concrete
instruments of production when they are transferred from one
industry to another, assuming the total supply of each main type
of factors of production to be given. We are not concerned with
changes in the relative shares of the national dividend which accrues
to each of the broad classes of
factors of production due to the
changes in their relative total
supplies.

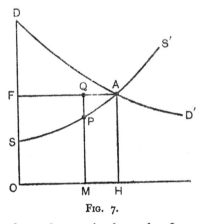

FIG. 7.

This can be seen clearly when
we turn to Marshall's well-known
diagram on p. 811 of the *Principles*
reproduced in Fig. 7. *DD'* is the
demand curve for the particular commodity and *SS'* is what
Marshall calls the " Particular
Expenses " curve, which for the
moment we will regard as the
marginal cost curve for the in-
dustry (excluding economies arising from changes in the scale of production). The forward rising *SS'* curve shows that as output is increased, factors of production less well-adapted to the production
of the commodity will be drawn into the industry, thus raising the
marginal cost and increasing the differential rent enjoyed by the
better-adapted factors of production. *OHAF* represents the total
producers' receipts from the output of *OH* and *OHAS*, the total

producers' expenses.   The difference between the two, the triangl e
FAS, represents the producers' surplus from that output.   *DAF* is
the consumers' surplus and at the equilibrium point *A* where
marginal cost is equal to price, the combined surplus from the
commodity is maximised.

Thinking in terms of the diagram, we usually take it for granted
that the triangles *FAS* and *DAF* are exact counterparts of each
other.[1]   This is, however, not strictly true for the following reason,
even assuming that related industries are optimally organised.   The
consumers' surplus triangle *DAF* is constructed on the assumption
that if this particular commodity was withdrawn from the market,
the consumers would have to fritter away their money outlay of
OHAF in increasing their marginal purchases of other commodities
from which they will obtain only a negligible amount of surplus.
(If we draw consumers' surplus diagrams for other commodities, this
will be shown by small triangular increments at the margin.)   This
is true even when there are substitutes for the particular commodity,
for in constructing the demand curve for it, Marshall had already
assumed that the consumers will take full account of the fact that
substitutes are available at given prices (op. cit., p. 131 and n.).
Thus (subject to the assumption of constant marginal utility of
money) the triangle under the demand curve measures the consumers' surplus on this commodity only because the money outlay
which yields a surplus in this particular use will become *marginal*
expenditure elsewhere.

Can we apply the same sort of reasoning to the producers' surplus
triangle *FAS* ?   That is to say, can we assume that the factors of
production which are receiving a differential surplus in the given
industry will become marginal factors in their next best uses ?   This
requires that the factors of production in question are specific
enough to lose all their differential advantages and earn no more
than " marginal reward " in other uses, but are at the same time
not specific enough to lose the whole of their earnings.   Before we
test the plausibility of this assumption, a brief explanation of the
term " marginal reward " is desirable.   When we are concerned
with producers' surplus due to special entrepreneurial ability,
marginal reward may be regarded as the " normal profit " or the
wage of management.   When we are concerned with quasi-rent [2]

---

[1] Marshall actually discouraged this view (cf. op. cit., p. 473 and n.).

[2] For the sake of generality we are here extending Marshall's argument.   Marshall
preferred to use the producers' surplus diagram only for long-term problems of rent
proper and not for short-term quasi-rent (see below and op. cit., p. 812).

on durable instruments of production, marginal reward (following Marshall) may be regarded as the pure time-preference rate of interest on the amount of savings embodied in these instruments. For simplicity's sake, we are obliged to ignore the fact that frequently what we regard as the " marginal " machine in an industry may be a worn-out machine retained in use, although it does not cover the overhead charges, just because it yields a little more than its running costs.   In this case, however, a greater part of the original capital value would have been amortised.   When we are concerned with rent from land proper marginal reward may be regarded as the reward of the " no-rent " land, which does not receive any residual share after the factors used together with it have been paid off according to their marginal products.

Now if the factors of production in question are highly specific, like specialised machines designed for the particular requirements of a given industry only, they would merely have scrap value in other uses and would thus lose the " marginal reward " of capital initially invested.   In such a case Marshall's producers' surplus triangle will be an inadequate measure of the financial loss of the owners of the machines if they were deprived of the opportunity of producing a given commodity, even if we measure their loss in terms of income and not in terms of capital value, although for the purpose of practical economic policy the latter may be the more relevant magnitude.   On the other extreme, it is theoretically conceivable (though practically unlikely) to have highly versatile factors which manage to retain constant differential advantages over the marginal factor in whatever industry they happen to be. This amounts to saying that their excess earnings are in the nature of pure scarcity rent and will not be reduced by their transfer from one industry to another so long as their total supplies remain constant relatively to the supply of other " ordinary " factors ; that is to say, so long as " the margin of cultivation " for the community in the Ricardian sense remains unchanged.

Ignoring these two extremes, it will be interesting to concentrate on middling cases where the factors of production in question will lose some of their differential advantages when transferred to their next best uses but will continue to earn some surplus in these uses. Such is the case of a rich agricultural land specially suitable for the production of wheat which will by no means become a no-rent land when its owner is obliged to turn it to the cultivation of barley. Such again is the case of a land site which is specially suitable for residential purposes ; it will lose a great deal of its differential advantages if there were a ribbon-development, but will continue to earn some site rent compared with the marginal land. Finally, we may take the case of a gifted entrepreneur who has a special aptitude for, let us say, the management of the cotton industry ; but he is likely to earn more than the wage of management if he were obliged to seek employment, say, in the rayon industry. In all these cases, then, the financial loss of the factors of production in question, if they were deprived of the opportunity of producing a given commodity, can be more accurately measured by the rent they are receiving in the given industry minus the rent they will receive in the next best industry relative to their qualifications.

This concept of the foregone surpluses has been used with great effect by Prof. Hicks when the related industries are not optimally organised [1] (cf. " Rehabilitation of Consumers' Surplus ", loc. cit., pp. 114–16). But our analysis as regards differential producers' surplus is valid even if related industries are optimally organised. For, in the first instance, related industries are at optimum on the assumption that the particular factors of production we are considering are being used in the given industry. When, therefore, due to reorganisation, these factors are released, so long as they retain some of their differential advantages, they will push some of the rent-receiving factors in the related industries to the latters' next best uses.[2] Thus optimum in related industries will have to be redefined due to a chain of readjustments, each displaced factor pushing that slightly inferior [3] to it to its next best uses down to the sub-marginal factors which now become marginal factors. Thus the total loss of producers' surplus from the point of view of the community will be the sum of the losses of the rent-receiving factors each of which has been pushed to its next best use in the readjustments following a given change.

The above analysis might appear too elaborate in the face of the fact that Marshall was usually concerned with small contractions of output such as that from OH to OM in Fig. 7. Thus it might be argued that since those factors originally displaced are themselves near-marginal factors, it is plausible to assume that they would earn next to no rent in their next best uses and that therefore in

---

[1] In this case, even when excluded factors are " marginal factors ", they will produce extra units in other industries which will be worth more than their marginal cost and thus generate an additional surplus which accrues to someone or other.

[2] This is a " jig-saw puzzle " process only in that we are rearranging the pieces in their next best fits. (Cf. Robinson, op. cit., pp. 106–7.)

[3] The epithets " inferior " or " superior " are always defined in relation to a given specific use.

Fig. 7, the triangle QAP is a reasonable measure of the loss of producers' surplus due to a contraction of output from OH to OM. This can be readily granted, but the significance of our approach remains not as much because it is a correction of Marshall's argument, as because it can throw some light on the theory of imperfect competition particularly when there are " private " factors used by each firm to produce a slightly different product from its competitors. The earnings of these " private " factors are in the nature of differential producers' surplus. It is because their earnings depend on the exact degree to which they are adapted to the production of a particular brand, that it is difficult to conceive a " normal " rate of earnings for them and to subsume this in the " average cost curve " of the firm. The concept of " normal " reward is plausible only if we can assume that these " private " factors are fairly homogeneous and that their earnings are in the nature of scarcity rent which will be unaffected by their transfer from one firm to another and can be determined in an open market purely on the basis of their given total supply in relation to the general demand of the industry or related industries (cf. J. R. Hicks, " Annual Survey of Economic Theory ", *Econometrica*, January 1935, pp. 8–11, for further discussion of this point).

To summarise our conclusions : Before we can use Marshall's producers' triangle as the measure of the loss of the producers, if they were deprived of the opportunity of producing the given commodity, the following qualifications should be kept in mind :

(i) We must take into account the possible producers' loss of satisfaction due to interference with their preferences as between one occupation and another (both for the marginal factors and the surplus receiving factors), which do not appear in the marginal cost curve for the industry.

(ii) Even when we are concerned with the purely financial loss (as distinguished from their loss in terms of Net Advantages) it will be more accurate to measure the loss in terms of foregone surpluses rather than in terms of the absolute surplus, which accrues to the producers just because they are producing so much of a given commodity at such and such a price.

These qualifications are, however, not criticisms of Marshall's original argument but merely safeguards against its misinterpretation, for (*a*) Marshall was normally concerned with small contractions in output where the ordinary producers' surplus diagram is not liable to great errors so long as related industries are optimally organised, and (*b*) Marshall normally preferred to use the diagram for the long-term problems of rent rather than for short-term problems of quasi-rent. The method of representing quasi-rents in terms of the producers' surplus triangle, he warned us, rests on " very slippery " assumptions [1] (op. cit., Appendix H, p. 812).

IV

Recent developments in the surplus analysis have not only put a sharper edge to Marshall's concept of the surpluses, but have also considerably extended the range of its application. In order to have a clearer view of these extended applications, it will be desirable, in the final section of this chapter, to give a brief account of how Marshall actually set about to demonstrate his famous proposition : viz. that it might be " for the advantage of the community that the government should levy taxes on commodities which obey the law of diminishing returns, and devote part of the proceeds to bounties on commodities which obey the law of increasing returns " (op. cit., Book V, Chapter XIII, p. 475).

It is interesting to recall that in the original context of Marshall's argument this proposition appears as the second limitation to the " general doctrine that a position of [stable] equilibrium is a position also of maximum satisfaction " " in the full sense of the term " : the first limitation being the differences in wealth between different parties participating in exchange (ibid., pp. 470–2). As we have seen in Chap. VII above, this distrust of generalisations and the search for exceptions to the general doctrine of free competition is a Neo-classical characteristic which can be found in the writings of English economists from Sidgwick onwards.

The second interesting thing to note is Marshall's warning that his analysis by itself does not " afford a valid ground for government interference ". Apart from " semi-ethical considerations " this seems to be motivated by the traditional fear that economic policy, particularly a policy of subsidy, however well meaning, might be " wrenched from its proper uses, to the enrichment of particular interests " (ibid., pp. 465 ; 473–5).

The third and most interesting point to note (and it is frequently forgotten) is that the main part of Marshall's case for subsidising increasing returns industries and taxing diminishing returns industries is based on consideration of *changes in consumers' surpluses only* ; considerations of changes in producers' surpluses play a

[1] Cf. sec. IV, below.

very minor rôle. This is partly due to the previous consideration that while consumers form the bulk of the community, producers might develop into " pressure groups " and partly due to the additional technical difficulties of the producers' surplus analysis.

Marshall started by showing that if a tax was imposed on a commodity obeying the law of constant returns, the loss of consumers' surplus would be more than the receipts in tax ; and conversely, if a subsidy was given to the same commodity, the gain of consumers' surplus would be less than the amount spent on subsidy. This can be seen from Fig. 8 (op. cit., p. 467 and n.).

To start from the case of a tax : let SS' be the supply curve of the commodity before the tax and ss' the new supply curve after the tax sS has been imposed. Let DD' the demand curve cut SS' at A and ss' at R. The consumers' surplus before the tax is DAS ; after the tax, it is DRs. Thus the loss of consumers' surplus due to tax is $sRAS$; the receipts from tax, the output being contracted from OH

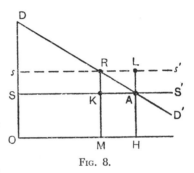

Fig. 8.

to OM is $sRKS$. Thus the former exceeds the latter by the triangle RAK, which represents a net loss to the community. To turn to the case of a subsidy : let ss' be the supply curve before the subsidy and SS' the supply curve after the subsidy. Assuming the demand curve DD' cuts them at R and A respectively, the gain in consumers' surplus is $sRAS$; but the amount spent on the subsidy, output having expanded from OM to OH, is $sLAS$. Thus the latter exceeds the former by the triangle RLA which represents a net loss to the community.

Marshall next considered the gain or loss of consumers' surplus due to a subsidy or a tax on the commodity obeying the law of diminishing returns. The result of a subsidy is clear. We have seen that even in the case of a commodity produced at constant cost, the gain in consumers' surplus would be less than the amount spent on subsidy. A fortiori, it would be much less in the case of the commodity produced under diminishing returns, since as output is expanded by the subsidy the cost of production would be raised and the consumers would have to pay a higher price for the commodity than under conditions of constant returns. The result of a tax on the commodity produced under conditions of diminishing returns is not quite so decisive. This can be seen by referring to Fig. 9, below (op. cit., p. 468, n. 2).

Let the old supply curve be *SS'* and let the imposition of tax raise it to *ss'* ; let *A* and *R* be the old and the new positions of equilibrium, and let straight lines be drawn through these points parallel to the two axes. Then the tax being levied, as shown in the diagram, at the rate of *RE* on each unit ; and *OM*, that is *CK* units being produced in the new position of equilibrium, the receipts from tax will be *TREF*, and the loss of consumers' surplus will be *TRAC* ; that is, the receipts from tax will be greater or less than the loss of consumers' surplus as *CKEF* is greater or less than *RAK*. In the figure as it stands it is definitely greater ; but if, however, we had

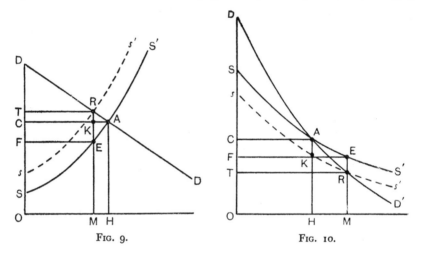

Fig. 9.   Fig. 10.

drawn *SS'* to indicate only very slight action of the law of diminishing returns, that is if it had been nearly horizontal in the neighbourhood of *A*, then *EK* would have been very small and *CKEF* would have become less than *RAK*.

Thus Marshall concluded that, in the case of a diminishing-returns industry, the receipts from the tax *may* be greater than the resulting loss in consumers' surplus and that they *will* be greater if the law of diminishing returns acts so sharply that a small diminution of consumption causes a great falling-off in the cost of production other than the tax (ibid., p. 468).

Marshall finally turned to the commodity produced under conditions of increasing returns. Here the result of a tax is quite clear. We have seen that even in the case of the commodity produced at constant costs, the loss of consumers' surplus will be greater than the receipts from tax. *A fortiori*, it would be much greater in the case of the commodity produced under increasing returns, since as output is contracted by the tax the cost of production would be raised and the consumers would have to pay a higher price for the commodity than under conditions of constant returns. The result of a subsidy is not quite so decisive ; as in the case of the commodity produced under diminishing returns, the net gain or loss will depend on the slope of the supply curve.

To illustrate, let us turn to Fig. 10, above (op. cit., p. 469, n. 3). Let SS' be the old supply curve and let it be lowered to ss' after the subsidy. Let A and R be the old and the new positions of equilibrium, and let straight lines be drawn through these points parallel to the two axes. Then the subsidy being given, as shown in the diagram below, at the rate of $RE = AK$ on each unit : and OM, that is FE units being produced at the new position of equilibrium, the amount spent on the subsidy will be $TREF$, and the gain in consumers' surplus will be $TRAC$. In the figure as it stands, $TRAC$ is very much greater than $TREF$; but if, however, we had drawn SS' to indicate only a very slight action of the law of increasing returns, that is, if it had been nearly horizontal in the neighbourhood of A, the case would not have been very different from a bounty on a commodity produced at constant returns, i.e. the amount spent on subsidy would have been greater than the gain in consumers' surplus.

Thus again we have the conclusion that in the case of an increasing-returns industry, the amount spent on subsidy *may* be less than the resulting gain in consumers' surplus and that it *will* be less if the law of increasing returns acts so sharply that a small expansion in consumption causes a great falling-off in the cost of production (ibid., p. 469).

It will be seen that so far Marshall's argument is quite tentative and runs entirely in terms of changes in the consumers' surplus. The function of the supply curves in the diagrams is merely to indicate the price which the consumers will have to pay when the output of the commodity is changed ; they are not meant to represent the changes in producers' surplus. It is true that, a little later, Marshall extended the argument and said that if the commodity obeys the law of increasing returns

an increase in its production beyond equilibrium point may cause the supply price to fall much ; and though the demand price for the increased amount may be reduced even more, so that the production would result in some loss to the producers, yet this loss may be very much less than the money value of the gain to purchasers represented by the increase in consumers' surplus (ibid., p. 472).

Yet this is not meant to be a systematic analysis of the changes in producers' surplus, for Marshall pointed out that in the practical applications of his analysis, besides the " semi-ethical questions " there will be other questions of " a strictly economic nature, relating to the effects which any particular tax or bounty exerts on the interests of landlords, urban and agricultural " and that these questions " differ so much in their detail that they cannot be fitly discussed here " (ibid., p. 473 ; cf. G. F. Shove, " Varying Costs and Marginal Net Products ", *Economic Journal*, 1928, p. 258).

Marshall's reluctance to discuss producers' surplus in diagrammatic terms is due to the difficulties of illustrating the economies which arise from changes in the scale of production. If these economies were taken into account, the method of drawing the new supply curve parallel to the old, after a tax or a subsidy, would be incorrect ; since the scale of output is different in the new position of equilibrium, the new supply curve should have a different shape from that of the old. This, in fact, is the crux of Marshall's distinction between the " Particular Expenses " curve which takes into account the economies to be obtained by producing a given scale of output and the normal supply curve which represents " the general conditions of production " of the commodity.

In the case of the industry working under diminishing returns it may be permissible to abstract from the economies relating to the scale of output and analyse changes in the producers' surplus on the basis of the marginal cost curve for the industry. In fact, Marshall himself made such a provisional abstraction and showed us in terms of a diagram how, if a tax was imposed in such an industry, the receipts from the tax would be less than the combined loss of the consumers' and the producers' surplus (op. cit., p. 473 n.). The diagram he used is substantially reproduced in our Fig. 4 above, where it can be seen that the combined loss of surpluses due to the imposition of the tax is *TRAEF* ; the receipts from tax being *TREF*, the net loss to the community is the triangle *REA*.

In the case of the industry working under increasing returns, however, a similar simplification is not possible.

To do so would be a contradiction in terms. The fact that the production of the commodity obeys that law implies that the general economies available when the aggregate volume of production is large are so much greater than when it is small, as to override the increasing resistance nature offers to an increased production of the raw materials of which the industry makes use (op. cit., Appendix H., p. 812).

The difficulties of a diagrammatic representation of the producers' surplus in an increasing returns industry may be seen from the fact that our Fig. 10 above, which is a substantial reproduction of the diagram Marshall used in his analysis of changes in consumers' surplus in such an industry, is, strictly speaking, not legitimate (cf. op. cit., p. 469, n. 2). If we interpret the SS' curve in that diagram as the marginal cost curve for the industry, the producers' surplus would have been negative for all outputs of the commodity and the commodity would not have been produced at all.

This is a convenient point to mention an important extension of the Marshallian analysis made by Prof. Pigou in his famous chapter on Discrimination and more recently by Prof. Hicks (Pigou, *Economics of Welfare*, Book II, Chap. VII ; Hicks, " Rehabilitation of Consumers' Surplus ", sec. v, loc. cit.). It consists in carrying Marshall's argument a step further to show that even under free competition, if the law of increasing returns operates in a given industry in such a way that producers' surplus is negative at all selling prices, the commodity in question would not be produced ; and this in spite of the fact that it may generate a consumers' surplus which will more than compensate the loss to the producers and yield a net gain of surplus to the community. This method of analysis is even more important when we come to a situation of general imperfect competition where the converse case holds. Here a commodity may be produced because the producer can obtain a positive surplus even though the combined consumers' and producers' surplus is less than the potential surpluses which the resources required in its production can generate in other uses This state of affairs is possible because, unlike under conditions of perfect competition, related industries are not optimally organised and prices are in excess of marginal costs. Thus the resources released from the production of the given commodity will produce extra units of other commodities which are worth more than their marginal costs and will thus generate surpluses for someone or other.

From this analysis Prof. Hicks has given us a general criterion : a commodity should be suppressed or introduced according as the consumers' surplus plus producers' surplus from it is smaller or greater than the potential surpluses which the resources used in its production will yield in other industries. In using this method of foregone surpluses, particularly with regard to the " new " commodity to be introduced, it is well to remember Marshall's warning that the list of demand prices for any commodity is highly conjectural except in the neighbourhood of the customary price and that " the best estimates we can form of the whole amount of utility of anything is liable to a large error " (op. cit., pp. 132–3). In the case of a " new " commodity, by the nature of the thing it has no customary price and the practical difficulties of estimating the total consumers' surplus from it should not be overlooked. Theoretically, however, there are no difficulties so long as it is clearly understood that the commodity is " new " only in the sense that so far the latent consumers' demand for it has not enjoyed a favourable chance of expressing itself effectively in the market and not " new " in the sense that it involves an entirely new want which has not existed in the *given* preferences of the consumers in a previous situation.

Perhaps the most important achievement of the method of the alternative surpluses is that it enables us to give a more comprehensive formulation of the optimum than is possible by using the marginal analysis alone. The marginal approach to the optimum starts from a given arbitrary list of the commodities existing in the initial situation and concerns itself with the problem of producing the " right " quantities of these commodities. The surplus analysis further enables us to consider whether the given list of the commodities is itself the " right " list and whether an *improvement* in the sense we have defined would not be possible either by suppressing any one of the existing commodities or by introducing a new commodity for which a latent demand exists.

CHAPTER X

PROFESSOR PIGOU'S "ECONOMICS OF WELFARE"

P ROF. PIGOU'S *Economics of Welfare* [1] occupies a unique position in the history of economic thought. It is the culmination of the great Neo-classical tradition ; and yet at the same time it marks a departure from it. For in his attempt to systematise his predecessors' concrete *ad hoc* approach to welfare economic problems Prof. Pigou has arrived at a concept of the general optimum ; and this concept of the optimum, although perhaps not as logically stringent as the Paretian optimum, represents a significant intermingling of the concrete particular approach of the English economists and the formal general approach of the continental economists. A brief study of so monumental a work as the *Economics of Welfare* must necessarily be selective and we shall concentrate here on the theoretical backbone of Prof. Pigou's system contained in Parts I and II of his book.

I

The Neo-classical element in Prof. Pigou's approach can be clearly seen from a strong admixture of those ideas which originate in the classical physical level of analysis.

Thus although Prof. Pigou defines economic welfare subjectively as quantities of satisfaction which can be brought into relation with the measuring rod of money, he goes on to explain that " economic causes act on the economic welfare of any country, not directly, but through the making and using of that *objective* counterpart of economic welfare which the economists call the national dividend or national income " (op. cit., 4th ed., p. 31). When we turn to his definition of the national dividend (taken over from Marshall) the influence of the classical physical productivity approach becomes apparent. He defines it as the flow of goods and services annually *produced* after *maintaining capital intact*, as opposed to Prof. Fisher who defines it as the flow of goods and services *actually consumed* during the year (ibid., p. 34).

[1] First published as *Wealth and Welfare* in 1912 ; considerably expanded and republished under the present title in 1920.

Now this definition of the national dividend is not very different from Ricardo's Net Revenue (plus wages) valued at appropriate prices, and the concept of *maintaining capital intact* on which it rests is a concept which belongs essentially to the physical level of analysis and cannot be transposed to the subjective level without raising formidable difficulties. Thus, J. S. Mill, thinking only in terms of the quantity of physical output which follows as a determinate technical function from a given stock of physical capital, had no difficulties in defining the net produce as

whatever is annually produced beyond what is necessary for maintaining stocks of materials and implements unimpaired, for keeping all productive labourers alive and in condition for work, and just keeping their number without increase (*Essays on Unsettled Questions of Political Economy*, p. 89).

When, however, we move to the subjective level of analysis and derive the value of capital from the expected value of income it will yield (instead of the other way round) the concept of maintaining capital intact merely by making good the physical wear and tear of capital goods becomes quite inadequate. We will now have to allow for a large item of depreciation due to obsolescence which will occur with changes in tastes and technique even if the capital goods are physically as good as new. Prof. Hayek following this logic of the subjective analysis has successfully attacked Prof. Pigou on this point and, despite many modifications Prof. Pigou has since introduced, it is fair to conclude that his concept of maintaining capital intact is capable of a precise meaning only at the physical level of analysis (cf. Hayek, " The Maintenance of Capital ", *Economica*, 1935 ; Pigou, " Net Income and Capital Depletion ", *Economic Journal*, 1935, and also a note in *Economica*, 1941). This does not, however, mean that we should discard the concept of maintaining capital intact from welfare analysis, for it is still plausible to argue that changes in the physical capital of a society would generally affect its economic welfare in the long run.

Again, recent developments in the Index Number theory have cast further doubts on Prof. Pigou's method of taking over the classical Net Product definition of the national dividend which is designed essentially as a measure of productivity and using it as the index of economic welfare. Prof. Hicks putting a sharper edge on Prof. Pigou's own analysis has shown that the national dividend as a measure of the subjective economic welfare is a different thing from the national dividend as a measure of productivity, except under perfect competition where prices are equal to marginal costs. In calculating economic welfare we use prices as the indices of marginal utilities while in the calculation of productivity we use them as the indices of marginal costs. Thus it would seem that Prof. Fisher's definition of the national dividend which measures current consumption is a more immediately relevant measure of economic welfare than Prof. Pigou's, which measures net productivity ; for current economic welfare directly depends on current consumption although here again productivity would affect economic welfare in the long run (cf. J. R. Hicks, " Valuation of the Social Income ", *Economica*, 1940, pp. 122–3 ; Pigou, op. cit., pp. 36–7).

Similarly there are many propositions in the *Economics of Welfare* which are rather perplexing until we view them against the background of the physical level of analysis. Such, for instance, is Prof. Pigou's argument that " a far-reaching economic disharmony " arises from the individuals' " irrational " premium on present satisfactions and discount on future satisfactions. Thus, apart from appealing to the ethical postulate that the State being a corporate body should make greater provisions for future generations than private individuals do, Prof. Pigou believes that the need for a discriminating taxation in favour of saving can be logically demonstrated on strictly economic grounds.

> Generally speaking, everybody prefers present pleasures or satisfactions of a given magnitude to future pleasures or satisfactions of equal magnitude, even when the latter are perfectly certain to occur. But this preference for present pleasures does not—the idea is self-contradictory—imply that a present pleasure of given magnitude is any *greater* than a future pleasure of the same magnitude. It implies only that our telescopic faculty is defective, and that we, therefore, see future pleasure, as it were, on a diminished scale (op. cit., pp. 24–5).

Here again Prof. Hayek following the strict logic of subjective analysis has pointed out :

> It implies a comparison between the present (absolute) utility of a future commodity and its future absolute utility, which is regarded as true utility. Such a comparison does not arise in any act of choice, since it is from the nature of things impossible to contemplate on anything at one and the same time as from present and as from future. All comparisons of relative utility are necessarily from one moment of time, so that all they express are the relations between present utilities of present goods and the present utility of future goods (" Utility Analysis and Interest ", *Economic Journal*, 1936, p. 49).

Prof. Hayek's criticism is deadly. Provided we are at the subjective level of analysis and provided we ignore the dynamic possibilities of divergence between the planned saving and realised investment, no economic disharmony can be said to arise from the individuals' allocation of their resources between present and future wants according to their time-preferences.   Their time-preference must be accepted as given just as much as their preference between any other two commodities.   Thus Prof. Pigou can only justify his argument by going back to the classical economists' first approximating assumption that physically identical bundles of products yield equal quantities of satisfaction at all times and places.   We then arrive at the classical proposition that savings should be increased until the physical marginal productivity of the indirect method of using resources is lowered by successive investment to equal that of the direct method.

Finally, let us take as our illustration Prof. Pigou's distinction between the Supply Price of a commodity from " the standpoint of the industry " and from " the standpoint of the community ". The Supply Price from " the standpoint of the industry " is the ordinary money expenses of production per unit of the commodity when its output is increased.   This would be the same as the Supply Price from " the standpoint of the community " if the price of the factors used in the production of the commodity remains constant with the increased demand for them.   If, however, the price of the factors changes with the expansion in the output of the commodity, then Prof. Pigou argues that the Supply Price from " the standpoint of the community " should be the money expenses of production per unit minus those elements of expenditure which are due to the changes in the price of the factors used.   Thus it will be seen that the function of the Supply Price from " the standpoint of the community " is to pick out the purely technical obstacles to be overcome in increasing the output of the commodity and to measure the strength of these obstacles by the variations in the physical quantity of factors required to produce per unit of the increased output.   " Quantities of resources in the physical sense were related directly to quantities of output " (op. cit., pp. 217–22).

Now it should be remembered that Prof. Pigou regards his distinction of the Supply Price from the two standpoints as fundamental to his proposition that the *economic welfare* of the community can be increased by subsidising the Increasing Returns industries.   The question thus arises whether the concept of the Supply Price from " the standpoint of the community " which is so reminiscent of the classical " quantity of labour embodied " measure of value can be justifiably used at the subjective level of welfare analysis.   To simplify the argument let us take an industry working under conditions of constant physical returns ; i.e. it continues to require the same amount of factors to produce each unit of the increased output. Let us, however, assume that the demand of this industry forms a considerable part of the total demand for some of the factors used so that their price rises with the expansion of the industry. Should we then include the increase in money expenses of production per unit of the increased output due to the rising price of the factors in the social cost accounting? Prof. Pigou answers no, because he considers the increased rates of payment to the factors merely as a transfer of income from one section of the community to another. He argues that the Supply Price from "the standpoint of the community" remains constant since the technical obstacles facing the community in the production of that commodity have remained unchanged. When we move from the physical to the subjective level of analysis, however, it becomes clear that the industry in our example has to pay a higher price for the factors it requires to expand its output because it is attracting them away from the production of other commodities the marginal utilities of which have risen as their outputs are reduced. Thus the increased price which our industry has to pay to attract further supplies of the factors is nothing but the measure of the increasing quantities of satisfaction which the consumers have to forgo elsewhere. Looked at in this way, therefore, what Prof. Pigou has dismissed as mere " transfer elements " are real elements of Social Opportunity Cost. To ignore them would be to ignore the principle of diminishing marginal utility and the whole economic calculus at the subjective level.

So much for the Neo-classical sub-stratum of physical productivity approach in Prof. Pigou's analysis. Let us now turn to those features of his analysis which represent a departure from the Neo-classical tradition. This departure takes place in two ways. Firstly, in the place of Marshall's Surplus analysis which deals with " chunks of economic welfare " Prof. Pigou introduces a Marginal analysis which is concerned with balancing the advantages and disadvantages of very small variations of output in different industries. After restating the difficulties of measuring the aggregate of surpluses for the community which we have noted above, Prof. Pigou concludes that any type of measure which involves the use of the surpluses should be ruled out of court (Pigou, op. cit., p. 57 ; cf. above, Chap. VIII, sec. I). He adheres to this resolution even in his analysis of Discriminating Monopoly and " lumpy investments " where by the very nature of the subject the surplus analysis would have been much more effective (op. cit., Part II, Chap. XVII ; cf. Hicks, " Rehabilitation of Consumers' Surplus ", loc. cit., p. 115).

Secondly, instead of concentrating *ad hoc* on particular cases of exception to laissez-faire as the Neo-classical economists had done, Prof. Pigou systematically subsumes all such possible conflicts between the private and social interest under his generalised concept of the Marginal Social Product curves. The result of all these is that, in the place of the older case-by-case concrete approach and the Partial Surplus analysis, we have a more systematic General Welfare analysis built round the concept of the Optimum which requires the equality of the Marginal Social Product of resources in all uses throughout the economic system.

These points of departure deserve to be specially mentioned to counteract a frequent tendency to lump the works of Pigou and Marshall together and to criticise the " Cambridge Welfare Economics " *in toto*. It is true that Prof. Pigou has taken over from Marshall, amongst other things, two fundamental ideas : viz. (i) the convention of drawing a boundary line between the Economic and the General Welfare by the measuring rod of money and (ii) the practice of assuming that the marginal utility of money is the same for different individuals so that quantities of satisfaction are proportionate to the quantities of money. It may also be admitted that Prof. Pigou is normally concerned with an economic system which is fairly competitive and where divergences between the private and the social products occur only rarely, so that in practice the Neo-classical method of selecting cases of exception to laissez-faire might have served quite as well as his more elaborate apparatus of separate Marginal Social Product curves. But, in spite of all these, the theoretical apparatus set up by Prof. Pigou is entirely different in character and range of application from the Partial Surplus analysis and the *ad hoc* Neo-classical approach. How different it is we can perhaps most clearly see in Mr. R. F. Kahn's extension of Prof. Pigou's methods to an analysis of an economic system working under conditions of general imperfect competition. Here, in its abstractness and severe formality, the Pigovian system of welfare analysis seems to be as far removed from the older Neo-classical tradition as is the Paretian Optimum (cf. Kahn, " Notes on Ideal Output ", *Economic Journal*, 1935).

II

Let us now turn to Prof. Pigou's celebrated cases of divergences between the Private and the Social products [1] (Pigou, op. cit.,

---

[1] These products are conceived in terms of money value and not in physical terms.

Part II, Chap. IX). We shall follow Prof. Pigou's classification of these divergences into three main types with certain modifications and examine each of these types of divergences by turn.

(i) Prof. Pigou's first type of divergences arises in connection with those wasteful forms of tenancy which do not provide adequate compensation to the tenant of land or other durable instruments of production, for the repairs and improvements which he may have undertaken during his tenure. Thus, " towards the close of his tenancy, a farmer, in his natural and undisguised endeavour to get back as much of his capital as possible, takes so much out of the land that, for some years the yield is markedly diminished " (ibid., p. 175). A similar wastage occurs when " concessions " are given to private companies to supply the town with gas, electricity, etc., on condition that the plants of these companies pass into the hands of the municipality after a certain time-limit without compensation (ibid., p. 176). It will be seen that all such type of wastes are due to a wrong and generally excessive rate of utilisation of the durable instruments of production made possible by loose forms of tenancy which fail to impose the " economic rent ". Thus natural resources required for hunting, fishing, grazing, etc., would be similarly over-exploited when there is no owner to charge rent and enforce " closed seasons ". The root of the trouble here is, therefore, not a divergence between the private and the social products but a failure to introduce the competitive pricing process to these parts of the economic system. Thus, what we need is not a correction of the private product to get the true social product, but merely a more accurate calculation of the private product from the standpoint of the owners of these durable instruments of production (cf. F. H. Knight, " Fallacies in the Interpretation of Social Cost ", *Ethics of Competition*, pp. 219–25).

(ii) Prof. Pigou's second type of divergences arises when the production of a commodity gives rise to incidental uncharged services or uncompensated disservices to a third party who is neither its producer nor consumer but who merely happens to be near the site of production. These divergences arising from neighbourhood conditions are well known. One might include under this category almost all the evils of lack of town-planning : from Prof. Pigou's smoky factory chimneys which pollute the air of the district to the uncontrolled building activity which swallows up the country-side surrounding most big cities. Here of course there can be no doubt about a genuine divergence between the private and the social products. Indeed, the trouble is that the divergences of this type have developed on so vast a scale that it seems hardly adequate to use Prof. Pigou's Marginal apparatus. The Marginal Social Product analysis, as its name implies, is concerned with a small increase or decrease of output at the margin. It can therefore merely modify the *existing pattern* of industrial location by small changes here and there and is thus too fine a toothcomb to clear up the Augean stable of the sprawling cities and their vast slums. Prima facie it is costly to society to have smoky chimneys in a residential district ; while Prof. Pigou's method of taxing factory owners in such a district might ease the situation, a complete remedy of the evil would seem to require the abandonment of the existing pattern of land utilisation and the introduction of a more rational pattern where all such harmful juxtaposition of industrial and residential sites are prevented as much as possible. In planning a new pattern of land utilisation it would be desirable to estimate the Social Opportunity Cost in broader terms by weighing up the overall advantage or disadvantage of using a certain locality for a certain set of purposes taking into account the " external economies " and other complementarities between different industries. It will be seen that the Marginal welfare analysis, however generously interpreted, cannot be equal to such a task. It is one of those problems where what Prof. Hicks calls the " Total Conditions " of the Optimum are more important than the Marginal Conditions (cf. J. R. Hicks, " Foundations of Welfare Economics ", loc. cit., p. 704). It is not sufficient to impose taxes or subsidies to equate the marginal private and the marginal social products of individual factories in each locality according to the existing pattern of land utilisation. We should find out whether no improvements could be made by completely abandoning that pattern and introducing a new one.

Speaking of " Total Conditions ", there are one or two cases of divergences which Prof. Pigou has included in his second category which do not strictly depend on neighbourhood conditions for their existence. Such is Sidgwick's case of the lighthouse which although it would benefit shipping is not built because no toll could be conveniently levied on ships. Such again is the case of scientific research the results of which " are often of such a nature that they can neither be patented nor kept secret, and, therefore, the whole of the extra reward they at first bring to their inventor is quickly transferred from him to the general public in the form of reduced prices " (Pigou, op. cit., pp. 184–5). Perhaps the more convenient way of treating such cases is to regard the services of the lighthouse or research worker as a " new commodity " for which latent consumers' demand exists and which can therefore generate a great deal of consumers' surplus but which is nevertheless not produced because the producers' surplus is negative or zero. Stated in this way, it can be shown that this " new commodity " should be produced if it yields a consumers' surplus which is greater than the combined producers' and consumers' surpluses which the resources required for its production is capable of generating in other alternative uses (cf. above, Chap. IX, sec. II).

(iii) We now come to Prof. Pigou's third type of divergences which is discussed separately in Part II, Chap. XI. Here Prof. Pigou maintains that the marginal social product of the resources employed in an industry with Decreasing Supply Price is greater than their marginal private product so that the output of such an industry is less than the optimum amount. For practical purposes Prof. Pigou's argument amounts to the same thing as Marshall's celebrated proposal to give subsidies to Increasing Returns industries, but he has arrived at the conclusion by a more arduous and perhaps less-acceptable route. It will be remembered that Marshall's case for subsidies rests entirely on considerations of changes in Consumers' surplus, changes in the Producers' surplus being left in the background (cf. above, Chap. VIII, sec. IV ; Marshall, *Principles*, Book V, Chap. XIII). On the other hand, Prof. Pigou, apart from using the Marginal in the place of the Surplus analysis, seems to attribute the divergences to the incidental services rendered to the persons " who are producers of the commodity " (Pigou, op. cit., pp. 174 ; 213). Further, Prof. Pigou's argument is complicated by the introduction of two debatable ideas : viz. (i) the distinction between the Supply Price of a commodity from the standpoint of the community and from the standpoint of the industry and (ii) the concept of the Equilibrium firm.

(i) As we have already seen Prof. Pigou's method of deriving the Supply Price from the standpoint of the community by deducting from the marginal cost of the industry the so-called " transfer elements " which are due to changes in the price of the factors used is valid only at the physical level of analysis. For there we are concerned with the changes in the physical quantity of factors required to overcome the technical obstacles of production per unit of the increased output. When, however, we come to the subjective level of analysis to which Prof. Pigou's argument purports to apply, the increase in the expenses of production, whether it is due to the increased quantity of factors required per unit of output or merely due to the higher price which has to be paid to attract the same quantity of factors from other uses, should be counted in the Social Opportunity Cost (cf. above, Chap. IX, sec. I).

(ii) Even ignoring this as a minor point we still have to face a second set of difficulties raised by Prof. Pigou's further distinction between the Supply Price from the standpoint of the industry and the Supply Price of the Equilibrium firm. Prof. Pigou has used the former (assuming the prices of factors to be constant) as the reciprocal of the Marginal Social Product and the latter, as the reciprocal of the Marginal Private Net Product of resources used in that industry. Thus, in an increasing returns industry where, in Prof. Pigou's terminology, the Supply Price from the standpoint of the industry is less than the Supply Price of the Equilibrium firm, the Marginal Social Product is greater than the Marginal Private Product. Now the concept of the Equilibrium firm, a variant of Marshall's Representative firm, is a perplexing concept. If what has been said about the Representative firm can be extended to the Equilibrium firm, it is a concept which does not command a general acceptance even among Cambridge economists and is one of those ideas which create more trouble than they are worth (cf. " Symposium on the Representative Firm and Increasing Returns ", by G. F. Shove, P. Sraffa and D. H. Robertson, *Economic Journal*, 1930, pp. 79 et seq. ; also L. Robbins " Representative Firm ", loc. cit., 1928).

However, whether we accept the Equilibrium firm or not Prof. Pigou's method of deducing the variation in the Marginal Social Product from the variation in the Supply Price of the industry has still to face a final difficulty : viz. there need not necessarily be any correlation between the forward-falling supply curve of an industry and the external economies it creates. Thus an industry may have a falling supply curve without creating any external economies, simply because it enjoys the economies created by other industries. Conversely, it is possible for an industry to have a rising supply curve and at the same time be creating some external economies. Here it is true that an industry generally cannot create external economies without enjoying internal economies itself and these internal economies may be counterbalanced by the increased price it has to pay for the " scarce factor " required for its expansion (cf. G. F. Shove, " Varying Costs and Marginal Net Products ", *Economic Journal*, 1928, p. 258 ; R. F. Kahn " Notes on Ideal Output ", *Economic Journal*, 1935, pp. 10–11). In fairness to Prof. Pigou it should be remembered that he assumes the prices of all factors to be constant when he uses the Supply Price of the industry as the reciprocal of Marginal Social Product. Nevertheless, for the purpose of calculating the Marginal Social Product, we need to know which industries really originate external economies and which merely enjoy them, and the shape of the supply curve of an industry remains an undecisive indication of its capacity to generate external economies.

III

Let us now consider how Prof. Pigou has worked these various cases of divergences between the marginal private and the marginal social products into the formal framework of his Optimum. He begins by defining the Optimum as a state of affairs where the marginal social products of resources are equal in all industries. Since, however, he is working on the basis of an economic system where the marginal private products in all industries are equalised automatically by competition and where the marginal private and the marginal social products diverge only rarely, the optimum output in each industry can be reached by equating its marginal private product to its marginal social product by a tax or a subsidy (op. cit., pp. 214–15). But the equality of the marginal private products to the marginal social products is not a fundamental condition ; it is merely a means of equating the marginal social products in different industries to each other. Thus in an economic system where there is a widespread divergence between the marginal private and the marginal social products so as to make it impossible to equate them to each other, the optimum can still be attained (theoretically at least) by equating the marginal private products in all industries and by making the marginal social products diverge from the marginal private products in an equal degree in all industries (ibid., p. 225). That would still equalise the marginal social products to each other.

Now Prof. Pigou's concept of the Optimum follows from the simple proportionality reasoning of ordinary economic theory, provided the following two conditions are fulfilled : (i) the Marginal Social Product is a justifiable theoretical concept and (ii) the Marginal Social Product curves are continuous and forward falling curves like those used in the Marginal Productivity theory. Let us examine these by turn.

(i) Prof. Pigou has defined the Marginal Social Product as " the total net product of physical things and objective services due to the marginal increment of resources in any given use or place, no matter to whom it may accrue " (ibid., p. 134).   To obtain the *value* of this Social Physical Marginal Product we multiply the main product and the incidental services or disservices rendered by their respective market prices.   For the sake of brevity we will use the term " marginal product " to mean marginal value product and will introduce the term " marginal physical product " when we want to refer specifically to the hotch-potch of physical things produced by a marginal unit of investment.

From this definition it will be seen that the prefix " Social " used by Prof. Pigou to qualify the marginal product does not imply an antithesis of the " Individual " and does not involve any ethical judgments about " Social Good ".   The Marginal Social Product is calculated by valuing the hotch-potch of physical things produced by a marginal unit of investment according to their given market prices determined by individual motivations.   It is thus merely an unusually complete summing up of productivity from the point of view of different individuals on the basis of data provided by the market ; it does not incorporate any further valuations made by Society as a central organic entity.

Granted this, the calculation of the marginal social product falls logically into two problems : (a) how to make an inventory of the hotch-potch of physical things produced by the marginal unit of investment and (b) how to reduce them into the common denominator of money.

(a) We have seen that incidental services or disservices are due either to neighbourhood conditions or to external economies and diseconomies.   The construction of an inventory for these incidental services or disservices is more difficult than it would seem at first sight.   Thus in the case of the smoky factory chimneys it might not be difficult to assess the increase in the laundry bill ; but what about the bad health and the many occupational diseases caused by these " satanic mills " and who would dare to assess these evils in money terms ?   Again, as we have seen, with regard to the external economies and diseconomies we will have to go behind the supply curves to find out which industries really originate and which merely enjoy them.

(b) Having obtained the inventory of physical things produced by the marginal unit of investment, the next step is to reduce these different items to a common money value, for money value is the bridge by which we pass from the physical to the subjective level of analysis.   Here Prof. Pigou's procedure is to take these physical items by turn, multiply them by their respective market prices and then add up the resulting sums of money, counting disservices as negative sums of money. The algebraic sum total of these money values is then taken as the measure of the size of the marginal social product due to the marginal unit of investment (ibid., p. 135).

In regarding the size of the marginal social product as the measure of the increase in subjective economic welfare due to the marginal unit of investment, Prof. Pigou is obliged to assume two things : (i) The marginal utility of money is identical to different individuals so that if they are willing to spend the same amount of money they will each obtain an equal quantity of satisfaction. By this Prof. Pigou ignores the differences in incomes. But this is only for the purposes of Production welfare economics for we are told at the outset that the transfer of income from the rich to the poor would increase economic welfare, provided it does not reduce the total size of the national dividend (op. cit., Part I, Chap. VIII). (ii) Prices of different commodities measure the absolute quantities of satisfaction obtained by their consumers so that money values of the different physical items produced by the marginal unit of investment can be added together to obtain a measure of the algebraic sum of the quantities of satisfaction and dissatisfaction due to that unit of investment. Here, methodologically speaking, we are in deep waters. In the formulation of the Paretian Optimum we have used the price ratio between each pair of commodities as the index of their relative marginal utilities or their marginal rate of substitution ; now we are obliged to use the price of each commodity as the measure of its absolute marginal utility. Further, in adding up the small increase in the quantities of satisfaction or dissatisfaction which different individuals obtain from the hotch-potch of physical things produced by the marginal unit of invest-ment, we are making interpersonal comparisons of utility.

This is perhaps the most serious weakness in Prof. Pigou's analysis. Theoretically, perhaps, Prof. Pigou's methodological diffi-culties can be overcome by extending the principle of Compensation which we have used in the surplus analysis. But in practice we must remember that we are dealing with very small increments or decrements of welfare in Prof. Pigou's marginal analysis. While it is worthwhile setting up the elaborate apparatus of Compensation in dealing with large chunks of economic welfare involved in the surplus analysis, the application of the principle of Compensation to marginal variations in economic welfare is so cumbrous as to be almost futile. If, however, we decide to follow Prof. Pigou across this methodological gap, his analysis may have one practical advan-

tage over the surplus analysis. In the surplus analysis we have
to find out the relevant range on the demand curve due to a given
change in the price and if the price change is great our calculations
are liable to serious errors. In the marginal product analysis we
merely use the prices and quantities given by the market ; we thus
dispense with the difficult problem of interpolating the required
range of the demand curve and merely take the given points on
the demand curves of the products produced by the marginal unit
of investment.

(II) Let us now turn to the second condition of Prof. Pigou's
Optimum which requires that the marginal social product curves
are continuous and forward-falling curves. At the outset it should
be pointed out that we cannot appeal to the ordinary principle of
non-proportional physical returns to fulfil this condition. When
Prof. Pigou speaks of a marginal unit of investment, he is not
thinking of a marginal unit of the variable factor assuming the
quantity of other factors used together with it to be constant. On
the contrary, he explicitly points out that the marginal unit of
investment " must be interpreted as the rth (physical) increment
of some sort of productive resources (e.g. labour of a given quality)
plus whatever additions to the quantities of the other sorts which
properly go with that increment ". The phrase " properly go with "
means that " the various factors of production must be combined
in such wise as to make their aggregate money cost a minimum "
(ibid., p. 173). Defined in this way, diminishing physical returns
means diminishing physical returns to scale and there is no *a priori*
reason why this should necessarily happen. Indeed, Prof. Pigou
himself seems to doubt the probability of diminishing physical
returns in this sense (ibid., p. 220). Thus the falling marginal
product curve in Prof. Pigou's sense must be derived ultimately
from the principle of diminishing marginal utility for the product
itself. The fact that due to the falling demand curve for the product the producer will obtain diminishing marginal receipts for
successive equal units of money outlay will ensure that the marginal
private product curves are falling at the point of equilibrium.
But what about the social marginal product curves ? For industries
working either under conditions of diminishing physical returns
or generating external diseconomies, there can be little doubt that
the social marginal product curves would also be falling. For an
industry enjoying the economies of large-scale production so that
its marginal private product is falling only very gradually and
which in addition is creating large external economies for other

industries, there is, however, a possibility that its marginal social product may be constant or even rising at the point of the equilibrium. Prof. Pigou realises this possibility, although he has stated it in a slightly different way. He also mentions a further possibility of increasing social marginal product when the introduction of a new commodity such as tobacco or music enhances the tastes of the consumers and enables them to obtain a greater satisfaction from it after a certain time (ibid., pp. 139–40). We will, however, have to exclude his second example as we are concerned in this part of the book only with welfare analysis based on *constant wants*. But the first case by itself shows that although the marginal social product curves would be generally falling, we cannot presume too confidently that they would necessarily be so. Thus, as Prof. Pigou explains, the Optimum obtained by equating the marginal social products may only be a position of *relative maximum* and not necessarily that of the *absolute* maximum :

even though the values of marginal social net products were everywhere equal or differed only in ways "justified" by the costs of movement, there might still be scope for State action designed to increase the magnitude of the national dividend and augment economic welfare (ibid., p. 141).

IV

From what has been said above it will be seen that Prof. Pigou's welfare analysis occupies an intermediate position between the highly formalised Paretian theory of the Optimum on the one hand and the " earthy " but less-systematic Marshallian surplus analysis on the other. We can best appreciate the advantages and disadvantages of the middle course Prof. Pigou has adopted by comparing his analysis with these two types of analysis at the opposite ends of the scale.

The Paretian and the Pigovian systems have two common features : (i) both give us a General welfare analysis based on a concept of the Optimum for the economic system as a whole and (ii) both use the Marginal apparatus to define the conditions of the Optimum. Here, however, the similarity ends, for they are designed to serve two different purposes.

The Paretian theory of the Optimum is concerned with the basic methodological problems of welfare economics rather than with its practical application. Its main purpose is to show that it is possible to formulate a stringently demonstrable concept of the Optimum which avoids the traditional bugbears of welfare economics, viz. interpersonal comparisons of utility and value judgments. In order to achieve its aim, however, it has to sacrifice realism and assume the ideal conditions of Perfect Competition with perfect mobility and divisibility of factors and perfect knowledge. The fact that Perfect Competition could never be attained in practice even under the most favourable conditions does not invalidate the concept of the Optimum. It does, however, mean that the normal feature of economic life consists in the deviations from, and not the attainment of, the Optimum. It has been a great achievement to formulate a stringent concept of the Optimum ; it is the necessary foundation of a scientific welfare economics and without it we cannot conceive the Deviations from the Optimum. Nevertheless, it is only a beginning of welfare economics and for the actual study of these deviations themselves we require a more realistic model than that of Perfect Competition which virtually assumes away all possible frictions and faults.

Prof. Pigou, on the other hand, is primarily concerned with the practical application of welfare economics rather than with its logical foundations ; " it is the promise of fruit and not of light that chiefly merits our regard " (op. cit., p. 4). Thus his distinction between the economic and the general welfare is not logically clear-cut ; it also obscures the necessity of assuming given and constant wants for the purpose of scientific welfare analysis (cf. op. cit., p. 139). But it is a reasonable expedient which few economists would reject in practice. Again, his method of calculating the marginal social product by adding up the market values of all the direct and indirect effects of a given unit of investment is another such practical expedient. It is difficult to find a workable alternative method ; but, as we have seen, in regarding the marginal social product as the measure of the marginal increment of subjective economic welfare to society Prof. Pigou is obliged to make interpersonal comparisons of utility which make his analysis unacceptable to the purist economist.

Fixing his eyes on practical application and yet at the same time desiring to preserve the formal framework of the competitive Optimum, Prof. Pigou has chosen a model of the economic system with a fair degree of competition. This is not to say that he ignores monopoly and imperfect competition (cf. op. cit., Part II, Chaps. XIV–XVII). It is merely that in working out the backbone of his analysis he assumes the " free play of self-interest " from which monopoly is explicitly excluded (ibid., p. 143 n.). Prof. Pigou's model of Free Competition, as contrasted with the Continental model of Perfect Competition, allows for some degree of friction, immobility, indivisibility and imperfect knowledge (ibid., Part II, Chaps. V–VIII). In a world where imperfect competition is not a rare phenomena but a normal feature and cannot be eliminated merely by abolishing institutional restraints on the free play of self-interest, Prof. Pigou's model is still unrealistic ; nor would he claim it to be otherwise. But we have come a step further in the process of successive approximation to reality and by means of his less abstract model we are able to take into account those important divergences between the social and the private marginal products. These divergences arising out of indivisibilities and rigid interrelations in the conditions of production would have been incongruous in the ideally fluid system of Perfect Competition. Besides, Prof. Pigou's analysis can be, and in fact has been, extended to deal with more and more imperfect models of the economic system. Before we go on, however, there are certain questions of principle relating to the " structural planning " of the economic system which may be conveniently cleared up in terms of Prof. Pigou's model.

Assuming there are no divergences between the social and the private products, Prof. Pigou has argued that the free play of self-interest will bring about the Optimum marked by the equality of marginal product of resources in all uses. He, however, allows for the possibility of deviations from perfect equality of marginal products due either to imperfect knowledge or to the cost of movement of factors from one use to another. Starting from an initial situation where the cost of movement is high or knowledge is imperfect, Prof. Pigou's Optimum is therefore quite compatible with considerable differences between the marginal products in different uses. The question thus arises whether the State should give bounty to lessen ignorance or to reduce the cost of movement. On purely theoretical grounds and in the absence of further extenuating circumstances Prof. Pigou would answer No to this question.

A cheapening of knowledge and movement to individuals, brought about by the transference of a part of the cost of these things to the State is quite a different thing and works quite differently from a cheapening brought about by a real fall in cost. The two sorts of cheapening have the same tendency to promote . . . increased equality among the values of marginal net products at different points. But, when the cheapening is due to transference, the resultant increase in equality is an increase beyond what, *relatively to existing conditions*, is most advantageous. Prima facie this sort of cheapening, though it will make the values of the marginal products more equal, is likely to injure the national dividend (op. cit., pp. 147–8).

This is the logical conclusion of applying the marginal calculus to the problem and it would at first sight seem to run opposite to the view held by many liberal economists that since anything which makes the economic system " more competitive " is desirable, structural planning promoting knowledge and mobility should be made " on principle ". But the reconciliation between these two views is not difficult in practice, for Prof. Pigou adds :

> To obviate misunderstanding two modifying considerations should be added. First, the presumption just established against the industry promoting mobility is merely a special case of the general presumption against the grant of a bounty to any industry. It may therefore be overthrown if there is special reason to believe that, in the absence of a bounty, investment in the industry in question would not be carried so far as is desirable. Secondly, when the State takes over the work of providing either information or the means of movement, and elects for any reason to sell the results of its efforts either for nothing or below cost price, we have, in general, to do, not merely with the grant of a bounty on these things, but at the same time with a real cheapening due to the introduction of large-scale methods. Even therefore though the bounty element in the new arrangement were proved to be injurious, it might still happen that the arrangement as a whole was beneficial (ibid., p. 148 n.).

This virtually supports the case for subsidising knowledge at least, for there are many reasons why knowledge should be regarded as a special commodity ! (i) The demand for knowledge cannot be properly reflected by the price system because the existing degree of knowledge about the advantages of greater knowledge is imperfect. (ii) The consumption of knowledge, unlike that of other subsidised commodities, is not confined to any particular section of the community but benefits everyone by a process of diffusion. (iii) In real life, especially under conditions of imperfect competition, divergences from the Optimum may be due as much to lack of knowledge as the deliberate distortion of knowledge by particular vested interests, which clearly calls for State interference.

The case for subsidising movement is less clear-cut and brings in a lot of complicating factors. In practice, mobility of labour might depend not merely on transport costs but on the various amenities available in the new neighbourhood. While there is a strong case for promoting mobility to cure " structural unemployment " and depressed areas, this is one of those questions where we have to take into account the overall advantages and disadvantages in terms of the " Total conditions " and not of " Marginal conditions ". Nevertheless, Prof. Pigou has shown us that it is possible to push analysis to find out how much resources should be devoted to structural planning instead of merely advocating it on principle.

Let us now very briefly examine Mr. R. F. Kahn's attempt to extend the Pigovian social marginal product analysis to an economic system in which imperfect competition is normal and widespread (cf. Kahn, " Notes on Ideal Output ", loc. cit., pp. 1 et seq.). Prof. Pigou, starting from a model of the economic system which is fairly competitive and in which the divergences between the social and the private marginal products occur rarely, could arrive at the Optimum merely by equating the social and the private products when they occasionally diverge. When, however, we come to an economic system in which imperfect competition has gone too far on an extensive scale, it is no longer possible to equate the social and the private marginal products in all industries. Here Mr. Kahn suggests that we should adopt an alternative method of attaining the Optimum contained in a proposition which Prof. Pigou has mentioned in passing : viz. to make the marginal social products diverge from the marginal private products to the same extent in all industries (cf. Pigou, op. cit., p. 255). This method fulfils the essential condition of the Optimum : for even with general imperfect competition the marginal private products of resources will be equal in all industries so long as there is free entry into industry ; and thus by making the marginal social products diverge from the marginal private products to the same extent in all industries, we equate the marginal social products to each other.

To this end Mr. Kahn suggests that we should arrange all industries in descending order of the amount of external economies they create and the degree of monopoly they enjoy (diseconomies being counted as negative economies and the degree of monopoly being measured by the gap between Price and Marginal Cost). " At a certain point represented by the ' average industry ' a line may be drawn. Then all industries above the line have to expand to reach ideal outputs and those below the line have to contract . . ." (loc. cit., pp. 6–7). When by means of taxes and subsidies all the industries in the economic system have been contracted or expanded to conform to the average degree of monopoly and average capacity to create external economies, the marginal social products would have diverged from the marginal private products to the same extent in all industries and the Optimum would be attained.

In this summary we are able to give only a very Bowdlerised version of Mr. Kahn's extremely ingenious and complex construction which must remain a little classic in its field. It is, however, sufficient for our purpose of appraising Prof. Pigou's social marginal product analysis in relation to a more realistic model of the economic system·with general imperfect competition. Mr. Kahn has shown that the Pigovian analysis is capable of being developed into a very elegant and theoretically satisfying system. But he has also brought out the various difficulties of using it as the basis of practical economic policy.

In Prof. Pigou's original model in which competition is assumed to be fairly effective and divergences between the social and the private marginal products occur only rarely, it is possible that we can approximate to the Optimum by his method of correcting these divergences by occasional taxes and subsidies. This is perhaps because Prof. Pigou's analysis in the context of his original model is practically a Partial analysis disguised in the form of a General welfare analysis. Thus although we are theoretically concerned with the Optimum for the economic system as a whole, in practice we need merely concentrate on *particular* sectors of the economic system where the divergences have actually occurred, assuming the rest of the system to be more or less optimally organised.

When, however, Mr. Kahn extends the Pigovian analysis to an economic system with widespread imperfect competition and divergences, there are at least two main practical difficulties which are almost insurmountable. In Prof. Pigou's model the " central value " to which the marginal social products of the different industries should conform is automatically given by free competition ; and taxes and subsidies are to be used only as " extraordinary restraints and encouragements " to correct occasional deviations from the competitive norm (Pigou, op. cit., pp. 213–14 ; 192). On the other hand, Mr. Kahn's analysis requires firstly the calculation of the average degree of monopoly and the average capacity to create external economies. These averages are formidable things and may well remain what Prof. Clapham has called the " Empty Economic Boxes " (cf. Clapham and Pigou, " Empty Economic Boxes ", *Economic Journal*, 1922). After this it also requires an extremely complex system of taxes and subsidies comprehensive enough to make all the industries in the economic system toe the " average line ". A proposal which contains two such extremely complicated requirements must surely prove unworkable in practice (cf. A. P. Lerner, *The Economics of Control*, pp. 103–4).

V

Finally, let us compare Prof. Pigou's welfare analysis with the Marshallian analysis. Both are constructed with an eye for practical application rather than for logical stringency and elegance ; but the method adopted by each is very different. Prof. Pigou uses the Marginal apparatus designed to deal with small variations in economic welfare while Marshall uses the Surplus analysis which deals with fairly large " chunks " of economic welfare. Again, while the Pigovian analysis is, formally at least, a General welfare analysis, the Marshallian analysis is a Partial welfare analysis in form and substance based on a concrete case by case approach. It will be argued that on both these counts the Marshallian analysis is likely to prove superior to the Pigovian analysis as a basis for practical economic policy, defining the purpose of " practical economic policy " as the immediate correction of deviations from the Optimum in an economic system in which private enterprise prevails to a greater or lesser degree.

The drawback of the Marginal apparatus as the basis of practical economic policy is perhaps due to the fact that it was originally designed to study the fairly responsive private reactions of individuals in a fairly competitive world in which rigidities, business conventions and other institutional factors are assumed to be at a minimum. On the other hand, practical economic policy relates to the slow corporate reactions of the State in a world of imperfect competition and rigidities, and of red tape and public opinion ; and here, far from being able to abstract from the institutional factors, the very form and working of the administrative machinery would depend upon them. In such a world of slips and time-lags, of conventions and rigidities, the somewhat bogus accuracy with which the Marginal Calculus works in a theoretical model has to be abandoned ; what we need is a much more rough-and-ready apparatus. The committee's intention " to leave no stone unturned " has become a joke ; and it is not possible (and will not be economic if it were possible) to balance delicately the loss and gain at the margins in " all possible avenues ". There are altogether too many possible avenues and to get a working procedure we will have to sacrifice some details and draw a short list of priorities for State interference arranged according to the magnitudes of possible gains or preventable losses. These gains or losses will be much bigger than marginal magnitudes and will have to be dealt with in a framework of Surplus analysis and Total conditions. Furthermore, they will not be susceptible of accurate calculation and will be in the nature of probabilities. But by comparing one rough magnitude of gain with another similarly rough magnitude, we may generally be able to tell which is the bigger one and thus obtain a determinate list of priorities of " glaring cases ".

The truth of the above reflections may be illustrated by examining the construction of Prof. Pigou's Marginal Social Product curves. In order to get a smooth marginal product curve Prof. Pigou has said that the size of the " marginal unit of investment " should be small (ibid., p. 133). The question is : How small? In ordinary economic analysis we take the marginal unit as that which produces an increment of product, very small compared with the total product, but large enough to overcome the *Minimum Sensibile* of the individuals concerned. As we have seen the *Minimum Sensibile* of the State is likely to be much larger and thus the marginal unit for the purpose of welfare analysis should be correspondingly larger. Here we come to a fundamental dilemma. If the divergences between the private and the social interests are small enough to be fitted into the Marginal analysis, they will also probably be too small to attract State interference, particularly when government is run on democratic lines and action is required for the whole expanse of the economic system. When, however, the divergences have grown sufficiently large enough for the administrative machinery to come to grips with them, the magnitudes involved would have been too " lumpy " and discrete to be fitted into the smooth framework of the Marginal analysis.

We have seen many of the important divergences Prof. Pigou has mentioned, e.g. bad town-planning, outgrowing the marginal framework and developing into problems which can be solved only by reorganisation of large sectors of the economic system by weighing up overall Total conditions rather than the Marginal conditions. Another such example is Mr. Kahn's attempt to calculate the marginal social product of an entrepreneur who under conditions of imperfect competition introduces a new brand of a given commodity for which " rational " consumers' preferences exist (Kahn, loc. cit., pp. 25-6). Perhaps the question of " rational " preference cannot be fully discussed until we come to the next part of this book in which we go beyond the assumption of " given wants ". For the moment, however, assuming that the latent consumers' demand exists for the new brand, the question whether or not this new brand should be introduced is a matter of Total conditions and not of Marginal conditions. The relevant magnitudes are the potential consumers' and producers' surpluses which this new brand will yield and the consumers' and producers' surpluses which the resources required for its production are yielding in alternative uses. These magnitudes involving the interpolations of large ranges of the relevant demand and cost curves cannot be accurately estimated. But on the workable procedure we have adopted if the former is probably sufficiently larger than the latter to allow a comfortable margin for errors then the case for the introduction of the new brand is established. Mr. Kahn, on the other hand, is able to analyse this question in terms of the marginal apparatus only by forcibly telescoping the essentially surplus magnitudes into his formula for the marginal social product of the entrepreneur, which is not helpful even if it is not actually misleading.

The above considerations, if accepted, seem to cast a serious doubt on the suitability of using the marginal analysis as the basis of practical economic policy. Prof. Pigou himself has pointed out that the Optimum is compatible with considerable divergences of marginal products in different uses if they are '' justified by the cost of movement ''. We now find that, in practice, given the limited capacity of the administrative machinery, the cost of trying to adjust the margins too finely *everywhere* may mean missing out *some* sources of large potential gains. For the gains to be obtained by tightening up the Marginal conditions in a near optimum situation are likely to be much smaller than those to be obtained by reorganising the Total conditions. To use a happy analogy of Prof. Pigou : '' A point *near* the summit of the highest hill may be higher than any summit except the highest itself '' (op. cit., p. 140). This does not mean we should abandon the margins altogether for even Surplus magnitudes have their margins somewhere. What we should do is to treat the margins as secondary guiding lines to be approached rather than to be reached, for, as is well known, an attempt to follow the economic calculus too finely may degenerate into a niggling and uneconomic behaviour.

Let us now turn to the relation between Prof. Pigou's General welfare analysis and the Marshallian Partial analysis. In making a short list of '' glaring cases '' based on Total conditions, we have implicitly rejected not only the Marginal but also the General welfare analysis as a primary basis for a workable economic policy To attempt to translate a General analysis into practice would frequently saddle us with such unwieldy '' empty economic boxes '' as those of the average degree of monopoly for the economic system as a whole, etc., and the most we could reasonably expect a practical administrator to do is to make a rough estimate of the probable gain or loss involved in a proposed *change* in a given sector of the economic system.

But although relegated to a secondary position, the General welfare analysis perhaps plays a more important rôle in practice than the margins themselves, for the following reason. In order to have a workable estimate of the gain or loss involved in a proposed measure, the practical administrator would require a fairly simple formula with a minimum of easily calculable variables or variables approximated by constants. Such a formula, if at all available, would be the result of considerable simplification and " isolation ". Now " isolation " does not mean severing a given sector from the rest of the economic system ; it merely means replacing all the possible interrelations between the two by a few significant key links, *assuming other things to be equal.* This is where the General welfare analysis comes in. By showing us all the theoretically possible interrelations between the " isolated " sector and the rest of the economic system, it enables us to check up whether in our selection of key links we have not overlooked some quantitatively important relationship. Thus in calculating the gain to be obtained by a new brand of a given product, we would be liable to serious errors if we concentrated on its consumers' and producers' surpluses alone, without taking into account the foregone surpluses which will depend on the degree of monopoly existing in the uses from which the factors required for its production have been withdrawn (cf. J. R. Hicks, " Rehabilitation of Consumers' Surplus ", loc. cit., p. 116). By referring to the General welfare analysis as a background map, therefore, sources of serious errors and inconsistencies are removed. However, on the same principle as that we should stop trying to reach the margins when the cost of " tightening up " outweighs the additional gain, we should stop broadening our Partial analysis when the gain in greater accuracy is outweighed by unwieldiness and complexity. On balance, it seems probable that a practicable method which can be used without serious errors in many of the " glaring cases " is nearer to the concrete simplicity of the original Marshallian approach than to the more elaborate and generalised forms of welfare analysis.

VI

We are now able to summarise our conclusions concerning the three main types of welfare analysis at the subjective level which we have studied in Part II of this book. Firstly, at the highest level of abstraction is the Paretian theory of the Optimum ; next, at the intermediate level is Prof. Pigou's system of Marginal Social Product analysis ; and lastly, closest to the ground, is the Marshallian Partial Surplus analysis. As we have seen, each type of analysis is adapted to deal with particular groups of problems, although perhaps these different groups of problems are not all of equal importance.

The Paretian theory fulfils the primary function of demonstrating that it is possible to formulate a methodologically stringent concept of the Optimum which avoids the interpersonal comparisons of utility and value judgments and which is valid for all types of economic systems. This is, of course, nothing short of putting welfare analysis on a scientific basis and it would have been meaningless to talk about the deviations from the Optimum without first establishing the concept of the Optimum on a logically secure footing. To achieve its purpose, however, it has to sacrifice realism and adopt the ideal model of Perfect Competition which assumes away almost all the divergences which economic policy has to deal with in practice.

The Pigovian Marginal Social Product analysis is of great interest from the point of view of the development of economic thought as it represents a confluence between the two great streams of thought, viz. the Continental General Optimum approach and the English Neo-classical approach. As we have seen, there are certain problems of interest relating to " structural planning " which may best be discussed within the Pigovian framework. The *Economics of Welfare* has reigned supreme as the book on the subject and there are few economists who would hesitate to accept most of Prof. Pigou's practical conclusions. However, concentrating on the theoretical backbone of Prof. Pigou's system contained in Part II of his book, and judging its purely technical properties as an instrument of analysis, one cannot help feeling that the Marginal Social Product analysis has somehow fallen between two stools. It is not methodologically as stringent as the Paretian Optimum ; and while it throws a great deal of light on issues relating to the intermediate level of abstraction, it is perhaps too elaborate and too delicate to be readily adaptable as a practical basis of economic policy. There is much to be said for having an intermediate Partial-General welfare analysis. But, as we have seen, a more promising line of approach to the problems of imperfect competition seems to be to generalise the Surplus analysis on the line of Hicksian foregone surpluses rather than to extend the Pigovian analysis on the lines suggested by Mr. Kahn.

Lastly, we come to the Marshallian Partial Surplus analysis. From our argument it has emerged as the thin end of the wedge through which welfare analysis can influence practical economic policy. The Surpluses are not only larger and more important than the economists' usual marginal products ; they are also large enough magnitudes for the administrative machinery to come to grips with and large enough magnitudes to outweigh even the very large margin of errors we must allow for the calculation of gains or losses in practice. Recent developments of the Surplus analysis by Prof. Hicks and others have done much to strengthen it as an instrument of analysis. These developments have not only overcome possible methodological objections which might have been levelled against Marshall's original formulation. They have also generalised the Surpluses beyond the rigid framework of the Partial analysis into Alternative or Foregone Surpluses able to take into account the interrelations between the markets for different products under imperfect competition.

PART III

ETHICAL LEVEL

CHAPTER XI

TOWARDS A BROADER CONCEPT OF WELFARE?

THE development of modern welfare economics has been punctuated by a series of methodological controversies, the highly suggestive term " welfare ", with its ethical overtones, adding fuel to the fire. The Classical economists took it for granted that the Art of Political Economy was their legitimate sphere and exercised it without any self-consciousness. However, with the Marginal Revolution and the rise of Continental schools of thought scrupulous about methodological purity, a distinction was drawn between the old broader concept of Political Economy and the new narrower concept of Economics as a pure science. It was then argued that scientific economics should restrict itself to the positive cause and effect analysis of Price economics and that Welfare economics was unscientific as it involved interpersonal comparisons of utility and normative value judgments.

In Part II we have shown how interpersonal comparisons of utility can be avoided by the Paretian formulation of the Optimum and the principle of Compensation. We have also pointed out that welfare analysis need not involve any normative value judgments so long as we take the wants of the individuals to be *given* and *constant* and confine our study to the purely mechanical efficiency of the economic system in satisfying these given wants. At this pure subjective level of analysis our propositions are logically as stringent as those of price economics. But, since we stop short at this neutral concept of mechanical efficiency, we are still on an intermediate plane of discourse and although our propositions deal with quantities of satisfaction they are in some ways still as inconclusive as those at the physical level as a guide to practical action. Thus when we have demonstrated that a particular pattern of allocating the resources satisfies the given wants better than others, this does not amount to a categorical imperative that this pattern *ought* to be adopted. To obtain that we need a further premise, viz. that these given wants are of the same ethical quality of goodness. It is easy to make the mistake of slipping this premise implicitly into the argument ; but, so long as we avoid this pitfall, there is a distinct scope for studying the purely mechanical efficiency of the economic system in performing its function of adjusting its means to ends without accepting the Utilitarian ethics (cf. above, Chap. VII, sec. IV ; Chap. VIII, sec. III).

Having thus struggled to a legitimate scientific existence, welfare economics at the pure subjective level has to face a further set of criticisms. These criticisms have been advanced with varying degrees of intellectual sophistication and knowledge of economics by an assorted collection of writers ranging from Ruskin to Herbert Spencer, from Veblen to F. H. Knight. The objections are originally directed not towards welfare economics as such but to economic theory in general. But, when extended, they all lead to the argument that a system of welfare economics restricted by the discipline of having to accept individuals' wants as given and constant, cannot be broad enough to be an effective study of " Social Welfare " in a significant sense.

In their more workmanlike form, the objections directed specifically towards the narrower welfare economics at the pure subjective level may be roughly summarised under three heads : (i) It is inadequate and unrealistic to concentrate only on the formal mechanism of satisfying *given* and *constant* wants : since, in real life, wants are not only continually changing ; it is in their nature to grow and change. Thus man's aim in life is not merely to satisfy given wants but to grope forward continually towards what he considers to be the *right* sort of wants ; the aim of activity is not merely to satisfy given wants but to search for further bases of new wants. (ii) A position of strict ethical neutrality cannot be maintained in a realistic study of human welfare : since both in the study of the " concrete content " of wants and in comparing two situations in which wants have changed, a criticism of the Standards of Values cannot be avoided. (iii) Individuals' wants are not given in a vacuum but are being continually moulded by their social and institutional environment, a large part of which lies outside the price system. We must therefore supplement, correct, and sometimes even replace the valuation of separate individuals measured in terms of money by the valuations made by society as a collective whole, which, though less accurately measurable, are nevertheless at least equally, if not more, important.

Faced with the vast critical literature directed not only towards the narrower welfare economics but also towards economic theory in general, we shall have to be severely selective. We shall be mainly concerned with the criticisms which have come from within the ranks of academic economists. This does not at all mean that the criticisms made by economists are intellectually " sounder " than those made by others. It is simply that in these days of deplorable specialisation a student of economics finds it much easier to follow the thought processes and terminology of fellow-economists than those of non-economists, particularly on the treacherous issues on the borderline between economics and sociology and ethics. Thus although these economists have themselves drawn their critical material largely from outside sources, we shall have to be content with studying the writings of the sociologists, philosophers and social reformers at second hand, translated into the language we are familiar with by those whose knowledge of economics at least is above question. Of the critical writings of academic economists we shall particularly concentrate on those of Profs. F. H. Knight and J. M. Clark, two leading representatives of that acutely social-conscious generation of American economists, who have given us the most systematic criticism of the narrower welfare economics. (Cf. Knight, *Ethics of Competition* and other essays and his Preface to the Reissue of *Risk, Uncertainty and Profit*, L.S.E. Reprint ; Clark, *Preface to Social Economics* and *The Social Control of Business* ; for a representative collection of the writings of other American economists of the same generation see *The Trend of Economics*, edited by Guy Rexford Tugwell, 1924).

However, before we consider Knight's and Clark's criticisms of the narrower welfare economics in detail, it will be helpful to have a sense of perspective by describing in general terms the main groups of various critics of economic theory out of whose works these later and more specific criticisms have developed.

I

To begin with, there were writers like Carlyle, Ruskin and William Morris whose objections to Political Economy were based largely on emotional, æsthetic and humanitarian grounds. Although one cannot but admire the protest of the sensitive against the brutal, it must be admitted that their attacks on the " dismal science " were vitiated by misconceptions concerning the nature of economic theory. Whilst some of the minor economists of that period might have been provocatively complacent, they were to be superseded by men like Sidgwick and Marshall, who were themselves great humanists and reformers with social sympathies so broad that they were never able to submit completely to the discipline of accepting a position of ethical neutrality and the narrow yardstick of money. As we have seen, Marshall believed that the development of human character through a series of new and more refined wants, generated by and adjusted to a series of new activities, was more important than the mechanical problem of satisfying given wants (cf. Chap. VIII, sec. III, above). Again he pointed out that no practical issues can be settled purely on the basis of economic theory and ultimately we must consult " our ethical instincts and common sense " to decide how far we would be scientists and how far we would be reformers. He however warned us that " as the imitators of Michael Angelo copied ·only his faults, so Carlyle, Ruskin and Morris find today ready imitators, who lack their fine inspirations and intuitions " (*Principles*, p. 780 n. ; also p. 28). Indeed, the development of English economic thought was so permeated with the broader tradition of Humanities that when Mr. Hawtrey declared that " economics *cannot* be dissociated from ethics ", this extremely provocative statement merely drew the following comment from Prof. Pigou : " There is, however, no difference in substance between Mr. Hawtrey and myself. We both take into account those variations of quality " in welfare (R. G. Hawtrey, *The Economic Problem*, p. 184 ; Pigou, *Economics of Welfare*, 4th ed., p. 17 n.). Here we should also mention the works of that great Humanist economist, J. A. Hobson, which have exerted a profound influence on Knight and Clark (cf. particularly Hobson, *Work and Wealth* and *Wealth and Life* ; Clark, *Preface to Social Economics*, p. 42).

Ruskin, in a sweep of vision, had once declared that all barriers between Political Economy and other social sciences and arts should be torn down (cf. Ruskin, *Munera Pulveris*, art. xl, and Hobson, *Work and Wealth*, 1933 ed., p. 11). We have next a group of writers headed by Auguste Comte and Herbert Spencer who developed this idea more systematically and in heavier tomes. They insisted that economics should give up its separate existence and be included in an all-embracing science of Sociology which studies Society as an indivisible whole. In England this Collectivism was closely associated with what Prof. Hayek has called the younger generation of the Historical school typified by Schmoller, Roscher, Ashley and Cunningham amongst others (cf. J. K. Ingram, *History of Political Economy*, Chap. VI).

Marshall, himself not unattracted by a biological concept of

" Social Organism ", has given us a shrewd but tolerant estimate of these writers. With regards to Comte's proposal to have a unified social science, he admitted the dangers of over-specialisation in the face of closely interconnected social phenomena, quoting Mill's dictum that " a person is not likely to be a good economist who is nothing else ". But he pointed out that

the whole range of man's action in society is too wide and too various to be analysed and explained by a single intellectual effort. Comte himself and Herbert Spencer have brought to the task unsurpassed knowledge and great genius ; they have made epochs in thought by their broad surveys and suggestive hints ; but they can hardly be said even to have made a commencement with the construction of a unified social science (*Principles*, p. 770).

On the question of the desirability of widening the scope of economics he wrote :

But every widening of its scope involves some loss of . . . scientific precision ; and the question whether that loss is greater or lesser than the gain resulting from its greater breadth of outlook, is not to be decided by any hard and fast rule. There is a large debatable ground in which economic considerations are of considerable, but not dominant importance ; and each economist may reasonably decide for himself how far he will extend his labours over that ground (ibid., p. 780).

Marshall, however, spoke more warmly of the Historical school. He traced the awakening of interest in sociological and institutional studies in England to J. S. Mill's *Principles* :

Mill's followers have continued his movement away from the position taken up by the immediate followers of Ricardo ; and the human as distinguished from the mechanical element is taking a more and more prominent place in economics. Not to mention writers yet living, the new temper is shown in Cliffe Leslie's historical inquiries, and the many-sided work of Bagehot, Cairnes, Toynbee and others ; but above all in that of Jevons, which has secured a permanent place in economic history by its rare combination of many various qualities of the highest order (ibid., pp. 764–5).

Incidentally, Marshall thought it significant that the sub-title of Mill's *Principles* was " with some Applications *to Social Philosophy* " and not to " *other branches of Social Philosophy* " (ibid., p. 765 n.). Marshall also mentioned the good service done by the German economists, particularly Hermann and Wagner, in emphasising the " breadth of those strains of human character with which economics is concerned " (ibid., p. 783).

Recently Prof. Hayek has given us a vigorous criticism of both the Collectivism of Comte and the Historism of Schmoller and his circle, describing them under the common heading of " Scientism " (F. A. Hayek, " Scientism and the Study of Society ", particularly

Parts I and II, *Economica*, August 1942 and February 1943). Since this part of Prof. Hayek's criticism is relevant to our study of the " Social Value " school later on, we shall attempt to summarise it very briefly.

According to Prof. Hayek, Comte and his followers have indiscriminately tried to transpose the methods of the Physical sciences to the Social sciences and this has merely resulted in sham science or " Scientism " for at least two main reasons.

Firstly, they have insisted on finding " real " or " objective facts ", whereas the " facts " of the social sciences are necessarily the *subjective* reactions or " opinions " of the individuals observed (and not the observer's opinions) on external things or on other individuals. These opinions and beliefs may or may not be strictly and objectively true, but nevertheless they have to be treated as data for the social sciences. It is only in the physical sciences which are concerned, not with man's mental reactions on things, but with the physical relations among things, that " objective facts " in a strict sense are obtainable (cf. Hayek, loc. cit., Part II, sec. iii ; also " The Facts of the Social Sciences ", *Ethics*, October 1943 and " Economics and Knowledge ", *Economica*, February 1937).

Secondly, they have naïvely accepted the popular conception of social " wholes " such as " society " and " capitalism " as if these were objective entities given like lumps of matter beforehand. On the other hand, the only raw materials given to the social scientist are the individuals and their relations to each other, out of which he has to *constitute* the " wholes " by building models which reproduce *some* of the relations between these familiar elements (ibid., Part II, sec. vii). The phrase " some of the relations " is important, since no model can ever hope to reproduce comprehensively all the complex relationships between these elements which we can simultaneously observe in real life. Thus the only practicable procedure seems to be to construct alternative models of analysis based on different judgments concerning what should be treated as *significant* relationships to be selected and reproduced. This should be kept in mind when we consider in later sections the legitimacy of the search for a broader welfare analysis based on relationships outside the price system.

Prof. Hayek then extends his attack to the younger generation of the Historical school. He argues that unlike the older members of the Historical school who have rightly treated each historical phenomenon as unique, to be accounted for by a patient study of all the forces that have gone into its making, Schmoller and his circles have succumbed to the mythical concept of social " wholes " like " Capitalism ", " Imperialism ", etc., and have tried to derive bogus " theories " or " philosophies " of history purporting to show how these " wholes " are bound to succeed each other in definite " stages " or " phases " according to " the logic of events " (ibid., Part II, secs. ix and x).

It is a short step from the Historical school to our next group of writers, the American Institutional school, led by that erratic genius Thorstein Veblen. Prof. Hayek's criticisms above can be readily extended to Veblen's insistence on an " evolutionary economics " which must be

a theory of process of cultural growths determined by the economic interest, a theory of cumulative sequences of economic institutions stated in terms of the process itself (T. Veblen, *The Place of Science in Modern Civilisation*, p. 77).

Thus Veblen also believed that economic institutions succeed each other in a definite order of " stages " and in spite of avowals of ethical neutrality necessary for a genetic study of the evolutionary process, he even classified these stages in terms of " higher " and " lower " (cf. Veblen, op. cit., pp. 75–6 ; also his review of Gustav Schmoller, ibid., p. 269). Thus criticising J. B. Clark's anti-trust writings, he wrote :

the monopolistic business against which Mr. Clark speaks is but a *higher and more perfect development* of that competitive enterprise which he wishes to reinstate . . . competitive business so-called being incipiently monopolistic enterprise (ibid., p. 217).

Veblen's attacks on academic economists are frequently shrewd and stimulating but are unfortunately marred by distortions resulting from his over-eagerness to expose their " philosophical precon-ceptions ". Thus he began by drawing a rather superficial distinc-tion between the " pecuniary " and the " industrial " standards. The former is concerned only with market values and more fre-quently than not, with predatory ways of making money ; the latter, on the other hand, is concerned with " the shaping and guiding of *material things and processes* " which form " the subject matter of physics and other material sciences " (ibid., p. 292). According to Veblen almost every academic economist up to his time had the " pecuniary " bias. Thus he told us :

The Classical economics, having primarily to do with the pecuniary side of life, is a theory of processes of valuations (ibid., p. 144).

Again,

> With Ricardo it is a pecuniary problem concerned with the distribution of ownership (ibid., p. 133).

After what we have seen of the classical economists' concern with the Physical level of analysis in Part I of this book, these statements are patently untrue. A glance at Ricardo's famous chapter " On Value and Riches " would have shown that Ricardo, of all the classical economists, was least open to such an attack and even Malthus, who paid more attention to " Value ", never forgot the physical basis of wealth. Veblen's knowledge of the English economic thought could not have been profound to overlook the continuous tradition of thinking in " real terms " from Ricardo, Mill, Marshall, Cannan down to Pigou.

Again, had he been not so obsessed with exposing the " preconceptions ", Veblen would have seen that his distinction between the " pecuniary " and the " industrial " employments was not dissimilar to the Classical (and the Physiocratic) distinction between the " productive " and the " unproductive " labour. Veblen, however, carried his concern with the physical productivity and technical efficiency much further than the classical economists, and in fact ended by advocating " technocracy " or the control of the entire industrial system by the engineers (cf. Veblen, *Vested Interest and the State of the Industrial Arts* and *Engineers and the Price System*). In this he obligingly provided Prof. Hayek with a complete illustration of the dangers of " scientism " and the " engineering type of mind " in economic studies (cf. Hayek, loc. cit., Part I, p. 269).

In spite of this, however, in the second generation, combined with the teachings of J. B. Clark, the Institutional school developed into the " Social Value " school. This latter school, on the other hand, has produced economists like J. M. Clark, who, avoiding many of the earlier mistakes, have much that is significant to say about broadening academic welfare economics.

Since we have so far been concerned mainly with the development of European welfare economics, it should be pointed out that there was an active interest in welfare studies in America since the early eighteen-eighties, when J. B. Clark wrote his famous articles for the *New Englander*, later incorporated into his *Philosophy of Wealth*. In that charming little book he told us how he revolted against the matter-of-fact complacency of the classical Price economics. This he thought had missed the structural changes of the economic system of his time which was tending towards predatory commercialism enabling shrewd men to create mere " exchange values " without a corresponding contribution of real wealth (op. cit., pp. 160–3). Clark's search for an economic theory " broad enough to include the entire social organism " was followed up and became one of the foremost issues in the pages of the *Quarterly Journal of Economics* between 1900 and 1920. By 1920, when Prof. Pigou published his *Economics of Welfare* in its present form, Prof. Frank Fetter was able to say that almost every outstanding economist in America, with the exception of the rather cautious Taussig-Harvard group and solitary extremists like Laughlinites and Davenport, had recognised the need for a Welfare economics (Fetter, " Price Economics versus Welfare Economics ", *American Economic Review*, 1920).

It is perhaps, however, fair to say that the American economists' enthusiasm for a broader Social Economics at that time had far outstripped their ability to develop a technique of welfare analysis. Discussions remained rather inconclusive since the central concept of " Social Value " was interpreted in many divergent ways by its leading exponents such as B. M. Anderson, Jr., Seligman, J. M. Clark and others ; Prof. Haney has given us a good detailed classification of its various versions (cf. L. Haney, " The Social Point of View in Economics ", *Quarterly Journal of Economics*, Vol. XXVIII, 1914, pp. 115 and 292 *et seq.*). Roughly, the main ingredients of the " Social Value " doctrines seem to be as follows :

(i) To begin with, there was Veblen's proposal to study the " cultural processes " as a whole combined with J. B. Clark's concept of " Society " as " an organic whole " or " one great isolated being " whose processes of valuations should be studied in terms of " a sort of higher social physiology " (cf. Clark, *Philosophy of Wealth*, pp. 81–3). As Haney remarked, the concept of " Social Organism " was frequently based " on mysticism, sometimes on biological analogy and sometimes on historical continuity " (Haney, loc. cit., p. 123).

(ii) Next there was Veblen's distinction between the " pecuniary " and the " industrial " employments reinforced by J. B. Clark's distinction between " production " and " predation ". As is well known, Clark believed that " institutional robbery " should be prevented and a " just " and " natural " system of distributing wealth maintained, by rewarding each factor according to its marginal product (J. B. Clark, *Distribution of Wealth* ; cf. also T. N. Carver, *Essays on Social Justice*). J. B. Clark's attempt to find a criterion of social justice in the marginal productivity theory, skipping lightly over the personal distribution of property, must appear rather naïve today ; but putting that aside, his idea that factors of production should receive just what they have contributed to the social fund of wealth is not dissimilar to Prof. Pigou's proposal to remove the divergences between the Social and the Private Marginal products. One might speculate whether Prof. Pigou's changeover from the Marshallian Surplus analysis to the Marginal Product welfare analysis was not in part due to Clark's influence (cf. *Economics of Welfare*, p. 133).

(iii) Finally, amidst attempts to fill up the formal framework of economic theory with institutional facts, there was also an attempt to search for the ideal " Social Value " which should not be dependent on the institutional set-up of the exchange economy but should also be valid for a socialist state. As Schumpeter pointed out, this idea may be traced to Wieser's concept of the " Natural Value " which would prevail in an ideal communist society with a central authority which serves as a real nerve centre (J. Schumpeter, " Social Value ", *Quarterly Journal of Economics*, 1909, pp. 416–20 ; also, F. v. Wieser, *Natural Value*, Smart translation). It is difficult to imagine how such a common " Social Value " might be found for societies with different systems of distribution of wealth and different social philosophies. However, as Schumpeter suggested, although such a concept of the " Social Value " cannot be accurately formulated, it might perhaps be used as a convenient fiction reminding us that things which have little market value under existing conditions might become very valuable with changes in laws and customs and vice versa.

Such briefly is the intellectual background of the two most considerable critics of the narrower welfare economics, F. H. Knight and J. M. Clark, with whose arguments we shall be mainly concerned in the following sections. These two deserve special study because they came to the conclusion of the need for a broader welfare economics, not merely out of natural morality like the English economists, but also after a more self-conscious examination of the methodological difficulties involved in stopping short at the assumption of given and constant individuals' wants. To prevent possible misunderstandings, it should be pointed out that F. H. Knight, perhaps too original and eclectic to belong to any school of thought, has been put side by side with J. M. Clark, the leader of the " Social Value " school, merely because Knight himself has indicated that on some of the issues with which we are concerned here, his approach most nearly resembles that of Clark (cf. Knight, *Ethics of Competition*, p. 21).

II

Let us now consider the three main objections directed towards the narrower welfare economics at the pure subjective level, in the order in which they have been summarised at the beginning of this chapter.

The first argument is that we can concentrate on the mechanical efficiency of satisfying *given* and *constant* wants only at the cost of making our analysis too abstract and formal to have any practical use and that, once we consider the " real content " of these wants, it will be seen at once that wants are neither given nor constant.

Of the aridity of the formal principle of choice, F. H. Knight has written :

> We can say that a man will in general prefer a larger quantity of wealth to a smaller (the principal trait of the economic man) because in the statement the term " wealth " has no definite concrete meaning ; it is merely an abstract term covering everything which men do actually (provisionally) want. The only other important economic law of conduct, the law of diminishing marginal utility, is almost as abstract ; its objective content is covered by the statement that men strive to distribute income in some way most satisfactory to the person at the time among an indefinite number of wants rather than to concentrate upon one or a few. Such laws are unimportant because they deal with form only and say virtually nothing about content (*Ethics of Competition*, p. 36).

To this J. M. Clark has added more pungently :

> Our old friend, the " economic man ", is becoming very self-conscious and bafflingly non-committal. Instead of introducing himself to his readers with his old-time freedom, he says : " I may behave one way and I may behave another, but what is that to you ? You must take my choices as you find them : I choose as I choose and that is all you really need to know." The poor thing has been told that his psychology is all wrong, and he is gamely trying to get on without any and still perform as many as possible of his accustomed tasks. He has become a symbol, rather than a means of description or explanation. Yet this noncommittal treatment of economic choices seems to be of immense import to those who have become accustomed to attach much of their thinking to this symbol (*Preface to Social Economics*, pp. 9–10 ; see also Veblen, op. cit., p. 175).

What happens when we try to fill up this symbol with a concrete content ? Then, wants become " the most obstinately unknown of all the unknowns in the whole system of variables ", for

> The purposes of men are inherently dynamic and changing ; want satisfying activity is not in the main directed toward gratifying existing desires sharply defined as data in the conduct problem ; it is largely explorative in character ; a repetitive experience is looked upon more or less as a necessary evil and its motive is a goad rather than an end. The problem of human life is less that of preconceived results than of finding out the results of actions and acquiring " better " wants (Knight, op. cit., p. 101 ; cf. also pp. 20–3).

Again J. M. Clark has reinforced this theory of the inherent dynamic growth of wants by pointing out the external conditions of imperfect competition and advertisement, under which business men do not merely direct pre-existing consumers' wants but actively set out to create new wants to build up markets for particular products (cf. *Economics and Modern Psychology*, Clark, op. cit., pp. 92–169). Here we are reminded of Veblen's dictum " Invention is the mother of necessity ".

The Knight-Clark theory of the inherent dynamic growth of wants in its extreme form is very destructive to scientific welfare analysis of all the types which we have studied in Part II.

(i) Once their argument is accepted we can no longer preserve the static framework of the Optimum theory by treating changes in wants as " exogenous changes in data ". Wants then become too inherently unstable to be treated as data in an ordinary scientific sense of that term.

(ii) When wants are assumed to be continually growing even the familiar principle of diminishing marginal utility breaks down, particularly when stated in the form that the individuals' marginal utility of his income diminishes as his income (or command over goods in general) is increased. Thus we cannot say that a man whose income has been increased from £500 to £700 will value £1 less than before ; by the very reason of his increased income he has opportunity to cultivate new wants, the satisfaction of which in his new situation may be as urgent as that of his more limited wants in his old situation. In Chapter VI we have pointed out that the Marginal Revolution introduced a second degree of approximation into welfare analysis by showing that consumers' satisfaction will increase less than proportionately to the increase in quantities of physical products. If we regard the assumption of growing wants as the third degree of approximation, it seems as plausible to say that consumers' satisfaction will increase more than proportionately, as to say that it will increase less than proportionately, to an increase in physical products. In the absence of further information, we might just as well steer the middle course and revert to the classical economists' first approximating assumption that consumers' satisfaction will increase more or less proportionately to the increase in physical products ; that is, if at all, quantities of satisfactions can be compared in two situations with different wants.

(iii) Finally, if we accept that wants are not precisely given to the individuals and that they are continually *exploring* for new and what they consider to be " better " wants, then it becomes difficult to avoid making criticisms of the individuals' standards of values. This leads us to the second objection against the narrower welfare economics, viz. it is not possible to maintain ethical neutrality in a serious and realistic study of human welfare. This will be considered in the next section.

How far can we salvage scientific welfare economics from this threatened wreckage? To begin with it does become very clear that if economics is to be " a study of mankind in the ordinary business of life ", it is inadequate to regard life merely as a mechanical process of satisfying given wants. As Marshall has suggested we must take life as a continuous process of development in which wants give rise to activities and activities in their turn give rise to wants, in overlapping cycles of mutual causation (cf. above, Chap. VIII, sec. III). However, in trying to come to grips with this essentially continuous process, our analytical apparatus has to break off the chain of mutual causation somewhere and take that as our starting-point. Thus if we have started from one arbitrary point, we may be inclined to consider the activities as being mainly directed towards the satisfaction of certain provisionally given wants. If, on the other hand, we have started from another arbitrary point, we may be inclined to think, as Knight and Clark have argued, that activities tend to create new wants rather than merely satisfy given wants. Therefore, the particular half of the mutual interaction which we have captured in our cross-section of the continuous process can merely be in the nature of a half-truth, and as J. M. Clark has well put it :

> Can it be that human nature is so built that it demands the clash of opposing half-truths in order to raise the issues from which it may work out a closer approximation to the truth? (Clark, op. cit., p. 21.)

Thus admitting that individuals' systems of wants have an inherent tendency to develop and change, there is nevertheless, at any given moment of time, a relatively definite and stable pattern of consumers' demand confronting the economic system as a whole. Without this relatively stable pattern of consumers' demand, the market organisation as we know it cannot continue to exist and perform its highly complicated tasks with some regularity and efficiency and the allocation of resources and the structure of production would have been in a complete state of chaos. Indeed, without some sort of a stable pattern of consumers' demand it is difficult to see how the economic system itself can exist and even Knight and Clark must admit that there is some such thing as an economic *system*.

Knight, in trying to illustrate the erratic nature of individuals' wants has pointed out how, amongst other things, human beings are torn between rival desires to be different from each other and to be like each other. In so far as the individuals try to conform to conventional patterns of wants, the social institutions and the "conventional necessities" which the Institutionalists emphasised so much must exert a considerable stabilising influence on their wants. Again Clark's argument that the growth of wants has been accelerated by advertisements which deliberately set out to create new wants for particular products cuts both ways. On reflection it will be seen that producers would not invest enormous sums of money in building up the markets for their particular products unless consumers' demands for these products are afterwards stable enough to be exploited for a considerable period of time.

Taking all these counter-objections into account, it is perhaps fair to conclude that it is almost as true or false to say that wants are given and constant as to say that they are never given and are rapidly changing. Knight and Clark have done a great service in pointing out the limitations of the conventional assumption of given wants ; but in their reaction against this, they seem to have erred in the opposite direction. If wants are not sufficiently stable to be treated as data in some sense by the economist, then they will not be stable enough to be treated as data by business men. Yet in real life, apart from a growing demand for " market research assistants ", business men have found it possible to organise the productive resources on the basis of anticipated consumers' demand and, whatever its defects, the complicated structure of the modern economic system has grown out of this process.

If that is so then, provided we know its limitations, there still remains a large element of truth in the assumption of given and constant wants ; and it is still possible to base our welfare analysis on it and yet be able to make a useful contribution towards the broader problem of human welfare. When wants have changed, however, it is no longer possible to restrict our analysis to the pure subjective level ; then we are left with the choice of either making no welfare propositions or making value judgments.

It should, however, be admitted that the Knight and Clark half of the truth is getting more and more important with rapid technical development and increase in productivity which have resulted in the expansion of consumers' demand from the primary products to the secondary and luxury products. In the sphere of luxury products, consumers' demand is certainly very unstable and elusive, " like streaks of lightning across the sky ". Even here we can extend our formal analysis and consider the divergences from the optimum due to over-investment in the less risky primary product industries and under-investment in the more risky luxury product industries (cf. A. G. B. Fisher, *The Clash of Progress and Security*, Chap. VI). However, our analysis remains rather undecisive since we do not know the exact magnitude of the risk to be discounted, although evidence seems to suggest that the error is on the side of over-cautiousness, particularly so if we accept the Keynesian concept of liquidity preference and its depressing effect on the level of employment as a specie of risk-aversion (cf. J. R. Hicks, " Foundations of Welfare Economics ", *Economic Journal*, Dec. 1939, p. 708).

While discussing the instability of demand for luxury products, however, we should not forget that even in this so-called age of plenty there still remains the larger section of the world population who have not even satisfied their wants for bare necessities, and in a balanced view of human welfare the wants of these people must command our foremost attention. There is thus still a very large scope for a welfare economics based on the assumption of given wants.

Finally, even the process of transition of the consumers' demand from the primary products to the secondary and luxury products follow a pattern definite and stable enough to admit of many significant generalisations (cf., for example, Colin Clark, *Conditions of Economic Progress*, Chaps. X and XIII). If this pattern of change in consumers' demand is stable enough, we can treat the future consumers' wants as their incomes are increased as a part of the given structure of wants, as data. Thus while our present welfare analysis is mainly concerned with the changes in the quantities of commodities bought with changes in their relative prices, we might have an alternative welfare analysis based on the changes in the quantities of commodities bought with changes in the consumers' incomes. It is true that an individual with an income of £500 a year may not know his precise wants when his income is doubled ; but taking a large group of such individuals a good sociologist may be able to forecast the budget of these newly rich people with a workable degree of accuracy. Besides, the increase of incomes due to technical progress is by no means as jerky as that.

III

We now come to the second objection raised against the narrower welfare economics : viz. that with all the scientific conscience in the world, it is not possible to stop short at a position of complete ethical neutrality in a useful and realistic study of the problem of human welfare.

Now it should be noted that no one has ever pretended that it is possible to make a *complete* study of the problem of *general* welfare without making value judgments. The real issues here are : (i) how far can we make a useful contribution towards the problem of *general* welfare while restricting ourselves to a scientific analysis of *economic* welfare on the assumption of given wants, and (ii) how far are we pushed down an inclined plane towards value judgments by the very nature of the subject-matter of welfare analysis.

These two points are very well brought out by the brilliant *tour de force* of Knight. Knight argues that like the assumption of given wants, the position of ethical neutrality can be maintained only when we confine ourselves to the formal husk of human wants. Once we try to describe the " concrete content " of these wants, the bulk of them, beyond bare necessities, will be found to be of social, æsthetic and sentimental character. This being so, these wants are not given in a precise sense to the individuals who are continually exploring new wants and sensations, using the present provisional set of wants as the base for " better " and more refined wants. Knight then maintains that a mere attempt to describe this process of exploration and development leads us into a universe of ideals, symbols and meanings, which are intractable to the apparatus of logical analysis ; and that we are here driven inevitably into making criticisms of standards of values. " For discussion of ideals cannot be confined to pure description—such description as is possible " ; " it describes what the observer ought to see, what he will see if he sees correctly " (Knight, Preface to the Reissue of *Risk, Uncertainty and Profit*, L.S.E. Reprint, p. xv). " Wants are culture products, to be judged by culture canons and understood and controlled through culture categories " (Knight, *Ethics of Competition*, p. 98 ; also p. 23).

It will be seen that a large part of this argument rests on the question of stability of wants which we have discussed in the previous section. However unaccountable and sentimental they may be, in so far as the wants can be provisionally pinned down at a given moment of time into a definite pattern of consumers' demand, the distinction between the scientific problem of economic welfare and the normative problem of general welfare still remains. The former is concerned with the *quantity* of satisfaction and the efficiency with which the provisionally given wants are satisfied ; the latter is concerned with the *quality* of wants and with the question how far the individuals succeed in living a good life. We need not pass from the former to the latter unless we wish to do so. If, on the other hand, wants are not stable enough to be treated as the data of a scientific welfare analysis, we cannot say whether the individuals are better off in one situation compared with another without making some sort of value judgments. In the previous section we have attempted to show that in spite of many important limitations of the assumption of constant wants which Knight and Clark have exposed, there still remains enough truth in that assumption to enable scientific welfare analysis to make a useful contribution towards the problem of general human welfare.

Knight's argument raises the further important point—how far we can keep separate the opinions, beliefs and wants of the individuals we are observing and our own (the observer's) opinions of these individuals' opinions and wants. Theoretically, the distinction between the two is clear-cut ; to say that such a distinction is not possible is to deny the possibility of a scientific approach to social problems. The real question, therefore, is how far we can attain this scientific ideal in practice and how far we can remain uninfluenced by our own prejudices.

This immediately raises the problem how far we can really describe and understand the individuals' acts of motivation from the outside without having a sympathetic perception of their inner beliefs and ideals. Here there is an undoubted danger of trying to carry the " objective scientific " approach too far into the realm of elusive human motives and idiosyncrasies. Thus let us take a very simple example. Assume that we find an individual preferring to buy a particular brand of a certain product while he could buy similar brands of the same product at a much cheaper price ; assume also that to us (the observer) the different brands are physically identical and exhibit no other objectively ascertainable differences. Shall we then accuse the individual of " consumer's inertia " and " irrationality " or shall we give him the benefit of the doubt and say that although we cannot find out, to the individual himself there is a certain significant difference between the brand he has chosen and other brands ? Here the problem is to draw a correct line between two alternatives : either of explaining away all cases of apparent consumers' inertia as being based on legitimate preferences, including an indolent preference for avoiding all the troubles involved in a careful choice or of dismissing all the consumers' idiosyncrasies and failure to conform to our preconceived " rational " pattern of behaviour as " inertia " and " irrational preferences ".

Mr. Kahn has suggested an interesting method of testing the rationality of consumers' preference for particular brands which does not involve value judgments : that is, to transfer compulsorily consumers buying one brand to another brand and find out whether they have lost some satisfaction from the change. If they have, their preferences have been " rational " ; if not, their preferences have been " irrational " (R. F. Kahn, " Notes on Ideal Output ", *Economic Journal*, 1935). Apart from the practical difficulties of conducting such an elaborate experiment, particularly that of finding enough consumers detached enough to report their experiences accurately, there is a theoretical objection to Mr. Kahn's scheme ; viz. the commonly observed phenomena that consumers prefer a particular brand simply because they are used to it. Thus it may be true that, in Mr. Kahn's experiment, consumers may initially suffer from some loss of satisfaction but may grow to like the new brand when they have got used to it. Methodologically, it is a ticklish question whether the process of having consumers " getting used " to a brand is compatible with the assumption of *given* preferences. Further there is a danger of carrying that type of reasoning too far, for in the long run consumers may get " used to " almost anything.

This will be sufficient to show how difficult it is to describe the significance of individuals' acts of motivation without a *sympathetic* perception of their inner beliefs and inspirations. Once this is recognised, it becomes very doubtful whether we can ever hope, in practice, to maintain a complete separation between the opinions, beliefs and wants of the individuals we are observing and our own (the observer's) opinions, beliefs and wants. This does not, however, mean, as Knight seems to conclude, that we should give up all attempt to make a scientific approach to the problem of human welfare and plunge ourselves completely into subjective value judgments. On the contrary, precisely because of these insidious difficulties, the need for maintaining scientific objectivity as much as possible becomes more important. A workable scientific approach should recognise that, human fallibility being such, we cannot hope to obtain a hundred per cent. objectivity in describing and analysing our fellow human beings and must therefore take extra precautions to purge our prejudices and preconceptions from our analysis. One practical safeguard is perhaps to make value judgments, boldly and without inhibitions, before we make our analysis and then use it as a basis of self-criticism of our scientific analysis. To disarm the critics we might even append the results of such a candid introspection to our scientific conclusions as an act of good faith.

The need for safeguarding the objectivity of our analysis may be illustrated by describing the possible preconceptions and bias which may have crept even into our workaday procedure of accepting the individuals' wants as given and constant.

Firstly, as we have seen, we cannot make a scientific welfare analysis (indeed, we can hardly make any type of economic analysis) unless the individuals' wants are given in a fairly stable and definite pattern. Thus the economists have a " vested interest " in the assumption of constant wants. The dangers of selecting and magnifying those aspects of economic life which can be turned into accurately demonstrable propositions while neglecting its other less malleable aspects have been pointed out by many economists from Marshall to J. M. Clark (Marshall, *Principles*, p. 850 ; J. M. Clark, *Preface to Social Economics*, p. 5). To facilitate analysis we may construct a theoretical model in which wants are more stable than they are in real life ; but in the same way as the ideal model of Perfect Competition differs from free enterprise in real life, we must always remember that our model has a " bias " towards over-determinateness. Thus in defending the assumption of constant wants, as we have done in the previous section, we must carefully check up whether some of our arguments in its favour are not uninfluenced by our " vested interest " in a determinate and logically demonstrable system of welfare analysis.

Secondly, we have pointed out that it is possible to study the purely mechanical efficiency of the economic system in satisfying *given* individuals' wants without accepting any value judgments, provided we remember that we are still at an intermediate level of analysis. Yet the critics have persisted in pointing out the " philosophical preconceptions " involved in this procedure. The less knowledgeable critics have accused the economists of Utilitarian philosophy and of denying the existence of the " higher " and the " lower " wants, while the more perceptive would probably point out a distinct correlation between the economists' insistence on methodological purity and their liberal philosophy.   The imputation of Utilitarian philosophy can be dismissed without much difficulty.   The more cautious modern reformulations of the Theory of Value and the Principle of Choice are ample evidence that economists nowadays are always on their guard against Utilitarianism.   However, the fact that " purist " economists are also frequently liberal economists cannot be dismissed so easily.

Veblen's erratic attacks have shown us the dangers of imputing " philosophical preconceptions " to other people and scientific caution requires that we should not deduce a causal relation from a correlation.   But it would prevent a lot of suspicion, and clarify the minds of all concerned, if the economists, in so far as they believe in the liberal philosophy, would boldly state that, apart from methodological reasons, they further prefer to accept the individuals' wants as given, amongst other things, for the following reasons : (i) because they believe that freedom of choice in itself is an ultimate good which ought to be defended at almost any cost ; (ii) because they believe that although all wants are not of the same ethical quality, the cost of suppressing freedom is generally too great to justify an interference with individuals' preferences, even when that is done " for their own good " and even if a common standard of values can be agreed upon ; and (iii) because they believe that with education, which essentially consists in free choice and learning from experience, the mass of mankind would gradually learn to appreciate the best æsthetic and moral standards which civilisation has to offer ; so that the free enterprise system is desirable not only for its final results in satisfying wants but also for its intermediate by-products, particularly that of promoting social and economic freedom.   Whether we were to agree with it or not, such a bold statement of fundamental ethical and political beliefs by a professional economist would be of considerable interest and value even from a narrowly scientific point of view (e.g., F. A. Hayek, *Road to Serfdom*).

Similarly, non-liberal economists, in so far as they believe in the usefulness of having a scientific welfare analysis at the purely subjective level, should explain why they use the assumption of given wants for the purpose of economic analysis, in spite of the fact that they do not accept the liberal doctrine of free enterprise. Here the critics who are inclined to impute " liberal preconceptions " to scientific welfare economics should be reminded that welfare economics started mainly as a criticism of liberal economics and that the modern renaissance in welfare economics has been largely initiated by the works of such Socialist economists as A. P. Lerner, H. D. Dickinson and O. Lange, not to mention the Socialist sympathies of that great master, Prof. Pigou. It should, however, be pointed out that all the above Socialist economists accept that the end of the economic system is to satisfy given individuals' wants, *provided incomes are equally distributed* (cf., for example, A. P. Lerner, *Economics of Control*, Chaps. I and III). As we have seen, although the theory of the General Optimum is concerned with the Productive efficiency of the economic system relative to a *given* Distribution of incomes, it does not imply the acceptance of the existing pattern of income distribution as sacrosanct ; indeed, there are as many positions of Productive Optimum as the number of possible patterns of income distribution and our optimum analysis is as valid in a free enterprise economy with unequal incomes as in a controlled economy with equal incomes (cf. above, Chap. VII, sec. I).

Finally, there may be other Socialist economists who strictly adhere to the labour theory, rejecting the entire subjective approach of modern academic economics. These economists may prefer to test the preliminary efficiency of the economic system, not at the subjective level described in Part II, but at the classical Physical level of analysis described in Part I of this book (cf., for example, M. Dobb, *Political Economy and Capitalism*, Chap. I, pp. 19–22). Such a method of testing is also provided for by our framework of scientific welfare analysis and if we accept that causes influencing physical productivity have as much influence on human welfare as those affecting the efficiency of allocating given resources to satisfy given wants and that the principle of diminishing marginal utility may not hold under conditions of growing wants, the test at the Physical level is as good as the test at the subjective level.

All this merely means that while a comprehensive system of scientific welfare economics provides economists of all shades of political opinions with the basic tools of analysis they require, its foundations and its methods are largely independent of the " philosophical preconceptions " of any group of these economists. Thus, in spite of Knight's brilliant *tour de force*, we may conclude that it is still possible to have a workably objective welfare analysis if we take care to see that there are no inhibited prejudices to colour our purely scientific analysis.

IV

Finally, we come to the third objection against the narrower welfare economics : viz. that it has followed the line of least resistance in restricting itself to the valuations of separate individuals which can be measured in terms of money, while a more comprehensive study of human welfare requires a revision and sometimes even a replacement of market values by the valuations of Society as a collective whole which although not so accurately measurable are more fundamental. The argument in this form has been developed particularly by J. M. Clark and not by F. H. Knight (cf. also Hobson, *Wealth and Life*, Part I, Chap. III).

Clearly the key question here is : what do we mean by " Society " ? In Parts I and II of this book we have freely used the terms " society ", " community ", and the " economic system " as approximate synonyms of each other. But we have never used them to describe " indivisible " or " organic " wholes ; they were merely convenient short expressions for a collection of separate individuals. This can be clearly seen by recalling our use of the term " social " in discussing the Pigovian divergences between the Social and the Private products. As we have seen, the Pigovian " social " product is not determined by a central organic social entity ; it is merely " an unusually complete summing up " of individual or private products. Thus the incidental services or disservices rendered to the third party are added to or subtracted from the value of the private product according to their respective market prices which result from the interactions of separate individuals' valuations (cf. above, Chap. IX, sec. III).

Clark recognises the value of the Pigovian divergences analysis which he calls the " theory of inappropriables " since it liberates our thinking from a particular institutional set-up and shows that things which do not normally have a market value under existing conditions might have one with a change in the laws and customs. But he wishes to go further and study not merely the value *in* society but also the value *to* society.

The theory of social value does not stop with the theory of inappropriables, which is merely an unusually complete summing up of individual values, utilities and costs, though this of itself is highly important to society as an organism. The ultimate question is : what is the value to society of these utilities consumed by individuals, or the cost to society of these costs which individuals bear ? (J. M. Clark, *Preface to Social Economics*, p. 49).

Before we discuss Clark's concept of " organic social values " it is important to recall Prof. Hayek's warning against the dangers of accepting too readily that popular concepts of social " wholes " exist and are given to us as data so that we can go and watch " Society " as if it were some large peculiar animal (Hayek, " Scientism and the Study of Society ", loc. cit., secs. vii and viii). As Prof. Hayek has pointed out, the only data directly given to the social scientist are the individuals as the centres of consciousness out of which he has to constitute the social " wholes " by building models which reproduce some of the relationships between these individual elements. For instance, the concept of society we have used in Part II is merely a model of analysis exhibiting the formal relationships between the individuals in the allocation of scarce resources, or to put it a little narrowly, through the structure of the price system.

That Clark is not guilty of a crude anthropomorphic interpretation of society may be seen from his statement that the concept of society " as the outgrowth of quasi-biological laws, inscrutable to the economist and independent of the desires that clash in the market " is due to overworking the analogy between social organisation and biological organism and that this doctrine is discredited among sociologists (Clark, op. cit., p. 62). Yet he frequently used such terms as the " social mind ", " organic social values " and " collective intelligence " and it is difficult to pin down his opinions on the subject to clear-cut statements (e.g., ibid., pp. 62, 48, 41). Broadly speaking, however, two main trends of thought seem to underlie most of Clark's arguments in favour of a concept of Social Value and his criticisms of the narrower welfare economics.

(i) The first trend of thought which underlies Clark's case for a concept of Social Value is closely linked up with his plea for broadening economics to include other social sciences, particularly psychology (cf. Clark, " Economics and Modern Psychology ", op. cit., pp. 92–169). Thus he maintains that " many matters truly economic cannot be contained in the pigeon-hole of exchange values " and that " it is less important to keep inside the traditional limits than to follow our natural questionings wherever they may lead and do whatever work we are specially fitted for and find undone ". " In doing this we should accept the authoritative results of other specialists in the fields of psychology, sociology and ethics " (ibid., pp. 60–1). Thus Clark concludes his essay " Toward a Concept of Social Value " with the following paragraph :

The whole problem of value to society is of course more than economic, and yet it seems to be one problem and not many separate ones. While its economic aspect is far from being exhausted, the chief thing to be striven for is that the central problem shall have all the light that can be thrown on it from all angles and that problems of exchange should be treated with this aim constantly in mind (ibid., p. 65).

Now it would save a lot of unnecessary controversy if Clark had clearly distinguished what is to be " broadened " to obtain a concept of Social Value : the intellectual equipment of economists as practical men of affairs or the logical boundaries of economics as a scientific discipline.

If Clark merely means that the intellectual equipment of economists as practical men of affairs should be broadened his argument would be warmly supported even by the champions of " pure " economics. Thus we may quote Prof. Robbins's reply to a similar argument made by Messrs. Hawtrey and Hobson :

> On the contrary, it is greatly to be desired that economists should have speculated long and widely on these matters, since only in this way they will be in a position to appreciate the implications as regards given ends of problems which are put to them for solution. We may not agree with J. S. Mill that " a man is not likely to be a good economist if he is nothing else ". But we may at least agree that he may not be as useful as he might otherwise be. Our methodological axioms involve no prohibition of outside interest ! (L. Robbins, *Nature and Significance of Economic Science*, p. 150.)

Here unfortunately it is true that while an average physical scientist, say a chemist, would at least have a working knowledge of physics, biology, etc., as a part of his general science course, no such claim can be made of an average economist's knowledge of psychology, social anthropology and ethics. Yet the fault does not entirely lie with the economist, for his allied subjects are less developed than those of a physical scientist. Thus a general " social science course " more frequently than not merely succeeds in conveying to the students a smattering of second-hand opinions on a hotchpotch of subjects which can hardly be called science. In the circumstances, the economist can hardly be blamed if he is reluctant to abandon the relatively stable foundations of economics for the shifting sands of psychology. Indeed, if we can accept, as Clark has suggested, the authoritative results of the specialists in the field of ethics, the most perplexing problems raised in this part of the book would have been solved without much ado.

However, it is one thing to say that the knowledge and outlook of the economists should be broadened, another to say that the scope of economic science itself should be broadened. Clark seems to maintain this further proposition also, particularly with regard to psychology. Thus he seems to think that economists have not gone far enough into psychology, " not far enough, in fact, to secure an adequate and sound equipment of psychological assumptions " (Clark, op. cit. p. 60).

On this question of broadening the scope of economic theory, we may again recall Prof. Hayek's fundamental argument that social " wholes " are not directly given to us and that the only method available to the social scientist is to constitute the " wholes" by building alternative models of analysis each of which select and reproduce *some* of the relationships between the individual elements. If this argument is accepted (and it is difficult to see how it could be refuted), then we should rule out of court the Comtian dream of constructing an all-embracing and objectively comprehensive theory of Society as an indivisible and organic whole. Again in spite of many reactions against it there is much to be said for the " purist " view that it is vital to have a pure economic science, independent of any particular psychology and ethics, which is applicable to all situations involving the disposal of scarce resources. While it is generally recognised that research in physical sciences may sometimes be nearest to practical applications at its most abstract level, the same possibility is denied to research in social sciences. Yet at least one good example of this truth can be given out of the subject matter of this book. Thus welfare economics, which is perhaps more " practical " than any other branch of economic theory, owes its present secure logical foundations to the Indifference Curve technique and the Hicks-Allen reformulation of the theory of Value which was concerned to begin with only with the most abstract formal and methodological problems, apparently without any practical significance.

Without therefore belittling the value of " pure " theory as a long-term investment, we might, however, attempt to go a little beyond the conventional attitude that economists should call in the aid of other branches of knowledge only with reference to a particular concrete problem of *applied* economics. When we look upon economics not merely as a pure science disclosing uniformities in diverse social phenomena but also as a tool for solving practical problems, the easy distinction between " pure theory " and " applied economics " is perhaps too wide to be helpful. There seems to be room for speculating whether it might not be useful to have a " combined operation " between the relevant social sciences to solve a particular set of urgent social problems which are too concrete to be solved by pure theory and yet having a much wider range of application than applied economics in the usual sense.

In Part II when dealing with the problems of economic welfare in a narrower sense, we seem to have found just such a method of intermediate level of abstraction in the Partial Surplus analysis. The success of the Surplus analysis is, however, due to two conditions : (a) In a situation with given resources, wants and distribution of income, we can obtain unanimous agreement on what should be considered the most urgent economic problems by selecting and arranging the " glaring cases " of divergences from the Optimum according to the measurable quantities of losses or gains of economic welfare they involve.   (b) The cases of divergences from the Optimum to be dealt with by the Surplus analysis are of a fairly uniform character.   Thus we can have a fruitful co-operation between economics, psychology and sociology to develop a common set of statistical methods to derive the relevant demand and cost curves.

How far can we extend this principle and obtain an agreement on what are to be considered the most urgent social problems in the broader sense to be solved by a combined operation between different sciences, social and physical ?   At this stage of our knowledge, a final answer cannot be given to this difficult question. However, a partial answer to it may be obtained in examining the second part of Clark's plea for a concept of Social Value.

(ii) Here Clark seems to argue that a co-operation between the different social sciences will bring to light common standards of Social Values prevailing in a given society at a given time ; and that the economist, " accepting whatever standards are in force ", can revise the market values according to these standards, while himself maintaining an attitude of ethical neutrality (op. cit., p. 58, n. 13).

Thus he believes that " there is ample proof that society does not wholly acquiesce in the idea that the desires of rich and poor should all have economic weight in proportion to the respective purchasing powers of these classes as they stand under the present distribution of incomes " (ibid., p. 49). Again he argues that " while men are unselfish and recognise many kinds of obligations to their fellows beyond the letter of the law, their unselfishness is not carried into business relations and extra-legal responsibilities are not business responsibilities, except such as have become so firmly established in business morals as to have the binding force of laws ". " We are not in business for health " (ibid., p. 77). At this point Clark's argument seems to develop into a criticism not only of the price mechanism but also of the political machinery of democracy, particularly the difficulty of making the weak and diffused majority will overcome the active and concentrated minority will (cf. ibid., p. 55).

We shall not attempt to discuss how far the capacity of democracy to express the latent will of the majority has been impaired (like the growth of monopolies in the economic system) by the " lobbying " of " pressure groups ". Assuming, however, that the existing laws of society do not fully express the obligations which its members feel towards their fellow-beings, how far can we find an extra-legal common ethical code which should decide what are the most urgent social problems ?

At first sight a search for a common code in the melting-pot of ethical values appears quite futile (cf. Hayek, *Road to Serfdom*, p. 44). It should, however, be pointed out that it is not impossible to find the common denominator among different standards of value and that although this important truth is quite trite when explicitly stated, it is frequently forgotten in the abstract discussions of the Ultimate Good. This may be found in the fact that while few could agree on what should be regarded as Positive Welfare there is an almost unanimous agreement on the point that lack of the elementary necessities of human life causes Negative Welfare or " Illfare " and that Positive Welfare either for an individual or for a community cannot be generally attained without first removing the causes of Negative Welfare. Common men have expressed this idea in terms of common humanity and Christian or Buddhist ethics. The same idea underlies Mr. Hobson's concept of " human cost ", Mr. Hawtrey's distinction between the " protective " or " utility " products and " creative " products and Prof. Pigou's advocacy of a National Minimum Standard of Real Income (J. A. Hobson, *Work and Wealth* ; R. G. Hawtrey, *Economic Destiny*, Chap. XIII ; and Pigou, *Economics of Welfare*, Part IV, Chap. XIII).

If, therefore, we are willing to accept this common denominator of ethical values, we have an agreement on what should be considered the first on the list of urgent social problems. The problem is concrete and quantitative if we follow Prof. Pigou and define the minimum standard of life by a certain set of absolute objective conditions requiring " some defined quantity and quality of house accommodation, of medical care, of food, of leisure, of the apparatus of sanitary convenience and safety where work is carried on, and so on " (Pigou, op. cit., p. 759).

Further, this problem also offers us a basis for co-operation between different sciences. Amidst the mutual distrust between the different types of social scientists, and the greater distrust between the social and the physical scientists, the success of a " combined operation " between sciences working for a common goal as shown by the T.V.A. scheme is a very encouraging step. Whether the pattern of co-operation between different sciences on the T.V.A. model will be successful in raising the standard of living of other depressed areas of the world, however, remains to be seen (cf. D. E. Lilienthal, *T.V.A.*, Chap. VIII ; also Foster and Bacon, *Wealth for Welfare*).

As we go beyond this basic step of preventing negative welfare, however, we meet increasing difficulties in following Clark's proposal to revise the market values by common social values.

To begin with, beyond the objectively determinable physical minimum of life, even if we can find a common ethical code held by a majority of individuals in a given society, they would be given frequently in the form of abstract qualitative statements. Thus it might be generally that quack-medicines are bad and that liberty is good or that Shakespeare represents a " higher " want than Sexton Blake. But how are we to revise the market values without a further agreement on a method of translating these abstract and qualitative value judgments into concrete rules stating how far quack-medicines should be suppressed or how many copies of Shakespeare and Sexton Blake should be printed each year ?

Again, before accepting the avowed values of a given society it is desirable to find out whether these values are really subscribed to by the majority of its members. In the absence of a comprehensive and accurate survey of the private opinions of the Public, the so-called " given " Social Values can be only obtained from the public statements of public men. Here none but the completely ingenuous must admit that unfortunately there is a great deal of truth in James Burnham's thesis concerning the gulf between the avowed social and political ideals and " Realpolitik "(cf. J. Burnham, *The Machiavellians*). For instance, we might bear in mind Keynes's dictum that " in the long run we are all dead " while appraising some of the " long-term " projects to develop the economically backward countries of the world.

Further, Clark's easy supposition that the economist would be able to accept with complete impartiality whatever standards of value that are in force in a given society is not convincing. We may recall Knight's penetrating argument in the previous section showing how difficult it is to remain completely impartial even when describing the concrete contents of individuals' wants for ordinary commodities. In describing their ethical values, *a fortiori* it would become impossible to maintain ethical neutrality, particularly in assessing the quantitative weights of different standards of value.

Finally, even if such an impartial assessment were possible, it is difficult to see how the economist can escape moral responsibility in advocating that Market Values should be corrected by Social Values even if the latter values were held by the majority of people in that society. Here, perhaps, it is possible to argue in theory that in the same way as we provisionally accept the given individuals' wants and conduct our welfare analysis at the purely subjective level, we may provisionally accept the social values and conduct a preliminary test of the efficiency of the economic system using a different set of weights. Clark has, however, never clearly distinguished analysis at an intermediate level with final social policy, and the term " Social " as he has used it has a penumbra of strong ethical approbation. Further, as we have seen in the previous section, even when the market values were given to us in a concrete and precise sense, it required all our powers of self-criticism to maintain a workable degree of scientific impartiality in our narrower welfare analysis. Once we enter the more elusive sphere of " social values " which are certainly not (and will never be) " given " in the sense in which the market values are given, it is difficult to accept the analogy. The difference in degree seems to have developed into a difference in kind and we cannot keep ethical values out of our study of human welfare in the broader sense.

On a closer examination, therefore, Clark's plea for a concept of Social Value boils down to an argument for introducing ethical values into our narrower welfare analysis, an argument which we have considered in the previous section. The concept of " Social " Value has been useful in suggesting that we might be able to find the common denominator of different values prevailing in a given society. But it also has its dangers : (*a*) it seems to give a pretence of " scientific " sociology to arguments which essentially belong to the ethical level and (*b*) it may lead to a transfer of moral responsibility from the individual to the vague collective term " Society ". Strictly speaking, everyone should share the moral responsibilities of the values which prevail in the society in which they live and a value judgment does not automatically become better or ethically more desirable simply because a large number of people subscribe to it, although it is but human nature to derive strength from the fact that our own notions and beliefs are shared by a large number of our fellows.

Ultimately, therefore, when the economist leaves the narrower welfare analysis at the intermediate level and enters the realm of practical economic policy and takes into account its effects on human welfare in the broader sense, he must either explicitly make use of his own ethical values or share the moral responsibility of accepting the ethical values of the majority of people in the society in which he lives, which he can observe (with perhaps a great deal of inaccuracy). The latter alternative does not enable him to maintain a position of ethical neutrality ; he merely implicitly accepts the following value proposition : viz. that it is better to rely on the common sense of the majority of common men rather than accept the moral guidance of the minority intelligentsia, himself included.

CHAPTER XII

CONCLUSION—DIFFERENT LEVELS OF WELFARE ANALYSIS

IN Part I we have shown how welfare analysis may be conducted at the Physical level, by assuming the quantities of economic welfare to be proportional to quantities of physical products. The Physical level of analysis is closely related to the labour-theory outlook which conceives the Economic Problem as the struggle between man and nature in which the success of man is to be measured by the quantity of his net physical product.

In Part II we have shown how welfare analysis may be conducted at the Subjective level, by assuming the quantities of economic welfare to be proportional to quantities of satisfaction of given and constant individuals' wants. The subjective level of analysis is closely related to the Scarcity approach which conceives the Economic Problem as the allocation of given resources to obtain the maximum satisfaction of given wants.

Finally, in Part III we have seen how the various criticisms directed towards welfare analysis at the purely subjective level may be ultimately reduced into the plea for supplementing the ethically neutral analysis of Economic welfare in the narrower sense with a study of the problem of Social welfare in the broader sense at the Ethical level. The approach to the welfare problem at the ethical level is, of course, related, not to the economic concept of relative value, but to the normative concept of absolute value. It is not concerned with the quantitative measurement of success in achieving given ends, but with the appraisal of the ethical *quality* of the ends themselves.

Looking back we shall see that these three levels of welfare analysis are not competitive but complementary; each has its rightful place in a comprehensive study of human welfare. The important thing is to be perfectly clear about the level of analysis at which we are conducting our argument and about its possibilities and limitations. Thus a logical gulf separates the narrower economic welfare analysis at the physical and the subjective levels with the broader problem of social welfare at the ethical level. The first two levels are capable of yielding scientific welfare propositions which are logically demonstrable and are concerned with quantities which can be put under the category of greater and less. But their scope is limited to showing the implications of a given action and to comparing the relative efficiency of attaining *given* ends by alternative methods. Thus if we wish to pass from scientific welfare analysis to practical social policy we are obliged to enter the ethical level and to make normative judgments concerning whether or not the given ends ought to be pursued. In doing this, however, our arguments have lost the authority and precision of scientific analysis ; for it is not possible to demonstrate by logic that a given end is good or bad, or to apply the quantitative calculus in appraising the ethical quality of the ultimate ends.

Let us, however, return to scientific welfare economics at the first two levels of analysis. Once it is accepted that economic welfare in the narrower sense consists of quantities of satisfaction of *given* individuals' wants, a strong degree of complementarity existing between these levels of analysis can be clearly seen. The central problem of each level of analysis is what is put into " the pound of *ceteris paribus* " at the other level. Thus welfare analysis at the Physical level provisionally assumes that quantities of satisfaction are proportionate to quantities of physical products and concerns itself with the possibilities of increasing the satisfaction of given wants by increasing the quantity and/or physical productivity of the resources. On the other hand, welfare analysis at the subjective level provisionally assumes that there is no possibility of increasing the quantity or productivity of the *given* resources and considers how these given resources may be more efficiently allocated among alternative uses to increase the satisfaction of given wants.

From this, two propositions follow which should serve as guiding principles for a practical approach to the economics of welfare : (i) A complete study of economic welfare cannot be attained without making use of both levels of analysis simultaneously. Exclusive preoccupation either with the physical level or the subjective level of analysis is bound to result in misleading exaggerations often developing into serious errors. (ii) *A priori*, there is no way of telling which of these two levels is the more important one, since economic welfare in the sense defined above will be increased all the same, either by an increase in physical output (with a given degree of allocative efficiency) or by a better allocation of resources (with a given level of physical productivity). In a given situation, the significance of each level of analysis (and also the different types of analysis at the same level) should be judged by its probable *quantitative* influence on the satisfaction of given wants.

The dangers of thinking exclusively at the Physical level and a consequent confusion between the " technical " and the " economic " problem is too familiar to be discussed at length. In its most harmless form it leads to a substitution of economic analysis by trite discussions of factory organisation, industrial psychology, technical education, etc., which make the old-fashioned text-books so dreary (cf. Robbins, op. cit., p. 65). In its more pernicious form, it may lead to those errors of " misplaced concreteness " : e.g. utopian projects to increase output by the aid of physical sciences alone, brushing aside consumers' preferences, existing distribution of knowledge and other " obstacles " to production in the economic sense ; the technocratic doctrine that all economic evils would be cured if only the engineers were allowed to run the economic system ; a naïve worship of elaborate up-to-date capital equipment without asking the question whether the construction of these sumptuous durable capital goods is justified by the individuals' subjective time-preferences (cf. Hayek, " Scientism and the Study of Society ", loc. cit.).

On the other hand, exclusive preoccupation with the subjective level of analysis is also not without its dangers.

Firstly, the subjective level of analysis seems to have a static bias since the formal principles of allocating resources and maximising the satisfaction of given wants can be most clearly brought out on the assumption of *given* resources and technique. This is frequently associated with an ascetic tendency to regard the quantity of resources, the state of technique and other factors influencing physical output as data in the ultimate sense governed by " exogenous " causes outside the equilibrium framework over which the economist has no control. The second proposition is very arguable. To begin with, even accepting that some of the causes influencing physical productivity cannot be analysed by the economist, it is the function of the welfare economist at least to know their quantitative effect on economic welfare. Accepting certain factors as data is not an excuse for ignoring their quantitative significance. Further, is it really true that the determinants of physical productivity, such as the size of population, the rate of capital accumulation and technical progress cannot at least be partly controlled by appropriate economic policies ? Here we may recall that the classical economists regarded the " tightening " up of the allocative efficiency within a given static framework merely as a minor method of increasing economic welfare. According to them much larger gains of economic welfare can be obtained by

" widening " the framework of the economic system (*a*) by extending the scope of division of labour and exchange thus increasing physical productivity by specialisation, and (*b*) by increasing capital accumulation and population.

Thus let us just consider the two most important factors governing physical productivity, viz. technical progress and capital accumulation. Although technical progress at first sight appears as an independent variable, it is an open question whether specific inventions might not be " induced " by economic policy, or more generally whether the existing system of rewards for invention leads to the optimum allocation of resources for scientific research including both the long-term pure research and the short-term applied research. Again, the classical productive labour doctrine which in effect advocates capital accumulation up to the point of zero profit has been criticised for neglecting the subjective time-preferences of the individuals. While it is important to emphasise that time-preference is a real element of economic calculus and should not be dismissed as " irrational ", it does not, however, follow that we should accept the rate of capital accumulation as given. If we accept the Keynesian analysis that liquidity-preference which is a specie of risk-aversion raises the rate of interest above the time-preference rate and thus retards investment, there would seem to be a large scope for the creation of new capital goods " artificially " by lowering the rate of interest and other policies. Apart from its effect on the level of employment, this would in fact bring the allocation of resources between present and future uses nearer to the optimum amounts (cf. J. R. Hicks, " Foundations of Welfare Economics ", *Economic Journal*, 1939, p. 708 and n.). Further, in discussing Optimum accumulation we should take into account not only the increased physical productivity of the " roundabout method " in a particular plant but also indirect increases of productivity in related sectors of the economic system due to external economies and overcoming of technical indivisibilities. This was in fact, foreseen by Adam Smith (*Wealth of Nations*, Cannan ed., Vol. I, p. 88 ; also Allyn Young, " Increasing Returns and Economic Progress ", *Economic Journal*, 1928).

Secondly, by concentrating too much on the subjective level of analysis, economists are frequently inclined to judge the merits of a complicated economic policy only in terms of loss of satisfaction due to interference with the equilibrium mechanism in the product market (implicitly assuming that the level of physical productivity remains the same). Thus a more balanced appraisal of the efficiency

of the Soviet Collectivist Economy would have been to take into
account not only losses at the subjective level due to interference
with the price-mechanism but also the gains at the physical level,
such as the increased rate of capital accumulation possible in a
collective economy and the vast gains to be reaped by large-scale
technical substitutions possible under a collective method of production (cf. K. Wicksell, *Lectures*, Vol. I, pp. 211–12). Recently
Prof. Schumpeter has suggested that a different light might be
thrown even on the textbook example of wastes due to maldistribution of resources, viz. monopoly, if we take into account its effects
on productivity (cf. J. Schumpeter, *Socialism, Capitalism and Democracy*, sec. ii).

Finally, there remains the belief that the subjective level of
analysis is superior to the physical level of analysis, because while
the physical analysis at its best is based on the crude assumption
that quantities of satisfaction are proportionate to quantities of
physical products, the subjective analysis takes into account the
refinements introduced by the principle of diminishing marginal
utility. This, however, depends on the purpose for which we want
to use our analysis. For the purpose of pure theoretical analysis,
the subjective level of analysis is certainly superior to the physical
level of analysis. Further, it is only by a clear understanding of
its formal principles that we can avoid the fallacies of the extreme
physical approach and allow for the margin of error involved in
the legitimate use of the physical level of analysis. Nevertheless,
as we have seen, for the general purpose of economic policy, however,
the most effective analysis is that which is designed to deal with
obvious sources of loss or gain involving large quantities of economic
welfare. For these larger-scale projects of social engineering the
rake is more frequently a superior instrument to the toothcomb.
Preoccupation with small quantities of welfare or the fallacy of
" misplaced refinement " should be avoided as well as that of
" misplaced concreteness ".

This leads us to our second guiding principle of practical welfare
analysis, viz. the significance of each level of analysis and each type
of analysis at the same level should be judged by its quantitative
effect on economic welfare.

Adopting this quantitative criterion, the classical proposition
that the potential gains to be obtained by increasing physical productivity and the volume of economic activity is greater than that
to be obtained by tightening up the allocative efficiency of the *given*
resources becomes one of the most important welfare propositions

and needs a systematic examination in the light of present-day economic conditions. The type of problems which may be conveniently dealt with at the Physical level of analysis may be put under three main heads :

> (i) The problem of optimum supply of labour, capital accumulation and rate of technical progress, with an emphasis on the relation between physical productivity and the latter two variables.
> (ii) Assuming given resources and technique, the possibilities of increasing productivity by overcoming technical indivisibilities and by making use of technical complementarities which form the basis of plans for regional economic development on the T.V.A. model.
> (iii) The problem of unemployment and unused capacity.

To obtain a quantitative estimate of the effect of each type of the above problems on economic welfare there is an urgent need for empirical research on the lines indicated by that great pioneer work, Colin Clark's *Conditions of Economic Progress*.

The type of problems which can be dealt with at the subjective level of analysis depends on the type of analysis at that level. In spite of its extreme abstractness, the formal theory of the General Optimum has two important functions to fulfil : (i) it enables us to put welfare analysis on a secure scientific basis by showing how the various methodological difficulties may be overcome, and (ii) it is only by a firm grasp of its formal principles that we can avoid the errors and excesses of both the physical level of analysis and the Partial Surplus analysis at the subjective level. However, if it is accepted that for the large-scale projects of social engineering the rake is more useful than the toothcomb, the Partial Surplus analysis emerges as the most immediately useful type of analysis at the subjective level. It is only in terms of the Surplus analysis that we can conveniently tackle those " glaring " cases of deviations from the Optimum which involve large quantities of economic welfare and it is only by paying more attention to the " Total Conditions " as distinct from the " Marginal Conditions " that we can effectively utilise the potential increase in productive capacity by determining a correct list of commodities to be produced according to given consumers' preferences, both those preferences which have been exhibited in the market and also those which are merely latent.

So far, we have been concerned only with the first two levels of scientific welfare analysis in the narrower sense on the assumption of *given* individuals' wants. What about the transition to the broader problem of social welfare at the third or the Ethical level, where scientific analysis is no longer possible and where we have to abandon our quantitative calculus and appraise the quality of welfare ? Here we have shown (i) that in spite of the tendency of human wants to grow and change, scientific welfare analysis based on the assumption of given wants still has an important contribution to make since, at any given moment of time, a relatively definite and stable pattern of consumers' demand can be found and (ii) that in spite of the many insidious difficulties of keeping separate our own opinions and the opinions of the individuals we are observing, it is vital for the existence of economic science to maintain scientific impartiality and ethical neutrality and that with sufficient care this is possible to a reasonable degree.

Having carefully disciplined ourselves to the requirements of scientific welfare analysis, however, it is desirable to step boldly and consciously into the Ethical level for at least two reasons : (i) One of the best ways of maintaining scientific impartiality is to make deliberate and uninhibited value judgments and to use them as a basis of self-criticism in our purely scientific analysis. (ii) A more important reason is that ultimately economic theory can only justify its existence by practical application, and in the sphere of practical social policy the economist, like any other citizen, must make his own value judgments or else share the moral responsibility for the standards of values prevailing in the society in which he lives. When this is recognised, however, we may recall Marshall's advice that each economist may reasonably decide for himself how far he will extend his activities beyond pure economic analysis (*Principles*, p. 708). The ideal economist is one who keeps his value judgments clearly apart from his scientific analysis without at the same time allowing his ethical instincts and " the native hue of resolution " to be " sicklied o'er with the pale cast of thought ".

SELECT BIBLIOGRAPHY

BOOKS

BOWLEY, M. *Nassau Senior and Classical Economics.*
CAIRNES, J. E. *Leading Principles of Political Economy.*
CANNAN, E. *Theories of Production and Distribution.*
—— *Review of Economic Theory.*
CLARK, C. *Conditions of Economic Progress.*
CLARK, J. B. *Philosophy of Wealth.*
—— *Distribution of Wealth.*
CLARK, J. M. *Preface to Social Economics.*
—— *The Social Control of Business.*
DOBB, M. H. *Political Economy and Capitalism.*
EDGEWORTH, F. Y. *Mathematical Psychics* (L.S.E. Reprint).
GIDE, C., and RIST, C. *A History of Economic Doctrines.*
GRAY, A. *Development of Economic Doctrine.*
HANEY, L. *History of Economic Thought.*
HAWTREY, R. G. *The Economic Problem.*
—— *Economic Destiny.*
HOBSON, J. A. *Work and Wealth.*
—— *Wealth and Life.*
INGRAM, J. K. *History of Political Economy.*
KEYNES, J. M. *The General Theory of Employment, Interest and Money.*
KEYNES, J. N. *Scope and Method of Political Economy.*
KNIGHT, F. H. *Ethics of Competition.*
—— *Risk, Uncertainty and Profit* (L.S.E. Reprint).
LERNER, A. P. *The Economics of Control.*
MALTHUS, R. *Principles of Political Economy* (L.S.E. Reprint).
MARSHALL, A. *Principles of Economics.*
MILL, J. S. *Principles of Political Economy,* Ashley ed.
—— *Essays on Unsettled Questions of Political Economy.*
PARETO, V. *Manuel d'economie politique* (2nd ed., 1927).
PIGOU, A. C. *Economics of Welfare,* 4th ed.
—— *Memorials of Alfred Marshall.*
RICARDO, D. *Principles of Political Economy* (Everyman's ed.).
ROBBINS, L. *Nature and Significance of Economic Science.*
ROLL, E. A. *History of Economic Thought.*
SAY, J. B. *Traité d'Economie politique.*
SCHUMPETER, J. *Socialism, Capitalism and Democracy.*
SENIOR, N. *Science of Political Economy* (Library of Economics).
SIDGWICK, H. *Principles of Political Economy.*
SMITH, A. *Wealth of Nations,* Cannan ed.
TAUSSIG, F. W. *Wages and Capital* (L.S.E. Reprint).
—— *Principles of Economics,* Vol. I.
THÜNEN, J. H. v. *Der Isolierte Staat* (ed. H. Waentig, 1930).
TUGWELL, G. R, ed. *The Trend of Economics.*
237

VALK, L. *The Principles of Wages.*
VEBLEN, T. *Place of Science in Modern Civilisation.*
VINER, J. *Studies in the Theory of International Trade.*
WALRAS, L. *Éléments d'economie politique pure* (1874).
WICKSELL, K. *Lectures on Political Economy,* Vol. I.
WIESER, F. v. *Natural Value* (Smart ed.).

ARTICLES AND ESSAYS

BARNA, T. " Note on Productivity of Labour ", *Bulletin of Oxford Institute of Statistics,* No. 8, July 1946.
BARONE, E. *Ministry of Production, Collectivist Economic Planning,* Hayek ed.
BURKE, A. " Alternative Formulations of Welfare Economics ", *Quarterley Journal of Economics,* 1937.
CAIRNES, J. E. " Laissez-faire ", *Essays on Political Economy, Theoretical and Applied.*
EDELBERG, V. " Ricardian Theory of Profit ", *Economica,* 1931.
FETTER, F. " Price Economics versus Welfare Economics ", *American Economic Review,* 1920.
HANEY, L. " The Social Point of View in Economics ", *Quarterly Journal of Economics,* 1914.
HARROD, R. F. " Scope and Method of Economics ", *Economic Journal,* 1938.
HAYEK, F. " Scientism and the Study of Society ", *Economica,* 1942, 1943, 1944.
HENDERSON, A. " Consumers' Surplus and Compensating Variations ", *Review of Economic Studies,* 1941.
HICKS, J. R. " Leon Walras," *Econometrica,* 1934.
―― " Foundations of Welfare Economics ", *Economic Journal,* 1939.
―― " Valuation of Social Income ", *Economica,* 1940.
―― " Rehabilitation of Consumers' Surplus ", *Review of Economic Studies,* 1941.
―― " Consumers' Surplus and Index Numbers, *Review of Economic Studies,* 1942.
―― " The Four Consumers' Surpluses ", *Review of Economic Studies,* 1943.
HOTELLING, H. " The General Welfare in Relation to the Problems of Taxation and of Railway and Utility Rates ", *Econometrica,* 1938.
KAHN, R. F. " Notes on Ideal Output ", *Economic Journal,* 1935.
KALDOR, N. " Welfare Propositions and Interpersonal Comparisons of Utility ", *Economic Journal,* 1939.
KEYNES, J. M. " Robert Malthus ", *Essays in Biography.*
LANGE, O. " Foundations of Welfare Economics ", *Econometrica,* 1942.
LERNER, A. P. " The Concept of Monopoly and the Measurement of Monopoly Power ", *Review of Economic Studies,* 1934.
PARSONS, T. " Marshall ", *Structure of Social Action,* Chap. IV.
ROBBINS, L. " Interpersonal Comparison of Utility ", *Economic Journal,* 1938.
SCITOVSKY, T. " A Note on Welfare Propositions in Economics ". *Review of Economic Studies,* 1941.
SHOVE, G. F. " Varying Costs and Marginal Net Products ", *Economic Journal,* 1928.
―― " The Place of Marshall's Principles in Economic Theory ", *Economic Journal,* 1942.
YOUNG, A. " Increasing Returns and Economic Progress ", *Economic Journal,* 1928.

INDEX OF AUTHORS

Anderson, B. M., Jr., 207
Ashley, W. J., 202

Barone, E., 91, 104, 115 n.
Boulding, K. E., 89
Bowley, M., 4, 6
Burke, A., 115 n.
Burnham, J., 226

Cairnes, J. E., 56, 69, 121, 127, 129
Cannan, E., 77, 122, 124–5, 206
Carlyle, T., 201–2
Carver, T. N., 207
Clapham, J. H., 192
Clark, C., 14 n., 213, 234
Clark, J. B., 91, 107–8, 120, 123, 129, 132, 137, 206–8
Clark, J. M., 140, 201–2, 206–12, 215, 217, 220–7
Comte, A., 202–3, 223
Condillac, E. B. de, 105
Cournot, A., 99, 121
Cunningham, W., 202

Dickinson, H. D., 219
Dobb, M., 2 n., 16, 219

Edelberg, V., 80, 105
Edgeworth, F. Y., 69, 93, 97, 99–100, 102, 145

Fetter, F., 207
Fisher, A. G. B., 213
Fisher, I., 173
Foster and Bacon, 226

Gide and Rist, 61
Giffen, 11

Haberler, G., 111
Haney, L., 207
Hawtrey, R. G., 202, 222, 225
Hayek, F., 174–5, 202–6, 218, 221, 223
Henderson, A., 143 n.
Hicks, J. R., 63, 97, 99, 111 n., 114, 115 n., 118–19, 139, 142, 149–52,

Hicks, J. R.—*contd.*
156, 165, 171, 174–5, 177, 180, 196–8, 232
Hobson, J. A., 202, 220, 222, 225
Hotelling, H., 143 n.

Ingram, J. K., 202

Jevons, W. S., 90, 120, 134, 137

Kahn, R. F., 178, 182, 191–2, 194–5, 198, 216
Kaldor, N., 103, 155 n.
Keynes, J. M., 30, 34, 48, 138, 226
Knight, F. H., 140, 142, 149, 179, 200–220, 208–12, 214–16, 219–20

Lange, O., 115 n., 219
Lauderdale, J. M., 70–1
Lerner, A. P., 1 n., 219
Lilienthal, D. E., 226
Longfield, M., 6

Malthus, T. R., 6, 8–10, 16–8, 21, 26, 30, 32, 34–44, 46–53, 62, 64, 77, 79, 82, 84–7
Marshall, A., 53–4, 65, 71, 90, 93, 97, 99, 104, 107–8, 122–4, 132–71, 173, 177–8, 193, 196–8, 201–3, 206, 211, 217, 235
Menger, K., 107, 120
Mill, James, 33
Mill, J. S., 2, 9–13, 65, 68–9, 71, 82–3, 92, 120–1, 125–7, 129, 174, 203, 206
Morris, William, 201–2

Pareto, V., 91, 99–100, 103–4, 111, 115 n., 117, 187, 197
Parsons, T., 134 n.
Pigou, A. C., 53–4, 90, 92–3, 119, 124, 130, 139, 146, 171, 173–98, 206–8, 219–20, 225

239

Ricardo, D., 6–9, 16–18, 26–33, 35, 45–6, 49–50, 52–3, 55, 62–8, 79–81, 84–5, 87, 105, 145–6, 174, 206
Robbins, L., 1, 108, 111, 126, 142, 149, 182, 222
Robertson, D. H., 182
Robinson, J., 160 n., 164 n.
Roll, E., 26
Ruskin, J., 200–2

Say, J. B., 6, 33, 71, 105
Schumpeter, J., 208, 233
Sčitovsky, T., 1 n., 104 n., 156
Seligman, E. R. A., 207
Senior, N., 6
Shove, G. F., 133, 182
Sidgwick, H., 13, 119, 122, 124–32, 139, 166, 201
Smith, Adam, 3–7, 12, 17–26, 34–5, 45–6, 55–62, 72–82, 85, 94, 104, 133, 232

Spencer, H., 200, 202
Sraffa, P., 182

Taussig, F. W., 53, 71, 207
Thunen, J. H. v., 105
Tugwell, G. R., 201

Valk, L., 107
Veblen, T., 200, 205–6, 218
Viner, J., 65

Wagner, A., 143
Walras, L., 97–8, 103–4, 106–7, 109, 120, 123, 129, 137
Wicksell, K., 103, 107, 109, 111–12, 233
Wicksteed, P. H., 109
Wieser, F. v., 91, 107, 111, 208

Young, A., 3, 53, 59, 124, 232